News Hole

In recent decades, turnout in US presidential elections has soared, education levels have hit historic highs, and the Internet has made information more accessible than ever. Yet during that same period, Americans have grown less engaged with local politics and elections. Drawing on detailed analysis of 15 years of reporting in more than 200 local newspapers, along with election returns, surveys, and interviews with journalists, this study shows that the demise of local journalism has played a key role in the decline of civic engagement. As struggling newspapers have slashed staff, they have dramatically cut their coverage of mayors, city halls, school boards, county commissions, and virtually every aspect of local government. In turn, fewer Americans now know who their local elected officials are, and turnout in local elections has plummeted. To reverse this trend and preserve democratic accountability in our communities, the local news industry must be reinvigorated – and soon.

Danny Hayes is Professor in the Department of Political Science, George Washington University.

Jennifer L. Lawless is the Leone Reeves and George W. Spicer Professor in the Department of Politics, University of Virginia.

T0371365

Other Books in the Series:

(Continued after the Index)

News Hole

The Demise of Local Journalism and Political Engagement

DANNY HAYES

George Washington University

JENNIFER L. LAWLESS

University of Virginia

CAMBRIDGE
UNIVERSITY PRESS

CAMBRIDGE
UNIVERSITY PRESS

University Printing House, Cambridge CB2 8BS, United Kingdom

One Liberty Plaza, 20th Floor, New York, NY 10006, USA

477 Williamstown Road, Port Melbourne, VIC 3207, Australia

314–321, 3rd Floor, Plot 3, Splendor Forum, Jasola District Centre,
New Delhi – 110025, India

103 Penang Road, #05–06/07, Visioncrest Commercial, Singapore 238467

Cambridge University Press is part of the University of Cambridge.

It furthers the University's mission by disseminating knowledge in the pursuit of
education, learning, and research at the highest international levels of excellence.

www.cambridge.org
Information on this title: www.cambridge.org/9781108834773
DOI: 10.1017/9781108876940

First published 2021

A catalogue record for this publication is available from the British Library.

ISBN 978-1-108-83477-3 Hardback
ISBN 978-1-108-81984-8 Paperback

Contents

Figures

Tables

Acknowledgments

We have been working on this book for a long time. We began collecting the data during the second term of the Obama administration. We submitted the final version of the manuscript in the final days of the Trump administration. We sketched the broad contours of the book in person, at coffee shops and restaurants in Washington, DC. We drafted most of the chapters while quarantined in different cities, with more phone calls than we can count. We celebrated receiving a contract for the book with drinks at a fancy bar. We commemorated its completion with drinks on Zoom.

Presidents and public health crises weren't the only changes we endured. The local news environment continued to evolve as we were studying it. When we started this project in 2014, newspaper circulation and the number of newsroom employees had been declining for decades. But by the time we finished, circulation was down another one-third, advertising revenue had fallen by half once again, and thousands of newsroom employees no longer had a job. Within the first six months of the coronavirus, dozens of newspapers closed up shop. (So did our favorite coffee shop, a staple in the neighborhood where we both lived in 2014 and the site of our first conversation about this project.)

Suffice it to say that writing a book about local news smack-dab in the middle of a pandemic and amid a roiling local news environment has been eventful. But as dizzying as this period has been, many people who helped us along the way made our task so much easier. We are grateful for the feedback we received from Mike Barthel, Dave Brady, Josh Darr, Johanna Dunaway, Mo Fiorina, Richard Fox, Paul Freedman, Kim Gross, Matt Hindman, Dan Hopkins, Gary Jacobson, Eric Lawrence, Adam Levine, Hans Noel, Erik Peterson, Jeremy Pope, Adam Schiffer,

Lee Shaker, John Sides, Sean Theriault, Emily Thorson, Marc Trussler, Mike Wagner, Antoine Yoshinaka, and Thomas Zeitzoff, all of whom read and commented on conference papers, drafts of journal article submissions, or presentations. We are also indebted to two Cambridge University Press reviewers whose advice helped sharpen the manuscript.

We also benefited from comments we received from various conference and research seminar audiences. We thank participants at the annual meetings of the American Political Science Association and the Midwest Political Science Association, the Local Journalism Research Conference at Duke University, and at research seminars hosted by American University, Georgetown University, the Harris School at the University of Chicago, the Hewlett Foundation, Northwestern University, Pennsylvania State University, Temple University, Stanford University, Stony Brook University, and the University of Maryland.

We could not have completed this book without generous funding from the George Washington University Facilitating Fund, the Columbian College of Arts and Sciences Dean's Research Chair, the University of Virginia, and the Women & Politics Institute at American University. We also thank several colleagues who generously shared data with us: Tom Holbrook, Gary Jacobson, Hans Noel, and Aaron Weinschenk.

Many research assistants worked tirelessly on various components of data collection, and we are deeply indebted to them. Gail Baitinger collected and coded tens of thousands of newspaper articles about congressional elections and state and local politics. She was so efficient that our access to one archival database was restricted until we could prove she was not a bot! Marx Wang, Rocket Claman, Samantha Guthrie, Mila Ho, Jessica James, Grace Jennetta, Richa Kanani, Paulina Kiehm, Alexandra Kurtz, Veronica Riccobene, Shooka Saket, Julia Salvatore, Kavya Samudrala, Jon Weakley, and Harrison Weeks completed tedious data collection with care and cheer. And we'd be remiss not to thank the staff at the Library of Congress, who helped us locate obscure materials and didn't mind that we set up shop there in the summer of 2017.

Perhaps the most fun part of this endeavor was conducting exit polls in the 2018 midterm elections in Arlington, Virginia, and the 2019 off-year elections in Charlottesville. We could not have done it without the help of an army of enthusiastic undergraduate exit pollsters. For the 2018 exit poll, we had the help of George Washington University students Eduardo Abascal, Lily Barrett, Dylan Basescu, Jack Broderick, Rachel Cousins, Margot Dynes, Adriana Feijoo, Sara Garcia, Chad Gilmartin, Abby Gipe, Matthew Girardi, Isabella Gonzalez, Tucker Guinn, Betel Hailemariam,

Gabrielle Hangos, James Harnett, Trent Hunter, Xinyue Ji, Sarina Kaplan, Jaimee Kidd, Molly Lienesch, Megan McDonough, Jill McInerney, Adelaide McNamara, Eimee Mendez, Aliana Michals, Noah Miller, Jordan Mullaney, Justyn Needel, Airon-Lin Newsom, Charlie Oberst, Anastasiya Parvankin, Ricardo Rauseo, Jessica Reed, Justin Scott, Irma Soriano-Diaz, Anavi Subramanyam, Claudia Teti, Alex Togneri-Jones, Karen Toledo, and Joshua Xiang. These students weathered unseasonably cold temperatures and torrential downpours, yet managed to interview more than 1,000 voters.

Students from the University of Virginia conducted the 2019 exit poll. The weather was gorgeous that day, but we still very much appreciate the efforts of Essey Abebe, Rawad Alnaas, Ama Amissah, Juhee Baek, Emily Barksdale, Maria Barrera, Ian Baxter, Hibah Shems Berhanu, Kathon Betterton, Kayla Cabrera, James Carey, Rosalind Chavier, Trent Chinnaswamy, Pauline Chong, Rheyanna Clemens, Irene Lujan Climent, Kate Colgan, Katie Cox, Noah Curtiss, James Davis, Caroline Dibble, Abby DiOrio, Jena Elshami, Leah Erwin, Mark Gray Felice, Kayla Fyock, Sarah Gill, Rodrigo Giron, Joanna Goodman, Emily Graffeo, Sean Gramley, John Green, Halina Gregg, Robert Grier, Benjamin Hadlock, Robert Haggart, Madeline Halgren, Catherine Hall, Kristin Hamman, Lauren Harris, Jayla Hart, Benjamin Hazelton, Thomas M. Hennessy, Victoria Hodge, Katherine Huiskes, Victoria O. Hume, Alexandra Iamonaco, Elizabeth Irwin, Brandon Jackson, Elsa Jensen, Komal Kamdar, Allison Kammerman, Ryan Keane, Devan Keesling, Patrick Kern, Shemya Key, Christine Kim, Grace Kim, Kiwi Kiwinda, Matthew Knox, Victoria Kunberger, Lily Lin, Connor Loughran, Adrian Mamaril, Murray McGovern, Quentin Milligan, Annelise Miranda, Denzel Mitchell, Shannon Mooney, Kaylee Moore, Andrew Mutch, Morgan Negron, Matthew Newberry, Katie Novak, Carrie O'Foran, Samantha Owens, Shannan Parry, Ellanie Pasamonte, Morgan Patterson, Spencer Philps, Phoebe Retta, Jeanne Rockwell, Emma Ross, Peter Rossano, Matt Ryan, Grace Sacripanti, Katya Sankow, Noah Shahinian, Julia Shea, John Shivers, Lucy Shoemaker, Brittany Shook, John Sipher, Erica M. Soderberg, Tiffany Thai, Meagan Thompson, Caleb Tisdale, Deven Upadhyay, Hunter Wagenaar, Amaya Walthall, Sylvia Wang, Sean Wells, Hannah Williams, Hatley Wood, Megan Wyatt, Amelia Young, and Ellie Young. Together, they surveyed 2,999 voters.

The dozens of journalists we quote throughout the book generously gave of their time to answer our questions about their experiences in local newsrooms across the country. We thank them for their observations and candor. Diana Witt, who created our highly navigable index in record time, was a pleasure to work with. And we owe a debt of gratitude to our editors at Cambridge University Press. Robert Dreesen enthusiastically believed in this project from its inception, and Sara Doskow saw it through to its completion.

As always, we were supported and encouraged by our families, even in the strangest and toughest of times. For Danny, his parents, Dan and Charlotte Hayes; sisters, Janie and Cindy Hayes; and brother-in-law, Jimmy Bisese, have continued their enthusiastic cheerleading. At home, in lockdown or not, it is impossible to imagine life without Nikki Raspa. Her capacity for love, resilience, and extremely large numbers of burpees never ceases to amaze. And although Gio doesn't yet know it, his arrival was the most joyful moment of his parents' life. Scout, barking at squirrels all the way, couldn't agree more.

Jen also thanks her parents, Marjorie and John Lawless, who still get the local newspaper delivered and with whom she quarantined from the onset of the virus. Indeed, most of these pages were written from her childhood bedroom (although the Michael J. Fox posters are no longer on the walls). Together, they weathered an absolutely horrific year. But along the way, they became Instacart's best customers, spent more money on fancy masks than anyone ever should, and realized that jigsaw puzzles make them angry. Richard Fox was a constant sounding board – for everything personal, professional, and political – even when Jen was an absolute pill. And Viola, the most supportive and stunning of bulldogs, will never know how much her snoring, snorting, and wiggling brighten the darkest of days.

I

The Local Political Engagement Puzzle

In 2014 the city of Los Angeles found itself facing a civic crisis. After decades of declining voter turnout, officials were desperate to boost citizen participation in municipal elections. Forty years earlier roughly two-thirds of the city's registered voters regularly showed up at the polls. But turnout in the most recent elections had hovered between an abysmal 18% and an anemic 23%.[1] In a proposal fit for the show business capital of the world, the Los Angeles Ethics Commission suggested turning the democratic process into something of a game show. Randomly selected voters would win a cash prize – up to $50,000 – for casting a ballot.[2] Perhaps owing to the obvious ethical and legal issues associated with paying people to vote, the proposal never got off the ground. And participation remained low. When turnout in the 2017 mayor's race – 20% – narrowly managed to avoid the city's worst showing ever, one writer wryly mused, "Do we get a trophy here or what?"[3]

Picking on Los Angeles is easy, but the city is not alone. In recent decades, citizen participation in local elections across the country has

---

[1] Mike Maciag, "Voter Turnout Plummeting in Local Elections," *Governing*, October 2014. www.governing.com/topics/politics/gov-voter-turnout-municipal-elections.html (August 26, 2020).

[2] David Zahniser, "Low Turnout Prompts L.A. to Consider Offering Prizes to Vote," *McClatchy News*, August 15, 2014. www.governing.com/news/headlines/mct-los-angeles-voting-prizes.html (August 26, 2020).

[3] Tim Loc, "Final Election Tallies Put Voter Turnout at 20%, So It Wasn't L.A.'s Worst Ever," *LAist.com*, March 21, 2017. https://laist.com/2017/03/21/final_election_tallies_put_voter_tu.php (August 26, 2020).

plunged. The 24% turnout in New York City's 2013 mayoral race[4] might have seemed an embarrassment until Dallas voters two years later managed just 6%, roughly the equivalent of a show of hands.[5] Graphs plotting municipal turnout since the mid-twentieth century in places such as Chicago and Philadelphia look like the screaming descents of amusement park roller coasters. The trends in smaller cities and towns are less steep but no less concerning.

It's not just voter turnout that's plummeted. By a number of other indicators, Americans' knowledge of their local government has also been declining for years. In 1966, for instance, 70% of voters could name their city's mayor.[6] Fifty years later, that number was down to less than 40%. One-third of respondents to a 1979 poll could accurately call to mind the name of their local school superintendent.[7] Fast forward to 2016 and 83% couldn't even hazard a guess. When asked in 2019 whether their county government was doing a good job, fully one-quarter of the nation's residents could not render a simple thumbs-up or -down.[8]

The declines in local knowledge and participation are puzzling. Throughout the last 25 years, turnout in presidential contests has increased. Education, one of the strongest predictors of political engagement, is at its highest level in US history.[9] The Internet has made accessing information about public affairs easier than ever. And while local government has always been central to Americans' lives, that's been especially true in recent decades. States and localities since the 1990s have been the frontlines of battles over the implementation of welfare programs, immigration policies, health care reform, and climate change, to name just a handful of issues. As the federal government stepped back amid the 2020 coronavirus pandemic, local governments became the first responders. By all accounts, these circumstances should have led to more political engagement close to home.

[4] "New York: Voter Turnout Appears to Be Record Low," *New York Times*, November 6, 2013. www.nytimes.com/news/election-2013/2013/11/06/new-york-turnout-appears-headed-for-record-low (August 26, 2020).

[5] Stephen Young, "Dallas Had the Worst Big City Mayoral Election Turnout in the U.S. in 2015," *Dallas Observer*, January 26, 2017. www.dallasobserver.com/news/dallas-had-the-worst-big-city-mayoral-election-turnout-in-the-us-in-2015-9119070 (August 26, 2020).

[6] Gallup 1966.

[7] The Kettering Foundation 1979.

[8] These figures come from our surveys of respondents in the 2016 and 2019 Cooperative Congressional Election Studies.

[9] Erik Schmidt, "For the First Time, 90 Percent Completed High School or More," *United States Census Bureau*, July 31, 2018. www.census.gov/library/stories/2018/07/educational-attainment.html (April 11, 2019).

Why has the opposite happened? Multiple factors play a role. Long-term changes in society, including suburbanization and economic pressures, have weakened civic ties in local communities. Electoral reforms that dismantled political machines – long the engines of voter mobilization in major cities – have decreased participation. And as the Republican and Democratic parties have polarized, voters' political attitudes have "nationalized," becoming closely linked to debates in Washington, DC, and less connected to local concerns. These major developments undoubtedly help explain Americans' waning interest in local politics.

But they are only part of the explanation, because they don't account for the most dramatic change in the civic life US communities have experienced in the last 20 years: the decimation of the local news media. As the Internet has undermined the business model of American newspapers, the industry has nearly collapsed. Once-proud, prizewinning papers have withered away in the face of declining advertising revenue. Hundreds have closed and nearly all the remaining ones have cut their editorial staff. With fewer reporting resources and a shrinking news hole – the amount of space for editorial content – newspapers have reduced coverage of local elected officials, city halls, school boards, county commissions, and virtually every aspect of local government. And all of this predates the coronavirus, which further decimated local newsrooms.[10]

The story of this book is that the hollowing out of daily newspapers, long the nation's most vibrant and indispensable sources of community information, has had profound consequences for local political engagement. With access to less local reporting, Americans are now less knowledgeable about their local governments, less interested in the actions of their local officials, and less likely to participate in local elections. These effects have been widespread, touching big cities and small towns, red states and blue states, and voters of all kinds. At a moment in history when information on seemingly any topic is bountiful and available with a click, the tale of local politics is quite the opposite. It is one of increasing scarcity – of both public affairs journalism and citizen engagement.

---

[10] Kristen Hare, "The Coronavirus Has Closed More than 50 Local Newsrooms across America. And Counting," *Poynter*, August 20, 2020. www.poynter.org/locally/2020/the-coronavirus-has-closed-more-than-25-local-newsrooms-across-america-and-counting/ (August 26, 2020).

LOCAL POLITICAL ENGAGEMENT AND ITS DOWNWARD SLIDE

It's hard to overstate the significance of local politics in the United States. Owing to the system of federalism set up in the US Constitution, 90,000 local governments – cities, towns, counties, and school districts, among others – wield vast taxing and regulatory power. Every year, they collect and spend billions of taxpayer dollars on roads, public safety, education, parks, trash collection, and almost any other public service you can name. Every day, they make decisions that determine whether Americans can start new businesses, renovate their homes, smoke in bars, or carry guns in churches. Yet most of the work of this "hidden Leviathan" happens without the public's knowledge, and elections for most of the nation's half million local elected officials rarely draw much attention.[11] Despite the importance of local government to the nation's founding and functioning, participation in local politics "is like family farming – romanticized in the political culture but practiced by few."[12]

Low levels of engagement stem, at least in part, from structural features of local politics.[13] Many city, county, and school board elections are not held concurrently with national contests, meaning that voters in some years are asked to show up to the polls multiple times. Unless a controversial candidate or issue appears on the ballot, many voters lack the motivation to turn out in these off-year elections.[14] The fact that some local elections are nonpartisan and that power in many localities is vested in appointed rather than elected officials may also contribute to disengagement. The result is that local politics is often dominated by the most politically interested, who tend to be highly educated, wealthy, and white, leaving the poor and people of color with less effective representation.[15]

But these structural factors have been a feature of politics in many US communities for decades, so they cannot explain why local civic engagement is even lower now than it once was. Two prominent scholarly accounts have taken up that trend. In his influential book *Bowling Alone*, political scientist Robert Putnam describes how social capital – the interpersonal networks and social trust that promote civic engagement and make democracy work –

---

[11] Oliver, Ha, and Callen 2012.
[12] Baybeck 2014.
[13] See Warshaw 2019 for a review.
[14] Anzia 2014; Hajnal 2009.
[15] Einstein, Palmer, and Glick 2019; Hajnal and Trounstine 2005; Schaffner, Rhodes, and La Raja 2020.

eroded in the latter years of the twentieth century.[16] As modern life became more individualized and less communitarian – a function of suburban sprawl, reductions in free time, the growth of women in the workforce, and generational change, among other factors – Americans stopped signing petitions, joining civic associations, and showing up at the polls. In Putnam's telling, the public's disengagement from local politics is a story of macro-level societal changes and the disappearance of a generation whose commitment to civic democracy was forged in the fires of the Great Depression and World War II.

A second, more explicitly political, account emphasizes the growing "nationalization" of American politics. Articulated most thoroughly by political scientist Daniel J. Hopkins, the nationalization thesis contends that voters' political behavior has become increasingly influenced by the debates, party positions, and political figures at the center of national politics.[17] National partisanship, more than local conditions or candidates, drives voters' choices in elections and attitudes about issues. With people's social identities now linked more closely to national partisan attachments, their connection to politics in their communities has weakened. As a result, voters have become less knowledgeable and less interested in local public affairs.

Neither of these accounts, however, is well suited to explain how the collapse of local newspapers has directly affected local engagement. That's not to say that they don't carve out a role for the media. Putnam sees television as a major villain because of its "privatization" of leisure time. Why bowl with your neighbors when you can stay home and be entertained alone? He also details the strong association between newspaper readership and civic participation. But Putnam's incisive account, written in the 1990s, couldn't foresee the scope of the local news disaster looming on the horizon. Hopkins, meanwhile, devotes substantial attention to changes in the media environment. He argues, however, that the decline in local engagement is more likely due to consumer behavior – people seeking out national news sources instead of local ones – than to a reduction in the reporting capacity of local news outlets. "It is not that newspapers . . . have changed dramatically; instead, what people watch, listen to, and read have," Hopkins writes.[18]

---

[16] Putnam 2000. See also Skocpol 2003.
[17] Hopkins 2018. See also Fiorina 2017; Zingher and Richman 2019.
[18] Hopkins 2018, p. 199.

The diffusion of television and the dramatic expansion of the media environment are surely responsible for some reduction in local political engagement. Indeed, the explosion in the number of consumer options for media content – news and entertainment alike – is a key cause of newspapers' current financial woes. But there are compelling theoretical reasons to expect that the reduction of coverage of local public affairs in the nation's daily newspapers has driven down political engagement on its own. In other words, audience demand may be part of the problem, but so is the dwindling *supply* of information that citizens need to keep apprised of their elected officials' actions and behavior.

WHY THE DECLINE OF NEWSPAPERS MATTERS AND HOW TO PROVE IT

Our argument arises from decades of research showing that when citizens lose access to political information, they become less knowledgeable about their elected officials and less likely to vote. Getting informed and participating in politics is costly – it requires some level of investment, whether time, money, or effort.[19] News media provide an information subsidy that reduces the costs of that investment.[20] Indeed, numerous studies have found that when the cost of information goes up – as when news becomes scarce or access becomes more difficult – fewer citizens are willing to bear it, and political engagement falls.[21]

That large body of research strongly suggests that widespread newspaper cutbacks and closures will negatively affect Americans' knowledge about local government and participation in local elections. That's because newspapers have long been the primary source of local government reporting in cities and towns across the country.[22] Studies have shown that newspaper coverage of local politics is far more thorough and substantive than the reporting in other outlets.[23] Indeed, the vast majority of what appears on local TV newscasts is crime, weather, and sports, not city council meetings. Newspapers are often the lone source for mundane information, critical for civic participation, such as polling

[19] Downs 1957; Lassen 2005.
[20] Baekgaard et al. 2014; Barabas and Jerit 2009.
[21] See, e.g., Althaus and Trautman 2008; Cohen, Noel, and Zaller 2004; Delli Carpini, Keeter, and Kennamer 1994; Gentzkow 2006; Hoffman and Eveland 2010; McLeod, Scheufele, and Moy 1999; Mondak 1995; Moskowitz 2021; Schulhofer-Wohl and Garrido 2011; Shaker 2014; Snyder and Strömberg 2010.
[22] See Schudson 1981 for a historical overview of American newspapers.
[23] Fowler et al. 2007; Martin and McCrain 2019; Stevens et al. 2006.

places and notices of political meetings.[24] In some smaller communities, the newspaper is the only entity that covers local politics at all. And even when they face competition from other media outlets, newspapers tend to set the agenda – meaning that newspapers' influence on the information environment goes well beyond what appears on their own pages.[25]

The importance of newspapers for political engagement is not just about their informational role. Newspapers have historically functioned as the connective tissue of American cities and towns, creating a shared sense of community among local residents.[26] Studies conducted a half century apart – in both the 1940s and 1990s – found that newspapers were so enmeshed in the fabric of residents' lives that when people missed their daily newspaper, they experienced a sense of "social and psychological trauma."[27] That may be one reason that newspaper readers report strong ties to their local communities – while TV watchers give the finger to their neighbors on the road.[28] Given these realities, it is no exaggeration to describe newspapers as the beating heart of civic communities throughout the twentieth century. And as newspapers have cut back, shrunk, and closed altogether, it would frankly be surprising if Americans' engagement with local politics did not decrease as well.

Despite the logical appeal of this argument, a variety of methodological challenges have limited the evidence linking the decline of local newspapers in the last two decades to a decrease in local engagement. We develop a new approach that tackles these issues in the existing literature and allows us to put our argument to a comprehensive test. We detail the extent to which the decline of newspapers has affected citizens' access to information about local government, how that reduction in access has shaped local engagement – and how to reverse the trend.

Documenting the Decline in Local News

In order to demonstrate that the demise of local newspapers contributes to declines in citizen engagement, an essential first step is to document the reduction in the availability of local political news across the country and over time. Yet this has mostly proven elusive in the existing literature. While a great deal of work surveys the local news landscape, most is

---

[24] Gimpel, Dyck, and Shaw 2006.
[25] Atwater, Fico, and Pizante 1987; Nielsen 2015; Vliegenthart and Walgrave 2008.
[26] McLeod, Daily, and Guo 1996.
[27] Bentley 2001, p. 2; see also Berelson 1949.
[28] Putnam 2000, p. 233.

based on studies of single cities, a small subset of political units (such as congressional districts), specific categories of candidates (such as incumbents), or a particular region. Moreover, it often covers just a single year or a couple of election cycles.[29] Some of the most prominent recent accounts are mainly anecdotal.[30]

The research that has adopted a wider scope and time frame faces limitations of its own. The most well-known is the University of North Carolina's series of "news deserts" reports, which detail how hundreds of counties across the United States have been left without newspapers.[31] This valuable project has shone a spotlight on the particular struggles of weekly newspapers, which represent the vast majority of closures since the early 2000s.[32] But throughout the last 20 years, the phenomenon most commonly affecting communities is not the death of a newspaper but the hollowing out of the dailies that survive. Understanding the consequences of that development thus requires data on how coverage of local politics has changed in the news outlets that remain. The handful of studies that have taken up this charge, however, draw conflicting conclusions, likely a result of measurement differences.[33] The upshot is that although the existing research offers insight into the local news environment in particular places, at particular times, or when a paper closes, there is less consensus on how the roiling of the media landscape has affected coverage of local politics, whether reductions have been more severe in some places, and why.

To offer a fuller account of the changing local news environment, we rely in Chapters 2 and 3 on an original database that includes measures of the amount of various types of local political coverage spanning three decades, more than 200 newspapers, and every state. Across the board, we find a dramatic reduction in the volume of reporting about local

---

[29] As examples, see Arnold 2004; Clarke and Evans 1983; Delli Carpini, Keeter, and Kennamer 1994; Durkin, Glaisyer, and Hadge 2010; Fogarty 2013; Fowler et al. 2007; Gershon 2012, 2013; Goldenberg and Traugott 1984; Hayes and Lawless 2015, 2018; Larson 1992; Manheim 1974; Martin and McCrain 2019; Napoli et al. 2017; Orman 1985; Ryfe et al. 2012; Snyder and Strömberg 2010; Tidmarch and Karp 1983; Vermeer 1987; Vinson 2003.
[30] Sullivan 2020.
[31] Abernathy 2020.
[32] See also Ferrier, Sinha, and Outrich 2016.
[33] For instance, Peterson (2021) shows that staff cuts at local newspapers between 2007 and 2015 significantly reduced the volume of local political coverage. Hopkins (2018), however, finds no clear time trend in coverage of state and local politics in big city newspapers between 1981 and 2013. One reason for the discrepancy could be that Hopkins focuses on the ratio of local (or state) to national coverage, rather than the total volume.

government. Although papers of all sizes suffered, the reductions were most severe at the smallest outlets, which often serve rural, less affluent communities. We also show that reporting cuts were the largest in the beats that publishers and editors viewed as least profitable, such as county government and schools. And drawing on data from dozens of local television stations and hundreds of local internet start-ups, we demonstrate that other outlets have largely failed to fill the void when newspapers have pulled back. Together, these data, plus interviews with three dozen journalists grappling with these changes in newsrooms around the country, illustrate a profound gutting of the local information environment since the late 1990s.

Establishing a Relationship between Local News and Citizen Engagement

Although the decline in local government coverage seems almost certain to have reduced political engagement, this argument has proven difficult to test. The existing research on the relationship between news coverage and civic participation falls into three categories. One class of studies identifies correlations between citizens' news usage and various measures of political knowledge or participation.[34] While suggestive, such data do not provide evidence that media coverage *causes* political engagement, since some third factor – say, political interest – could drive both news consumption and engagement.

A second approach examines the relationship between political engagement and local media market characteristics, such as the size or structure of television markets, the overlap between media markets and political districts, or the diffusion of new communication technology.[35] Market characteristics determine how much news content is available to local consumers, and so should affect the distribution of knowledge or levels of participation. Although this body of research produces better causal evidence, it typically relies on an assumption – not a demonstration – that the availability of news coverage itself is actually the mechanism that drives engagement.

---

[34] See, e.g., Hoffman and Eveland 2010; McLeod, Scheufele, and Moy 1999.
[35] See, e.g., Althaus and Trautman 2008; Cohen, Noel, and Zaller 2004; Delli Carpini, Keeter, and Kennamer 1994; Gentzkow 2006; Mondak 1995; Moskowitz 2021; Peterson 2019; Schulhofer-Wohl and Garrido 2011; Shaker 2014; Snyder and Strömberg 2010.

The third and most persuasive set of studies on the effects of the recent local journalism crisis relies on a quasi-experimental exploitation of newspaper closures. For instance, research has found short-term reductions in civic engagement after the shutdowns of the *Cincinnati Post*, *Seattle Post-Intelligencer*, and *Rocky Mountain News*.[36] But case studies of single cities naturally raise questions of generalizability, and the short time frame makes it hard to estimate the long-term effects. In a broader project, researchers demonstrated that the closure of more than 100 newspapers in counties across the United States led to decreases in split-ticket voting, perhaps because voters had less information about local candidates.[37] Even here, though, the findings speak only to what happens when a community loses a news outlet. Studies of shuttered newspapers cannot detect the effect of more insidious declines in coverage at surviving papers.

To provide a more comprehensive assessment, in Chapters 4 and 5 we analyze a wide array of data – aggregate and individual-level, cross-sectional and panel – to leverage longitudinal variation in both news coverage and numerous indicators of political engagement. Our use of polling data, election returns, and online search behavior together provide compelling evidence that reductions in local newspaper coverage have depressed citizen engagement at the local level. We also demonstrate that the effects have been widespread, reducing knowledge and participation not just among the least politically interested but for virtually everyone. Because the local media environment is far less diverse than the national landscape, when newspaper coverage falls away, all citizens – even the segment of the population who wants to follow local news and keep abreast of local politics – find themselves with few alternatives for local political information.

Reinvigorating Citizen Interest in Local News

With local news dwindling and citizen engagement following close behind, it is clear that communities across the United States are facing an information crisis. But that doesn't mean these trends are irreversible. In recent years, industry innovators and numerous philanthropic organizations have found ways to shore up newspapers' finances, create new revenue models, and begin to rebuild their decimated reporting capacity. In a few big cities, successful local news start-ups have emerged. While

[36] Schulhofer-Wohl and Garrido 2011; Shaker 2014.
[37] Darr, Hitt, and Dunaway 2018.

there is no magic bullet, these collective efforts have helped stave off wholesale industry extinction. But for the local news business to provide citizens with the information they need to carry out their democratic responsibilities, more needs to be done.

One way to address local news' supply problem – not enough money or staff to cover local government – is a demand-side solution. This is essential because the root of the current crisis is a shrinking audience; newspapers are dying because many consumers have abandoned them.[38] Yet little research focuses explicitly on how to increase demand for local news. Part of the challenge is the scattershot nature of the message about why local journalism is worth saving. In many cases, journalists and reformers focus on what society would lose if local news disappeared – a strategy that may succeed in worrying consumers but fail to change their news habits. Moreover, political interest and news consumption tend to be stable, habitual, and resistant to change, making quite daunting the task of altering people's attitudes or behavior.[39]

But in Chapter 6, we argue that boosting citizen demand for local news doesn't necessarily involve changing people's minds. Rather, merely telling people about the importance of local government or reminding them that local politics is critical to the civic health of their communities may be sufficient to increase their consumption of local news. Using original survey data, we show that large majorities of Americans believe that local politics is important, relevant, and part of being a good citizen. For them, activating these attitudes so that they play a more pronounced role in shaping news habits can boost their demand for local news. For people who don't know what local government does or how relevant it is, informing them of its importance increases their motivation to follow local news. In a series of experiments – drawn from nationally representative samples, a multi-wave survey of Democrats, and exit polls with actual voters in two elections – we show that simple interventions can increase interest in local news. These efforts are successful with younger and older people alike, allowing us to close a large generation gap in local news interest that otherwise signals even more difficult days ahead for the industry. The challenges facing local news remain formidable, but reminding Americans about the importance of local government can create a virtuous circle that boosts both civic engagement and the local

---

[38] Hindman 2018.
[39] Arceneaux, Johnson, and Maes 2012; Prior 2019; Weinschenk and Dawes 2017.

news business – rather than the downward spiral that newspapers find themselves in today.

In *Democracy in America*, Alexis de Tocqueville famously observed that for democracy to work, communities need a shared source of information and sense of purpose. Otherwise, the prospects for collective civic engagement are dim. "Hardly any democratic association can carry on," he wrote, "without a newspaper."[40] Nearly two centuries later, the French scholar would recognize little about the modern media landscape, but his essential observation about the importance of local news sources remains true. Americans' engagement with local politics depends in significant measure on access to quality reporting about their local community and elected officials. The continued erosion of the nation's newspapers threatens democratic governance in cities, counties, and school districts across the United States.

The diminishing local news environment poses at least four problems for democratic governance. The first is that it makes it more difficult for citizens to hold government accountable. At the heart of the democratic process is, to use Abraham Lincoln's famous words, government "by the people." The public must have the ability to keep tabs on their local officials so that they can decide at election time whether to keep them in office or send them packing. Because most of the work of government happens beyond citizens' direct observation, residents rely on an independent news media to learn about local politics – from what goes on in city council meetings to policies being considered by the school board to the mayor's peccadilloes. Without local news coverage, the public has little ability or incentive to monitor their local government and hold their representatives accountable on Election Day.

Second, an impoverished news environment undermines incentives for elected officials to act competently, efficiently, and ethically. If the public isn't watching – because there's little in the way of news coverage – then politicians can misbehave without paying a price at the polls.[41] Indeed, regular coverage of municipal politics is associated with less fiscal mismanagement and government waste.[42] Sustained media coverage makes it

---

[40] de Tocqueville 1969, p. 518.
[41] Larreguy, Marshall, and Snyder 2020.
[42] Gao, Lee, and Murphy 2020.

more difficult for political leaders to inflate their salaries.[43] And in places with more local news outlets, politicians fall under pressure to reduce toxic emissions and improve the community's environment.[44] Part of the reason government officials respond to news coverage is that they worry about electoral challenges. But when newspaper coverage declines, so do the number of people running for local office, undermining one mechanism of accountability.[45] Although a robust local news media by no means ensures good government, its absence almost guarantees worse government.

Third, local news can help promote effective representation. Government works best, is viewed as more legitimate, and engenders more trust when citizens are widely engaged. When few people vote or when a large portion of the electorate is unaware of their elected officials' actions, government policies are unlikely to represent the public's will. We recognize, of course, that participation and representation have been less than universal in America's cities and towns for decades. But the weakening of the local news media may exacerbate existing inequalities. If coverage of local government grows even more scarce and engagement in local politics becomes even more concentrated among a minority of citizens, representation may fall even further from the democratic ideal.

Finally, the decline of local news and political engagement threatens the foundations of American federalism. When the Framers designed the US Constitution, their decision to vest power in state governments – and state governments' authority to give power to local governments – created a counterweight to the federal government. If national leaders took actions that ran contrary to the interests of states or localities, then local officials would have the power to push back with support from their own constituents. That process, however, only works if citizens can discern how federal policies affect their own community – how local law enforcement responds to federal immigration laws or how superintendents interpret Centers for Disease Control and Prevention (CDC) guidelines for reopening schools amid a pandemic. Without a vibrant local news media, it's unlikely that citizens can acquire that information. The US political system is sometimes convoluted and always complicated, but one of its

---

[43] Mary Ellen Klas, "Less Local News Means Less Democracy," *Nieman Reports*, September 20, 2019. https://niemanreports.org/articles/less-local-news-means-less-democracy/ (September 16, 2020).

[44] Campa 2018.

[45] Rubado and Jennings 2020.

virtues is the built-in tension between local and national forces. Without local news, that productive tension could turn to slack.

At a time when political observers worry – justifiably – about the health of the United States' national political institutions, threats to local democratic governance cannot be ignored. The local news media – by providing accurate information to citizens about what is happening in city halls, county governments, school boards, and other local political institutions throughout the country – constitute a vital link in the democratic process. Political representation and government effectiveness thus depend on reinvigorating the local news media and the citizen engagement that goes along with it. It can be done, but without a collective effort by citizens, journalists, and groups committed to strengthening local journalism, the long-term health of American democracy may be in peril.

2

The Great Gutting of US Newspapers

To be a resident of Denver, Colorado, in the latter decades of the twentieth century was to enjoy a feast of local news reporting. Home to two prizewinning newspapers, the *Rocky Mountain News* and the *Denver Post*, the city saw fierce competition to break stories about state and local government. The papers battled for scoops about malfeasance in the local police department, zoning fights in City Hall, and the aftermath of the Columbine school shooting. "We were two worthy adversaries," one former reporter said, "and the public benefited."[1]

But mounting financial pressure in the late 1990s forced the *News* and the *Post* into a joint operating agreement as a way to cut costs. The maneuver proved only a Band-Aid. In the wake of the 2008 financial crisis, the *News* shuttered its newsroom for good. Denver suddenly found itself with a single daily paper covering a metro area of 2.5 million people. And things were about to get worse. In 2010, the *Post* filed for bankruptcy and was purchased by a New York hedge fund. Major layoffs and cutbacks followed, damaging the paper's ability to cover the city. In 2018, the *Post*'s journalists revolted, publishing a scathing editorial and accusing the new owners of having "murdered" the paper. "We know

[1] Kevin Simpson, "Across the Battle Lines: How Rocky Mountain News Reporters Regarded the Angst – and Comedy – of Competition with the Denver Post," *Denver Post*, October 15, 2017. www.denverpost.com/2017/10/15/rocky-mountain-news-denver-post-rivalry/ (September 23, 2020).

meaningful work will not get done because talented journalists have left the organization," said the paper's editor.[2]

The story of Denver in many ways illustrates the local news crisis that we document in this chapter. Once the nation's preeminent news sources, daily newspapers have in recent years seen a massive reduction in their reporting capacity. As a result, residents of cities and counties across the United States now have access to less coverage of their local governments than at any time in modern American history. As the potential for new sources of local news, such as internet start-ups, remains uncertain, the prospect of an unprecedented information crisis looms on the local horizon.

THE RISE AND FALL OF US NEWSPAPERS

For the US newspaper industry, the middle of the twentieth century was a period of extraordinary popularity and profit. In the early 1940s, newspaper subscriptions stood at 41 million, a remarkably large share for a country of 133 million residents (see Figure 2.1).[3] And as the population and the economy continued to grow in the postwar years, so did the industry's fortunes. By 1950, one estimate put the newspaper household penetration rate – a measure of market saturation – at 124%. With more newspaper subscriptions than US households, newspaper owners regularly enjoyed double-digit profit margins.[4]

But the boom times wouldn't last much longer. With the invention and rapid diffusion of television, newspapers lost their monopoly and found themselves facing a fierce new competitor for consumers' attention. Indeed, although raw circulation continued to climb through the mid-1980s (peaking in 1984 at 63 million), that growth resulted primarily from an expanding population, not an increase in newspapers' popularity. By the time cable and satellite television gave Americans even more news and entertainment choices in the early 1990s, just 68% of US

---

[2] Sydney Ember, "Denver Post Rebels against Its Hedge-Fund Ownership," *New York Times*, April 7, 2018. www.nytimes.com/2018/04/07/business/media/denver-post-opinion-owner.html (September 23, 2020).

[3] Pew 2019a.

[4] Alan Mutter, "Are Newspapers Losing 'Mass Media' Mojo?" *Newsosaur*, November 4, 2013. http://newsosaur.blogspot.com/2013/11/are-newspapers-losing-mass-media-mojo.html (February 24, 2020).

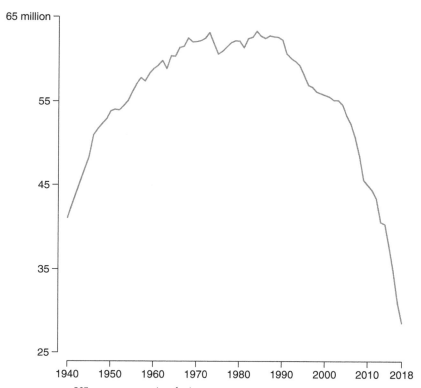

FIGURE 2.1. US newspaper circulation, 1940–2018.
Source: Pew Research Center 2019a. The data represent weekday circulation, including digital subscribers.

households subscribed to a newspaper.[5] As daily circulation fell throughout the decade, the alarm bells were ringing. But industry leaders were unprepared for what was next. "You couldn't get the attention of the major publishers," Kelly Fry, editor and publisher of the *Oklahoman*, told us in one of the dozens of interviews we conducted with journalists at newspapers across the country. "They couldn't see what was coming."[6]

What was coming was a revolution in the way people get information. When the Internet became widely available to Americans in the late

---

[5] Alan Mutter, "Are Newspapers Losing 'Mass Media' Mojo?" *Newsosaur*, November 4, 2013. http://newsosaur.blogspot.com/2013/11/are-newspapers-losing-mass-media-mojo.html (February 24, 2020).

[6] See Appendix A for a description of our sampling procedures, protocols, and interview questions.

1990s, consumers' choices for news and entertainment exploded. By 2000, more than half of Americans said they regularly went online. For the heaviest print news consumers – college graduates – it was more than three-quarters.[7] Although it would take years for the online news ecosystem to develop fully, internet-savvy consumers who wanted to keep up with current events could do so without paying for a newspaper subscription.

What happened next is well known: The newspaper industry fell off a cliff. Circulation plummeted so precipitously – with a not-so-gentle nudge from the financial crisis of 2008 – that by 2018, it had fallen to 28.6 million (down 55% from its 1984 peak). It's easy to read the line in Figure 2.1 as a giant frown from newspaper executives.

The increased competition from television, cable, satellite, and the Internet struck at the heart of newspapers' economic model – advertising – in two ways. First, smaller newspaper audiences reduced the value of advertising; fewer eyeballs meant fewer possible customers. Second, the Internet fundamentally changed the advertising landscape. Facebook, Google, and other online behemoths could use cookies, browsing histories, and other personal data to match advertisers with consumers in a way that newspapers never could. The Internet also created new forums for advertising. Sites such as Craigslist would allow people, at no cost, to sell their old furniture or rent their apartments. No longer would they have to pay newspapers to reach potential buyers.

The financial consequences of these changes began to become clear in the mid-2000s. Although newspaper advertising revenue grew steadily through 2005 (see Figure 2.2), it began to decline sharply in 2006. By 2018, advertising revenue was down 71% from just 12 years earlier, even accounting for newspaper websites' digital advertising. This "revenue issue," in the words of one reporter at a mid-sized paper in the Midwest, came to pose an existential threat. "People aren't picking up the print product, which has historically been the money maker. As we've moved online, the advertising dollars don't transfer equally, and so we need to be more efficient and more innovative and at the same time continue to cover the news," he told us. "That might be impossible to do." Jeff Parrott, who covers city politics and government for the much smaller *South Bend Tribune* identified the same problem. "People want to read online for free .... And that means there's no business model

---

[7] Pew 2019b.

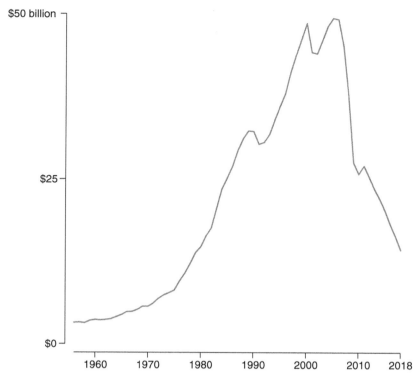

FIGURE 2.2. US newspaper advertising revenue, 1956–2018
Source: Pew Research Center 2019c.

anymore because advertising doesn't pay the same for online ads," he explained. Newspapers found themselves faced with a dilemma that was the opposite of a rap lyric: less money, more problems.

Faced with declining advertising revenue, newspapers across the country responded predictably: They shut down or shrunk. Since 2004, more than 2,000 US newspapers have closed.[8] The vast majority were small weeklies, but several prominent dailies, including the *Seattle Post-Intelligencer* and the *Youngstown Vindicator*, shuttered as well. The more common effect of the financial upheaval, however, has been staff reductions at the nation's 7,000 remaining newspapers.[9] In the last 12 years,

[8] Abernathy 2018a.
[9] As an indicator of the connection between newspapers' finances and their reporting capacity, the correlation between annual advertising revenue and the number of newsroom employees is 0.96.

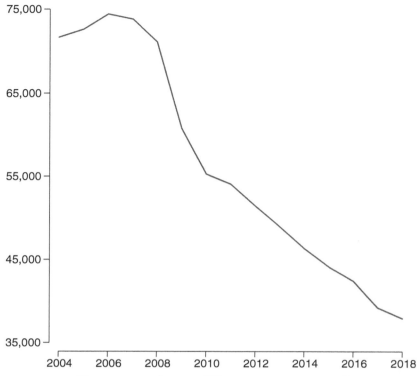

FIGURE 2.3. Newsroom employees at US newspapers, 2004–2018
Source: Pew Research Center 2019c.

the number of newspaper newsroom employees – reporters, editors, and photo and video staff – has fallen by 49% (see Figure 2.3).[10]

Some of that, of course, is due to newspaper closures. But the newspapers still in business now employ fewer journalists. In 2004, there were on average 8.1 newsroom staff for every newspaper operating in the United States. Today, that number is down to just 5.5.[11] The result has been a fundamental change to reporters' work lives. When Alex Rose started at the *Delaware County Daily Times* in 2004, for example, he recalls 12 to 15 full-time reporters, about 40 correspondents, and a group

[10] Peterson's (2021) analysis of staffing data from an annual newsroom census and newspaper directories reports similar trends.
[11] To arrive at this number, we divided newsroom employment data from the Pew Research Center by the number of newspapers in business, as identified by the News Deserts Project.

of summer interns. Fast forward 15 years and the newsroom is unrecognizable. "We don't really have beats anymore because we don't have the manpower," he explained. "We're down to two staff reporters and three others who pitch in for us when we borrow them from other local papers in our network." The *Toledo Blade* has three times the circulation as the *Delaware County Daily Times*, but has found itself in a nearly identical situation. "It's not the newsroom it was when I walked in the door [in 2000]," *Blade* Executive Editor Kurt Franck lamented. "We had 170 people then, and now we're at a little more than half of that. We used to have a Washington bureau, and we don't have that anymore." Darrell Ehrlick, a political reporter at the *Billings Gazette* couldn't say exactly how many colleagues he's lost over the years because he "quit counting after 30 rounds of cuts from layoffs." Said one reporter laid off from the *Philadelphia Inquirer* in 2007, "The guillotine has finally fallen."[12]

A closer look at a selection of 40 large regional papers provides another window into how the changing economic fortunes of newspapers has hollowed out newsrooms across the country. Most of these outlets are the "paper of record" for their city, and often for their state, constituting the primary source of information about the activities of local and state governments. Between 2000 and 2009, three-quarters reported cuts to their news executives and editorial management, according to figures compiled by the trade publication *Editor & Publisher* (see Figure 2.4). This includes positions like editorial page editor, city editor, arts editor, as well as some lower-level positions.

Among the 30 papers in this group reporting cuts, the average decline from the beginning to the end of the decade was substantial: 45%. In terms of raw numbers, this amounts to an average reduction of 12.8 newsroom managers – the equivalent of firing more than one person per year. Some publications – such as the *Detroit Free Press*, which cut 76% – slashed more severely than others. The *Newark Star-Ledger* in 2000 reported 40 news managers, but only 17 by 2009. Cuts by the *Providence Journal* – which was down from 29 newsroom managers in 2000 to 16 by 2009 – were typical. Just five papers saw increases during this period, and another five reported no change.[13]

---

[12] Katharine Q. Seelye, "Layoffs Imminent at Philadelphia Inquirer," *New York Times*, January 3, 2007. www.nytimes.com/2007/01/03/business/media/03paper.html (March 14, 2020).

[13] See Appendix B for a description of our source and method for collecting staffing data.

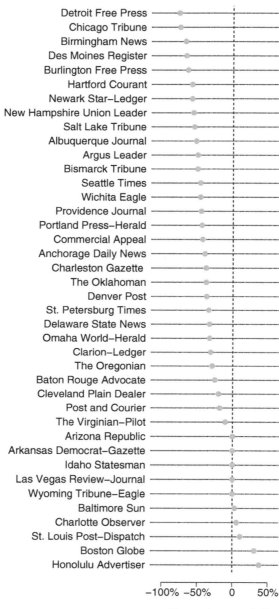

FIGURE 2.4. Changes in news staff at selected regional papers, 2000–2009
Note: See Appendix B for a description of our source and method for collecting staffing data.
Source: Data compiled from volumes of *Editor & Publisher's International Yearbook.*

These staff cuts didn't immediately bring newspapers to their knees. Publishers and editors restructured newsrooms, reassigned reporters, and publicly championed the idea of "doing more with less." Forced to prioritize, maybe newspapers could serve the interest of the public with a leaner and more nimble corps of journalists. Maybe these changes wouldn't diminish consumers' access to critical information about their local governments. Maybe it would all work out. But as we demonstrate in the next section, the reality, predicted in 2009 by former *New York Times* editor Bill Keller, was that "what you can do with less, is less."[14]

TRACKING LOCAL NEWS COVERAGE OVER TIME

Even as they suffer financially, newspapers remain the primary providers of local public affairs reporting across the United States. As recently as 2019, media scholars Philip Napoli and Jessica Mahone in a study of local media ecosystems characterized newspapers as "by far, the most significant providers of journalism in their communities."[15] Local television remains popular, and internet start-ups have tried to break into the business of local news. But when it comes to substantive reporting about local politics, those outlets provide just a fraction of the coverage that newspapers do – a point we return to later in this chapter. Accordingly, tracking changes in the local political coverage daily newspapers provide is essential for understanding the extent to which local communities are losing a key source of civic engagement.

Sample of Daily Newspapers

In order to measure local political coverage in newspapers across the country and over time, we first identified the largest circulating daily newspaper in each of the 435 US House districts.[16] These local outlets have the largest reach and thus the broadest consequences for citizens'

[14] Zachary M. Seward, "NYT's Keller: 'What You Can with Less, Is Less'," *Neiman Lab*, November 9, 2009. www.niemanlab.org/2009/11/nyts-keller-what-you-can-do-with-less-is-less/ (April 2, 2020).

[15] Philip Napoli and Jessica Mahone, "Local Newspapers Are Suffering, but They're Still (By Far) the Most Significant Journalism Producers in Their Communities," *Nieman Lab*, September 9, 2019. www.niemanlab.org/2019/09/local-newspapers-are-suffering-but-theyre-still-by-far-the-most-significant-journalism-producers-in-their-communities/ (March 14, 2020). See also Hindman 2018.

[16] This is based on 2014 circulation data.

political engagement. We then narrowed the sample to papers we could access through NewsBank, whose archives go back further in time than other databases. Because our research question demands a longitudinal analysis, we further restricted our list of papers to the 202 with consecutive coverage dating back at least to 2003. For 60%, or 121, of these papers, the full-text archives dated back to 1996. In addition to giving us at least one paper from every state, the diverse sample also captures the largest paper in each state. In 13 cases, the largest state paper was not available in NewsBank, so we accessed the archives through ProQuest. In the handful of cases in which a state's largest paper was unavailable from either database, we included instead the paper in the state with the second-largest circulation.[17] It is important to note that because of the way these electronic databases archive content, our data include content published on newspapers' websites as well as in their print editions.

The data set reflects coverage in different kinds of communities across the country and variation in the size of the paper as well as the size and characteristics of the markets. In our full data set, the smallest paper, the *Suffolk News-Herald* in Virginia, had a daily circulation in 2014 of only 5,012. At the other end of the continuum, the *New York Times*' daily circulation exceeded two million. Although our data set does not include many especially small newspapers (or any weeklies), the overall story we tell likely plays out in those as well.

Content Analysis of News Coverage

Once we assembled the sample of papers, we conducted a content analysis to collect three essential measures for detailing the decline of local news during the late 1990s and the first two decades of the 2000s. First, we tracked the amount of local political coverage in each newspaper. For each year, we identified in each paper the number of news stories that contained references to several major topics pertaining to local public affairs. Specifically, we collected data on coverage of mayors, city and town councils, local school boards, and county governments. US localities have a diverse set of political institutions, but these four constitute the key governmental bodies in the vast majority of communities. Thus, the way that newspapers across the country have covered these topics over time

---

[17] See Appendix C for a description of the sample and Appendix D for a list of the newspapers.

should reflect their attention to local politics more generally. Moreover, our four areas of focus have been identified as the primary topics of local political news coverage in research using methodologies different than ours.[18]

Second, we collected data to contextualize changes in local political coverage. By tracking news stories published about national politics (the president and Congress), the governor, and the four major professional team sports (basketball, baseball, football, and hockey), we can characterize not only how newspaper coverage of local government has changed in absolute terms, but also how that coverage has changed compared to other types of content.

Third, we created a measure of the "news hole" – an industry term that refers to the amount of space for editorial content once advertising has been placed. This includes news stories, but also entertainment, obituaries, and the many other items that appear in the paper. For each paper, we collected the total number of items it published each year, regardless of the topic. This measure is critical for an assessment of how publishers responded to their sinking financial fortunes. With increasingly limited space for news, what did they prioritize? The existing work on the decline of local news focuses on either changes to the overall volume of local politics coverage or the ratio of local to national coverage. Our measure of the news hole provides the first opportunity to determine whether coverage of local government suffered larger cuts than other newspaper content.[19]

THE CATASTROPHIC LOSS OF LOCAL NEWS REPORTING

We begin by describing the disappearance of the news hole over the last 25 years. Drawing on the 121 papers for which we have data stretching back to 1996, the drop in circulation and loss of advertising clearly shrunk the space newspapers had for editorial content (see Figure 2.5). In 1996, the papers in our sample published on average about 35,000 items per year – roughly 100 per day. Of course, there is a lot of variation. The *Los Angeles Times*' news hole 20 years ago was around 100,000. *The*

---

[18] Martin and McCrain 2019; Peterson 2021.

[19] Despite our fairly blunt method of analysis – keyword searches – we are confident that our approach effectively picks up stories specific to the individuals and institutions that comprise each category of news coverage. Appendix E includes details about our search procedures, as well as a discussion of the reliability and accuracy of our measures of local news content.

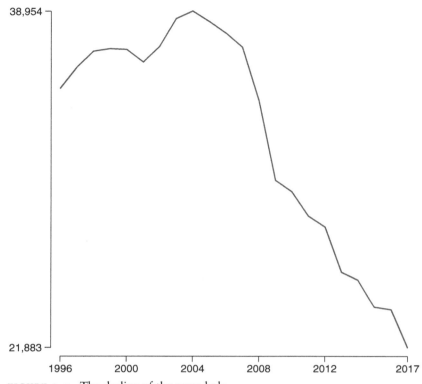

FIGURE 2.5. The decline of the news hole
Note: Results are based on the 121 newspapers for which we have content dating back to 1996 (see Appendix D). The measure of the "news hole" represents the total number of items a paper published each year, once advertising had been placed.

Spokesman-Review, in the considerably smaller Spokane, Washington, was publishing only about one-fifth of that. Other papers published even less. But on average, the news hole increased throughout the late 1990s and the early years of the 2000s, hitting a peak of about 39,000 in 2004.

And then the bottom fell out. By 2008, the news hole had in just four years decreased by 12%. This change was merely the start of what would amount to a catastrophic decline in the volume of news produced by local papers. By 2017, the news hole had contracted by 43% (compared to 2004). With advertising moving online and to other sources, local newspapers were shrinking to a degree that shocked almost anyone who had worked in the newspaper business in the halcyon days of the early 1990s.

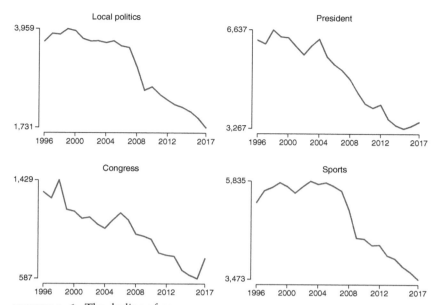

FIGURE 2.6. The decline of news coverage

Note: Results are based on the 121 newspapers for which we have content dating back to 1996 (see Appendix D). For specific search terms used to identify local politics, president, Congress, and sports stories, see Appendix E.

As size of the newspaper shrunk, the volume of news coverage withered. Consider first coverage of local politics. In the upper left-hand panel of Figure 2.6, we plot the average number of stories about local politics published each year in the papers in our sample. In the late 1990s, newspapers published on average about 4,000 stories about city hall, county governments, and other topics every year – roughly 11 articles every day. But beginning in the early 2000s, local government coverage began to fall, a decline that accelerated dramatically following the financial crisis of 2008. Between 1999 and 2017, the volume of local politics news dropped by more than half (56%). At the close of 2017, newspapers were publishing fewer than five local politics stories per day.

Reductions in coverage can't be divorced from the fact that reporters were disappearing from the newsroom. The experience of newspapers in some of Alabama's major cities is illustrative. Between 1996 and 2011, local politics coverage at the *Press-Register* in Mobile fell by about 10%. That meant fewer stories every day about the city council or Mobile County public schools. At the *Birmingham News*, local government

coverage fell by 24% over that same period. But when the two papers'
owner, Advance Publications, announced in the fall of 2012 the decision
to suspend print publication for all but three days each week and dismiss
hundreds of staff, things got even worse. By 2017, coverage of local
government in both papers was less than half of what it had been before
the layoffs. John Sharp, who covers the Mobile area for AL.com, the
umbrella site for the *Birmingham News* and *Press-Register*, told us that
the newsroom can still cover major local stories, but much less thoroughly
than the old days. "The difference between now and the early 2000s is
that we would have had more reporters to go around and cover different
angles [of the same story]," he said. "Now, it's pretty much me."

The lament is similar at papers all over the country. Twenty-five years
ago, the *New Hampshire Union Leader* published on average more than
seven local government stories each day. Now, with a dwindling team of
reporters handling multiple beats and scrambling to cover huge swaths of
the region, it's down to about four – a reduction of close to 40%. "This
afternoon, I'm going to a New England Patriots event about opioid
addition. I'm covering the Durham holiday parade and the need for a
menorah. I'm doing a feature on a woman who is going on a moose
hunt," Kim Haas, one of the paper's correspondents, told us in the fall of
2019. "And then of course, I need to see if there are any interesting arrests
or happenings in local government. And that's just this afternoon."
Reporters at other papers said that investigative reporting "is done," that
their stories are "undercooked," and that they can't talk to folks on the
street because "ground level reporting is too time consuming." At the
South Bend Tribune, Parrott was candid: "We're doing less coverage
overall, for sure. No one I know is willing to work without getting paid.
And we're not paid to work more than 40 hours."[20]

To be sure, newspapers didn't slash only their coverage of local politics. The remaining three panels of Figure 2.6 display the average number
of stories about the president, Congress, and sports. Although the trends
are slightly different for each topic, local newspapers carry significantly
less news about everything than they did two decades ago.[21]

These changes are closely related to the reduction of the news hole, as
illustrated in Figure 2.7. Start again with the upper left-hand panel, which

---

[20] See Peterson (2021) for more evidence of the way that newspaper staffing affects local
political reporting.
[21] We also measured attention to state politics (specifically, the governor), and the trend is
similar to the graphs displayed in Figure 2.6.

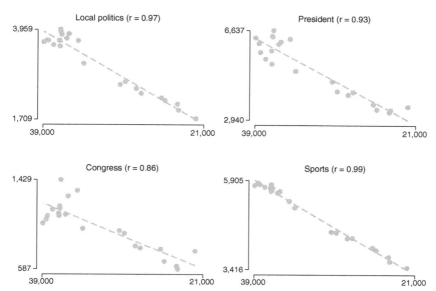

FIGURE 2.7. The shrinking news hole and the decline of news coverage
Note: Results are based on the 121 newspapers for which we have content dating back to 1996 (see Appendix D). Each dot represents a year, and the placement of the dot indicates the size of the news hole (on the horizontal axis) and the number of each type of news story (on the vertical axis) published that particular year.

plots coverage of local politics. Each dot in the panel represents a year, and the placement of the dot indicates the size of the news hole (the horizontal axis) and the number of local politics stories (the vertical axis) published that particular year. The diagonal line represents a summary of the average relationship. The downward slope indicates a strong correlation (0.97) between the two quantities: In the years when the news hole was small, papers published fewer stories about local politics. The same is true, with some variation, for the other topics as well. As advertising dollars disappeared, the news hole shrunk. And as the news hole goes, so goes news coverage.

What these correlations do not tell us, however, is whether the cuts to local politics were more or less severe than reductions of other topics. In other words, what content did publishers prioritize? Facing a steep drop in space for news – and perhaps more importantly, diminished reporting resources – publishers presumably had three options. First, they could cut everything equally across the board, reducing coverage of all topics by roughly the same amount. Second, they could cut national politics and sports more aggressively. Since that content was now available on cable news and the Internet, focusing on local politics coverage, which consumers couldn't get elsewhere, might be one way to capitalize on a product that local papers could still claim as a monopoly. Third, they could opt to preserve national coverage and sports reporting at the expense of local politics. Local public affairs reporting is relatively expensive, requiring a considerable amount of reporting staff and time. But coverage of national politics and (much) sports coverage could be drawn from wire service reporting. Once a newspaper subscribes to a wire service, there is no additional reporting cost, since a steady stream of content is available.

We consider these possibilities by examining the percentage of the news hole devoted to local politics, compared to other topics. By looking at the data this way, we can "hold constant" the available space for editorial content. If the share of the newspaper allocated to local politics declines more steeply than the share devoted to Congress or sports, for instance, it would suggest that publishers were less willing to commit resources to local government coverage in the face of a shrinking news hole. For this analysis, we focus on the sample of 202 newspapers for which we have data going back to 2003, the moment when the contraction of the news hole began in earnest.

Put simply, local government coverage was cut significantly more than other topics. The upper left-hand panel of Figure 2.8 plots the share of the news hole devoted to local politics from 2003 through 2017. At its peak, local government accounted for slightly less than 10% of the editorial content in the nation's daily newspapers. By 2017, that was down to less than 8%, representing a 20% cut. Even accounting for the shrinking news hole, publishers allocated one-fifth less of the paper to local government in 2017 than they had just 15 years earlier. These cuts were widespread: Seven out of 10 papers in our sample reduced the amount of the news hole devoted to local politics over this period.

At the same time, the trends for national politics and sports were very different. Between 2003 and 2015, presidential coverage, as a share of the news hole, declined by about 17%. But with the arrival of the 2016 election and the can't-look-away presidency of Donald Trump, stories about the president shot back up to 2004 levels. By 2017, they once again constituted more than 15% of the news hole. Perhaps more striking, the portion of congressional coverage actually grew over this period. Between 2003 and 2016, the percentage of stories mentioning Congress held steady, fluctuating no more than half a percentage point. But in 2017,

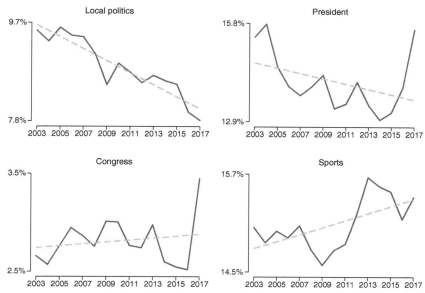

FIGURE 2.8. The decline of local politics and other topics as a share of the news hole

Note: Results are based on the 202 newspapers for which we have content dating back to 2003 (see Appendix D). Dotted lines are fitted linear estimates. For specific search terms used to identify local politics, president, Congress, and sports stories, see Appendix E.

that grew to 3.5%, higher than any year since 1998. It is impossible to say how much of this was the product of cost cutting by publishers or a reaction to the newsworthiness of the Trump presidency and Republican control of Congress. It is likely both. But it is clear that as the number of pages in the newspaper shrunk, news consumers found a larger percentage of them taken up with stories about politics in Washington, DC. Finally, the bottom right panel of the figure shows that as local public affairs reporting was de-emphasized, sports coverage became a growing share of the newspaper. In stark contrast to the widespread cuts to local politics, 53% of papers in our sample devoted *more* of their newsprint to sports in 2017 than in 2003.

In the early years of the twenty-first century, publishers had to make hard choices about what to save. In the aggregate, our data show that they chose to jettison the kind of public affairs reporting that sits at the heart of the democratic enterprise. With engagement in local politics declining at the same time, it is hard to imagine that the demise of newspapers wasn't at least partly responsible.

CAN LOCAL TV AND INTERNET START-UPS FILL THE VOID?

The counterpoint to our thus far gloomy assessment – Americans were losing access to essential local news from their most reliable source – is that the shrinking of newspapers coincided with an information revolution. As newspapers were imploding, electronic media were exploding, with new news and entertainment websites emerging seemingly every day in the early 2000s. Social media wasn't far behind. Moreover, local TV news remained, by some measures, the nation's most popular news source.[22] In that environment, the demise of newspapers might simply mean that consumers could stay informed by turning to the expanding array of other media sources.

In one respect, that's exactly what happened. Consumers interested in national politics, sports, and entertainment turned to cable stations and internet sites that could provide them more thorough and specialized coverage than even many of the best newspapers could. Even if consumers could no longer rely on their local papers for as much information about the New York Mets or President Obama's battles with Republicans in Congress, there were an increasing number of convenient other ways to get it. But for local politics, the options remained few. "It's not like the Huffington Post is going to show up at a Conway City planning commission meeting," said Tyler Fleming, a reporter at the *Sun News* in Myrtle Beach, South Carolina. As we will demonstrate, neither television nor the Internet have come to the rescue and stepped in to fill the hole left by legacy newspapers.

Local TV

One reason that local TV news might be viewed as a possible savior of local political engagement is that the industry has fared better financially in the last two decades than newspapers. In 2004, for instance, local TV advertising revenues were reported at $22.4 billion. In 2018, the number was $20.4.[23] Far be it for us to pooh-pooh a loss of $2 billion, but in the contemporary local news environment – and especially compared to

[22] Pew 2019c.
[23] Pew 2019c.

newspapers – this is not a dramatic drop. One reason for its relatively steady finances is that local TV remains popular, with a plurality of consumers telling pollsters that they get local news from TV broadcasts.[24] As a consequence, many outlets have avoided significant newsroom cuts; some have even grown.[25] And theoretically, the decline of local newspapers may have created an opening for local TV stations. By devoting more attention to local politics, they might be able to attract consumers who have grown dissatisfied with the diminished coverage their local newspapers provide when it comes to local government.

To investigate whether TV stepped up its public affairs coverage, we collected data from transcripts of local TV station archives in NewsBank. Electronically available broadcast transcript data are scarce, but we identified 31 stations with coverage going back to at least 2007 and over at least three consecutive years. The stations cover nine different markets in six states. For each of the 31 stations – local ABC, CBS, Fox, and NBC affiliates – we used the same search protocol we did for the newspaper content analysis to identify coverage that included discussion of local government (mayors, city government, and school boards).[26] We generated a measure of the news hole by calculating the percentage of transcripts for a given station in a given year that included discussion of local politics.[27]

The story from these data is clear: There is no evidence of a consistent uptick in coverage of local government. In Figure 2.9, each line represents the percentage of transcripts in which a story mentioned the mayor, city government, or the school board.[28] Let's say we consider it a change in local government coverage if stations in a market increased or decreased coverage by at least 1 percentage point from the beginning to the end of the time series. By that measure – a pretty minimal shift – our data show an increase in local politics coverage in three markets, a decline in four

---

[24] Wenger and Papper 2017.

[25] "Research 2019: Local TV and Radio News Strengths," Hofstra University Newsroom Survey. https://rtdna.org/article/2019_research_local_tv_and_radio_news_strengths (March 15, 2020).

[26] We could not include coverage of county government because there is exceedingly little of it on TV news.

[27] See Appendix F for a description of the content analysis of local TV news coverage.

[28] The overall percentages of local politics coverage are higher than in our newspaper data because these analyses are at the transcript (or broadcast) level, rather than the individual story level. If we calculated the percentage of newspaper editions (not stories) that included at least one mention of local politics, the number would almost certainly be several times higher than the percentages for local TV news.

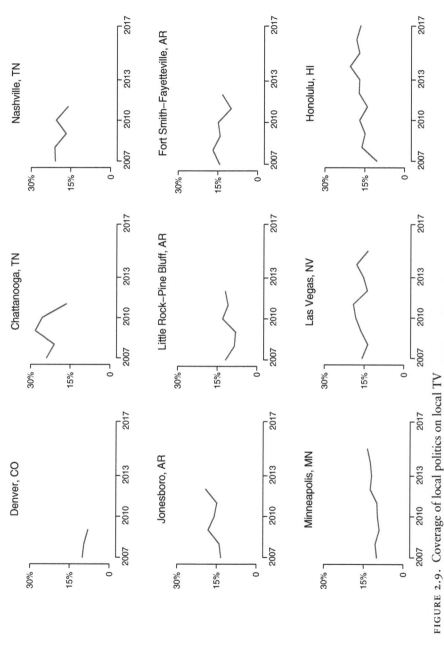

FIGURE 2.9. Coverage of local politics on local TV

Note: Results are based on transcripts of local TV stations' electronic archives in NewsBank. The sample includes 31 stations, which cover 9 markets, going back to at least 2007 and over at least 3 consecutive years (see Appendix F).

others, and no change in one. In the cities that saw increases, the changes are no more than 6 percentage points over 6–10 years. Although not nothing, these modest increases in local TV could hardly make up for declines in newspaper coverage that were sometimes 10 times the magnitude.

It's also worth noting that TV coverage of local politics tends to lack the depth of many newspaper articles. According to political scientists Gregory Martin and Joshua McCrain, "Mentions of local officials by name in news transcripts are rare . . .. That is, the average local news show mentions a state or local official by name about once every 6 months."[29] This may be why several of the newspaper reporters we interviewed said that they don't even consider the local TV stations as competition. In Ohio, for instance, the *Lima News* technically competes with one TV station but is not a true competitor because, according to reporter Josh Ellerbrook, "the network doesn't go very in-depth." *Honolulu Star-Advertiser* Kevin Dayton's assessment of the local television networks is similar. "TV has decided that government news isn't a priority for them," he told us. Columnist Linda Blackford said the same is true for the *Lexington Herald-Leader,* which competes with TV for advertisers, but "not for getting the local news scoop." Others mentioned that local television stations tend to be based in larger cities outside of their circulation area, so they don't even cover the specific community the newspaper reaches.

As newspapers have shed advertising revenue, slashed their newsrooms, and reduced local politics coverage, TV news has remained a profitable and popular source of news for many Americans. But our data offer no evidence that local stations in recent years have shifted their content in ways that could help bolster local political knowledge or participation. Indeed, local TV news is popular not because of its public affairs content, but because consumers like its staples: crime and weather.[30] It is an unlikely savior of citizens' political engagement.

Local News Start-Ups

If local TV isn't filling the void left by the decline of newspapers, what about the great informational hope of the twenty-first century – the Internet? Some observers have expressed optimism that local news

---

[29] See Martin and McCrain's (2019) appendix.
[30] Pew 2019d.

start-ups, crowd-sourcing, and the tools of social media would emerge to provide robust coverage of their local communities.[31] Not only could start-ups fill the gap left by the retrenchment of newspapers, but by positioning themselves as "hyperlocal," they might be able to cover their communities even more effectively than legacy news outlets. And with fewer expenses – no printing presses, limited distribution costs, and lean staffs – these outlets could thrive in the economic environment that has decimated mainstream news organizations.

To examine the plausibility of this argument, we draw on a data set of local news start-ups compiled by media scholar Michele McLellan.[32] To our knowledge, the list – known as "Michele's List" – is the most comprehensive current collection of local online-only news outlets.[33] To be included on the list, a start-up must be "devoted primarily to local news," update news reports "regularly," and meet a series of other standards common to news organizations, such as a commitment to accuracy. Although the list does not include every local internet site that occasionally posts news articles, it does account for exactly the type of sites that – if the Internet can step in where newspapers have stepped away – would inherit the mantle of substantive local news providers.

We started by examining the 462 sites based in the United States that, as of March 2020, had a working URL. We classified each site as including news or politics, or not. Our coding was generous; if any content touched on local news, we coded it as a "yes." This includes health care or business sites that provide information about elections, new ordinances or regulations, and the like. Sites we deemed devoid of politics included not even a modicum of anything resembling local news coverage.[34]

Overall, 400 sites (87% of those on the list) provided at least occasional coverage of news or politics. But delving deeper shows that over the course of the 2000s, online news organizations have not reached a point where they can be considered replacements for the journalism provided by thousands of local newspapers across the country. Few can even be considered supplements.

---

[31] Jimmy Wales and Orit Kopel, "The Internet Broke the News Industry – and Can Fix It, Too," *Foreign Policy*, October 19, 2019. https://foreignpolicy.com/2019/10/19/internet-broke-journalism-fake-news/ (September 22, 2020).

[32] "Michele's List." www.micheleslist.org/ (March 15, 2020).

[33] Hindman's (2018) analysis of online-only local news outlets is exhaustive, but it is based on data that are now a decade old.

[34] See Appendix G for a description of the content analysis of local news internet start-ups.

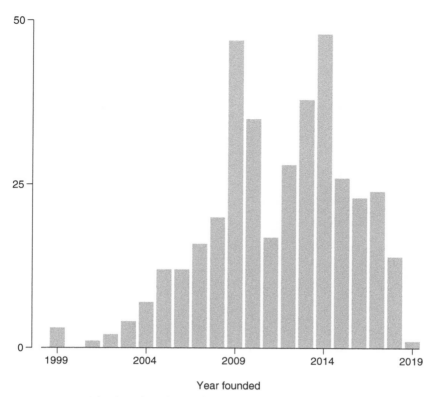

FIGURE 2.10. The founding dates of local news start-ups
Source: Michele's List, as of March 2020.

Consider first the year each site was founded (see Figure 2.10). The majority – 53% – listed a founding date of 2012 or later. Seventy-eight percent didn't exist before 2009. That means that most of these could have done very little to help recoup the loss of information left by the significant decline of newspapers in the first decade of the twenty-first century.

Not only does the timing suggest that local news start-ups haven't filled the void, but most of these sites are concentrated in a handful of (mostly urban) areas. In the Michele's List data set, fully 23% (95) are located in one state, New Jersey (see Figure 2.11). This is mostly a product of one large site with numerous affiliates (TAP). But it's not just New Jersey, or the TAP sites. Along with the Garden State, five other states with large urban areas and concentrated populations – California, New York, Pennsylvania, Massachusetts, and Texas – account for 50% of all the sites. The average number of local news start-ups in a state is nine, and

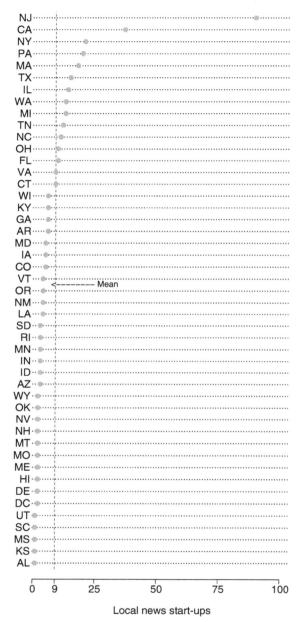

FIGURE 2.11. Local news start-ups, by state
Note: Dots indicate the number of local news start-ups as of March 2020. Data are from Michele's List.

most states have fewer. With a few exceptions, news start-ups are not serving the thousands of mid-size and small communities across the country that have traditionally been served by daily newspapers.

Even in the places where local news start-ups have established themselves, most have had a hard time gaining traction. In addition to infinitesimally small traffic numbers for all but a few, journalists we spoke with did not regard online news organizations as serious competition. Craig Brown, the editor of the *Columbian*, a small paper in Washington state, mentioned a couple of sites that, according to the paper's analytics, have "a loyal following, but not one that's growing." That's *Tulsa World* reporter Jason Collington's impression of the three or four websites that have sprung up in and around Oklahoma as well. "They try to do the news, although I have no evidence that they've grown an audience," he said. One reporter in Ohio referred us to an online news Facebook group – 419NewsNow – that has become popular. But when we visited the site – which has less than 6,000 members – we found not local news, but rather, links to national news stories about the coronavirus and an article about a Texas zoo that will name a rat after your ex and then feed it to a snake on Valentine's Day.[35] Tempting, for sure, but hardly the kind of thing that could allow news start-ups to meet the public service function that newspapers have fulfilled throughout US history.

CONCLUSION

The data presented in this chapter paint a portrait of a media landscape in which coverage of local politics has eroded substantially. Newspapers, facing tough financial times, had no choice but to scale back their reporting resources. Coverage of local politics took a disproportionate hit. As newspapers came to provide less and less reporting on their local governments, other venues did not step in to replace them. Whereas cable television and the Internet offer a steady stream of information about national politics, sports, and entertainment, the same isn't true for local political affairs. When newspapers stopped telling citizens what was happening in city hall or on their county commissions, there was no other place where citizens could find it. Thus, the retrenchment at local newspapers was most damaging to citizens' access to the kind of reporting that local newspapers were uniquely positioned to provide.

[35] "The New 419 News Now (Uncensored)." www.facebook.com/groups/1338687922887731/ (March 15, 2020).

Although the suffering at daily newspapers has been universal over the last two decades, cuts to local government reporting have not been the same at every outlet. Which kinds of papers, and what types of communities, have endured the biggest reductions in coverage of local politics? To what extent have newspapers deprioritized certain aspects of local government? And how have they made those decisions? Answering these questions is central for understanding the potential consequences that the erosion of local political coverage carries for citizen engagement. So these are the questions to which we turn in the next chapter.

3

Where Local News Has Suffered Most

As financial upheaval in the news business has cut a trail of destruction through newsrooms in recent years, the perilous state of local journalism has become a news story itself. Headlines have detailed the struggles of newspapers all over the country. National media outlets have recounted the fierce legal battles for control of big city papers such as the *Chicago Tribune*[1] and the *Los Angeles Times*,[2] as well the mighty challenges facing respected regional outlets such as the *Dallas Morning News*.[3] When the *New York Daily News* in 2018 became just the latest New York City paper to announce plans to cut its newsroom – in this case by half – one headline lamented, "The city that never sleeps finds that it's running out of reporters to report."[4]

Meanwhile, concern about the health of newspapers in the nation's smallest communities has been equally acute. Of the more than 2,000

---

[1] David Folkenflik, "Fresh Newsroom Cuts at Tribune Stir Mistrust as 'Vulture' Investor Looms," *National Public Radio*, May 20, 2020. www.npr.org/2020/05/20/859241046/ fresh-newsroom-cuts-at-tribune-stir-mistrust-as-vulture-investor-looms (September 28, 2020).

[2] Cerianne Robertson, "Where Do LA Times Staffers Go after They Leave the Paper? We Found Out," *Columbia Journalism Review*, May 30, 2019. www.cjr.org/business_of_ news/la-times-cuts-layoffs.php (September 28, 2020).

[3] Emily Goldstein, "Will Dallas Morning News Layoffs Imperil Key Beats?" *Columbia Journalism Review*, January 25, 2019. www.cjr.org/united_states_project/dallas-morn ing-news-layoffs.php (September 28, 2020).

[4] Paul Farhi, "The City that Never Sleeps Finds that It's Running Out of Reporters to Report," *Washington Post*, July 23, 2018. www.washingtonpost.com/lifestyle/style/the- city-that-never-sleeps-finds-that-its-running-out-of-reporters-to-report/2018/07/23/d4c94 10e-8e8f-11e8-bcd5-9d911c784c38_story.html?utm_medium=email&utm_source=next draft (September 28, 2020).

newspapers that have closed since 2004, the vast majority have been small
outlets in the "poorest, least educated and most isolated" parts of the
country.[5] While news organizations throughout the United States have
experienced financial distress, this has been "especially true in smaller
communities."[6] A 2018 *Bloomberg News* story declared, "Local News is
Dying, and It's Taking Small Town America with It."[7] Given these
headlines, a reader would be hard-pressed to tell whether big cities or
small towns have borne the worst of the local news crisis.

At the same time, it is also unclear how cutbacks have affected coverage of the different institutions of local government. A common refrain is
that profit-obsessed corporate chains and private equity funds adopted
scorched-earth policies that have left no corner of the newsroom
untouched. When the Tribune Company slashed 61 positions at the
Baltimore Sun in 2009, for example, the cuts "hit nearly every type of
job in the 205-person newsroom." A union representative described the
layoffs as "stunning, just the breadth of them across the board."[8] Writing
in the *Washington Post* in 2019, Steve Cavendish, president of Nashville
Public Media, said that Gannett's "slow-motion destruction" of
Nashville's local newspapers had decreased coverage of virtually everything – "sports scores, city council meetings, and major news."[9]

But the notion of uniform cuts – everything must go – stands in
contrast to the logic of a profit-driven industry. As newspapers were
"getting eaten away at every level,"[10] they found themselves under more
pressure to maximize their shrinking revenue. In trying to save the local
government coverage they viewed as most profitable, publishers may have

[5] Abernathy 2018b.
[6] "Town by Town, Local Journalism Is Dying in Plain Sight," *Associated Press*, March 10, 2019. www.cnbc.com/2019/03/10/town-by-town-local-journalism-is-dying-in-plain-sight.html (January 25, 2020).
[7] Riley Griffin, "Local News Is Dying, and It's Taking Small Town America with It," *Bloomberg News*, September 5, 2018. www.bloomberg.com/news/articles/2018-09-05/local-news-is-dying-and-it-s-taking-small-town-america-with-it (January 25, 2020).
[8] Lorraine Mirabella, "Sun Cuts 61 in News," *Baltimore Sun*, April 30, 2009. www.baltimoresun.com/news/bs-xpm-2009-04-30-0904290118-story.html (January 26, 2020).
[9] Steve Cavendish, "Local Newspapers Have Already Been Gutted. There's Nothing Left to Cut," *Washington Post*, January 25, 2019. www.washingtonpost.com/outlook/local-newspapers-have-already-been-decimated-theres-nothing-left-to-cut/2019/01/25/248fe102-200d-11e9-9145-3f74070bbdb9_story.html (January 26, 2020).
[10] "Town by Town, Local Journalism Is Dying in Plain Sight," *Associated Press*, March 10, 2019. www.cnbc.com/2019/03/10/town-by-town-local-journalism-is-dying-in-plain-sight.html (January 25, 2020).

sacrificed the beats and stories they viewed as less attractive to audiences – although not necessarily less important to the civic health of communities.

In Chapter 2, we showed that tectonic shifts in the media business decimated newspapers in the first two decades of the twenty-first century, leaving Americans with access to dramatically less reporting about their local governments. In this chapter, we turn our attention to how that reduced access to local politics coverage played out. Drawing again on our content analysis of more than 200 local newspapers from 2003 through 2017, we first investigate the extent to which the local news crisis has affected large versus small daily papers across the country. We then examine which parts of local government were the most likely to be ignored by local newspapers as their reporting ranks thinned. These analyses are critical because they shed light on the kinds of communities that lost the most coverage and the parts of local government most likely to go without scrutiny.

THE LOCAL NEWS CRISIS AT BIG AND SMALL NEWSPAPERS

Which kinds of newspapers have been hardest hit by the changing media landscape? It depends who you ask. One account suggests that small papers have suffered the most. The logic behind this story is straightforward. Because community newspapers typically operate with smaller budgets and a more limited financial cushion than their big-city counterparts, they were less equipped to withstand the loss of advertising and circulation revenue. As layoffs mounted and the news hole dwindled, small papers found it exceedingly difficult to maintain robust coverage of their communities. And although relatively few dailies shuttered altogether, the papers with small circulations were more financially vulnerable and would have been forced to cut their coverage more dramatically than larger papers with deeper pockets.[11]

An alternative account suggests that small-market dailies may have been able to maintain their local coverage more effectively than bigger papers. Media studies scholars Christopher Ali and Damien Radcliffe suggest that newspapers serving small communities provide a more "valuable, distinctive service,"[12] which puts them "in a stronger position than

[11] Of the newspaper closures identified since 2004 by the University of North Carolina's News Deserts Project, 90% are weeklies.

[12] Damien Radcliffe and Christopher Ali, "If Small Newspapers Are Going to Survive, They'll Have to Be More than Passive Observers to the News," *Nieman Lab*, February

their metro cousins."[13] Whereas readers expect small papers to cover local government and community affairs – their bread-and-butter – readers of larger metro or regional papers expect a mix of local, national, and international coverage. The audiences for small-market dailies also may have been more stable, as residents of small communities are more likely than people in larger urban areas to get their news from local outlets.[14] And because smaller papers historically have had high penetration rates, they may have been better positioned to maintain value for their advertisers.

Differences in the advertising markets served by large and small newspapers might have also worked to smaller papers' advantage. The emergence of the Internet and the proliferation of free online message boards and marketplaces – most obviously, Craigslist – robbed papers of reliable classified advertising revenue that had been a core part of their business model. By one estimate, the damage was $5 billion between 2000 and 2007.[15] But Craigslist and other sites appeared initially in large, urban markets, allowing newspapers in smaller communities to hang on to their classified advertising revenue longer. The more limited media ecosystem in small markets may have helped too, since businesses had fewer local outlets in which to advertise.[16] In major metropolitan markets, by contrast, advertisers enjoyed a growing number of (cheaper) ways to reach consumers, including geographically targeted digital advertising and social media. All of this may have somewhat insulated small dailies from the worst of the revenue crisis, allowing them to preserve more of their local coverage than papers in larger markets.[17]

Both perspectives are plausible, but previous efforts to determine which is true have not yielded a clear answer. Some work employs a qualitative approach, interviewing journalists and industry professionals

---

2, 2017. www.niemanlab.org/2017/02/if-small-newspapers-are-going-to-survive-theyll-have-to-be-more-than-passive-observers-to-the-news/ (January 25, 2020).

[13] Christopher Ali and Damien Radcliffe, "Small Market Newspapers in the Digital Age," *Columbia Journalism Review*, November 15, 2017. www.cjr.org/tow_center_reports/local-small-market-newspapers-study.php (January 25, 2020).

[14] Pew 2012.

[15] Seamans and Zhu 2014.

[16] Poepsel 2021.

[17] Margaret Sullivan, "The Local News Crisis Is Destroying What a Divided America Desperately Needs: Common Ground," *Washington Post*, August 5, 2018. www.washingtonpost.com/lifestyle/style/the-local-news-crisis-is-destroying-what-a-divided-america-desperately-needs-common-ground/2018/08/03/d654d5a8-9711-11e8-810c-5fa705927d54_story.html (January 25, 2020).

about how they have dealt with the crisis.[18] Other accounts focus on individual newspapers or just a handful of outlets to illustrate the types of papers and methods that have fared better or worse.[19] These approaches undoubtedly shed light on the strategic responses or newsroom practices adopted by journalists trying to continue to serve their communities. But a full account must also provide a systematic analysis of how reporting on local government has changed over time at different kinds of newspapers serving different kinds of communities.

The News Hole Shrinks, Especially in Major Dailies

In Chapter 2, we demonstrated that the news hole began to shrink in the early 2000s, falling precipitously as advertisers gravitated away from print and began to target consumers with search engine advertising and through social media. This meant less space for news in general, which meant less space for coverage of local government in particular. What we don't know is whether and how that pattern differed for papers of different sizes.

Using circulation data from the industry publication *Editor & Publisher*, we placed our dailies into four circulation categories: less than 25,000; 25,000–45,000; 45,000–90,000; and more than 90,000. These divisions represent quartiles from the group of papers for which we collected any data from NewsBank. Restricting the sample to papers for which we have the full 2003–2017 time series leaves us with 202 dailies – 41 papers in each of the smallest two circulation groups, and 60 in each of the two largest categories.[20]

Circulation data are of course only a proxy for a newspaper's overall readership in the internet age; they do not account for online readers and subscribers. But papers with larger print circulations also have larger readerships in all formats. And although newspaper size is not a proxy for the rural-urban divide, larger newspapers in our data set are far more likely than smaller papers to serve more densely populated, urban

---

[18] Christopher Ali and Damien Radcliffe, "Small Market Newspapers in the Digital Age," *Columbia Journalism Review*, November 15, 2017. www.cjr.org/tow_center_reports/local-small-market-newspapers-study.php (January 25, 2020).

[19] Deborah Fallows and James Fallows, "Our Towns: The Last Family-Owned Daily in Mississippi," *The Atlantic*, May 10, 2019. www.theatlantic.com/notes/2019/05/future-local-journalism-case-study-mississippi/588865/ (January 25, 2020).

[20] The full list of papers appears in Appendix D.

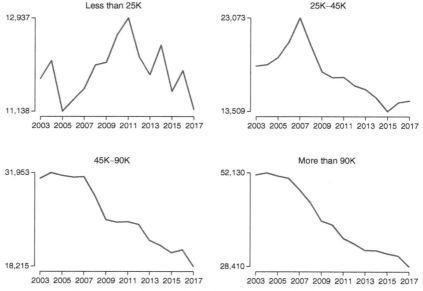

FIGURE 3.1. The size of the news hole, by newspaper circulation
Note: The news hole represents the average number of total items published in 202 daily newspapers in each year, broken down by circulation size.

communities.[21] Thus, differences in the news hole across newspaper size can tell us something about the magnitude of the reductions in coverage of local government in different types of communities.

Between 2003 and 2017, large papers experienced a more dramatic shrinking of the news hole than small ones (see Figure 3.1). As in Chapter 2, our measure of the news hole is the total number of items published by each newspaper in a given year; larger numbers reflect a bigger news hole, meaning more space for editorial content.[22] In the smallest dailies in our data set – those with circulations less than 25,000 (top left-hand panel) – the news hole generally increased through 2011, before beginning a slide over the next six years. In papers in the 25,000–45,000 range, the upward trend was more abbreviated, with things

---

[21] Based on US Census data, the home county for our smallest papers (less than 25,000 circulation) was on average 78% urban. It increases to 83% for the 25,000–45,000 circulation papers, 90% for the 45,000–90,000 papers, and 98% for the papers with a circulation of 90,000 or more.
[22] See Appendix E.

starting to get relentlessly bad around 2008. But the larger two categories of papers saw their volume of editorial content shrink as early as 2004 and move precipitously downward for the next decade-plus. These patterns are consistent with the argument that smaller newspapers were more insulated from the forces roiling the print advertising business in the early 2000s.

Because the size of the news hole varies significantly across the four categories of papers – the largest papers in 2003 had more than four times the number of stories as the smallest ones – the slope of the lines in the graphs doesn't indicate which set of papers saw the biggest drops, in percentage terms. But comparing the size of the news hole in 2017 to the peak year for each group of papers does. And that calculation makes clear just how devastating the local news crisis was for large metropolitan dailies. First, consider the smallest papers. At their peak (2011), papers below 25,000 circulation published on average 12,937 items. By 2017, that had declined by 14% (to 11,175 items) – certainly a massive loss of product for a business based on generating content. But for papers in the larger three categories, the numbers are even more severe. The news hole shrunk 37% at mid-market papers, and a whopping 43% and 46% respectively for the two largest circulation categories.

The journalists we interviewed suggested one reason for these huge losses is that large metro newspapers long had a bounty of content of all types – news, entertainment, sports, classified ads, special advertising inserts, and more. As advertisers began to take their business elsewhere, large papers simply had more to lose. Shane Fitzgerald, the executive editor at the *Bucks County Courier Times* in Pennsylvania, observed the differences from perches in newsrooms of various sizes over the last few decades. "I think the bigger newsrooms were – well, spoiled is the wrong word – but they got used to being well-funded and there was a little bit of a sense of entitlement," he said. Small papers, on the other hand, "didn't have a lot to start with." Already relatively lean, they were more insulated from the crash in part because they had a smaller volume of advertising to begin with. Jill Spitz, managing editor of the *Arizona Daily Star* in Tucson, told us that for dailies in major metro areas, "the real problem is the massive decline in retail advertising. And we as an industry didn't prepare for it, and we lost our competitive advantage." Elite papers, such as *The Washington Post* and the *New York Times*, have managed to maintain and even grow their audiences by building a national brand, but that isn't an option for local papers whose competitive advantage is necessarily limited by geography. "All papers our size are suffering and facing similar challenges," Spitz said.

TABLE 3.1. *The decline of coverage of local politics and other topics, by circulation size*

	Less than 25K	25K–45K	45K–90K	More than 90K
Local Politics	−27%	−48%	−53%	−54%
Other Topics	−9	−33	−41	−42

Note: Entries indicate the percentage point drops in coverage of local politics and other topics in 2017 compared to the peak year of coverage for each category of newspaper.

For newspaper readers in larger markets, the consequences of a thinner paper were predictable – and sometimes comical. One reporter at a large Southern daily lamented in an interview how little news the paper now produces: "The paper's not what it used to be." Over the years, the print product had grown so emaciated that it wasn't even heavy enough for delivery drivers to toss onto the reporter's property. "For a while, the carrier was sticking a *Wall Street Journal* in there so it would weigh down the paper, literally, to get it over the fence," the reporter told us. "I was getting a free *Wall Street Journal* just for the weight."

Cuts to Local Politics Are Severe, Especially at the Smallest Papers

The massive declines in the news hole at large dailies also translated into massive declines in the volume of published news, especially about local politics. Consider Table 3.1, which displays the reduction in coverage of both local politics and other topics, broken down by circulation category. Local politics refers to the number of published stories containing reference to the mayor, city government, county government, and school board. Other topics are national politics, state politics, and sports.[23]

Given the sizeable reduction in the news hole at the major dailies, it's no surprise that papers in the two largest circulation categories saw the biggest percentage-point drops in the volume of coverage between 2003 and 2017. As they bled resources – both editorial space and reporting staff – big-city dailies found themselves cutting their coverage dramatically. The typical reductions in local coverage at the biggest papers were twice as big as the reductions at the smallest papers. But reductions in local political coverage were substantially larger in papers of

---

[23] Details on the content analysis appear in Appendix E.

every size than the collective cuts to coverage of national politics, state politics, and major sports.

Perhaps more striking is that the smallest papers experienced the biggest proportional cuts to coverage of local government. While the absolute volume of reductions was largest at the big dailies, the very coverage that small newspapers can uniquely provide to their community – and that virtually no other outlets deliver – is exactly the coverage that suffered. Local coverage was reduced 300% more than other topics at the smallest papers, but only about 30% more at the largest papers. In response to fiscal pressures, then, smaller papers were actually less likely than bigger dailies to prioritize local coverage.

We can also get a sense of the content publishers prioritized and sought to preserve by calculating the percentage of the total news hole devoted to local politics versus other topics, and then tracking how those proportions changed over time. To do that, we divide the number of stories about local politics each year by the total news hole for that year. We do the same for our measure of other topics. In the two smallest categories of papers – those with less than 45,000 circulation – the share of the news hole devoted to local government fell by 23% between 2003 and 2017. In the larger dailies, the cuts were smaller, with the local politics share of the news hole dropping by about 17%. Large papers no doubt were slashing, but relative to the size of the news hole, the sweep of the blade wasn't as wide as it was at smaller dailies. Meanwhile, newspapers of all sizes in our sample either increased or held steady in how much of the paper they devoted to national politics, state politics, and sports.

The breadth of the cuts to local politics, especially in the smaller dailies, is evident in Figure 3.2. Here, we present the percentage of papers within each circulation category that cut the share of the news hole devoted to local politics and other topics between 2003 and 2017. Roughly three-quarters of papers in the three smallest circulation categories saw declines in coverage of local politics, compared to just 60% of the largest dailies. Small papers were also more likely to see declines in coverage of state politics, national politics, and sports. Within every category, more papers preserved their nonlocal government coverage.

These patterns are especially pronounced in the very smallest newspapers. Nine papers in our data set had circulations of less than 15,000. Among these, eight saw a decrease in coverage of local government as a share of the news hole between 2003 and 2017. (The one that saw an increase is the largest of the bunch, the *Wyoming Tribune Eagle*.) On average, these smallest papers reduced the share of the news hole devoted

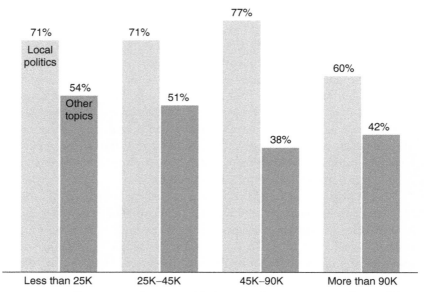

FIGURE 3.2. Percentage of papers with decreases in coverage as a share of the news hole, by circulation size

Note: Bars represent the proportion of daily newspapers in each circulation category that experienced a decline in coverage of local politics and other topics, as a share of the news hole, from 2003 to 2017.

to local politics by 25% over this period. That is the heftiest reduction of any group of papers in our sample.

Based on data from the US Census Bureau, Table 3.2 shows that the counties served by these nine smallest papers were less populous, more rural, slightly poorer, and older than the communities served by other papers.[24] In these markets, the local newspaper is the primary news outlet – and often the only one – that covers local government. Not only have residents of these communities lost a larger share of their local political news than other Americans, but in many cases they have no alternative venues to turn to as their newspapers have withered.

The story that emerges from our analyses is nuanced. Large newspapers were in some ways the hardest hit by the reduction of advertising revenue in the early 2000s. Because they had more to lose and faced

---

[24] We matched 2010 data from the US Census Bureau on population, population density, median income, and median age to the home county for each newspaper in our sample.

TABLE 3.2. *Characteristics of communities served by the smallest papers versus others*

	Population	Percent Urban	Median Income ($)	Median Age
Less than 15,000 Circulation	647,286	75	50,709	38
All Others	922,630	89	52,092	36

Note: Entries present averages for the home county for newspapers in each category based on 2010 US Census Bureau Data.

bigger cuts to their page counts, the reductions in the total volume of local news coverage in big cities around the country were dramatic. But critically, the communities that have suffered disproportionately – in terms of information loss – were the ones served by smaller papers. Even though the news hole declined less in these papers, the *share* of the news hole devoted to local news shrunk more than it did in larger papers. Contrary to the hopes of some, smaller papers haven't on the whole been able to maintain a stronger commitment to covering their local communities than have big-city papers.

THE TYPES OF LOCAL COVERAGE THAT GOT THE AX

Although smaller papers reduced their coverage of local government more aggressively than larger papers, newsrooms of every size were forced to grapple with the practical consequences of fewer resources. But within that environment, papers had choices. One approach might have been to make cuts with all the precision of a meat cleaver, effectively reducing staff and reporting capacity across the board. In some ways, this is the picture painted by many accounts of the local journalism crisis, which often offer a laundry list of beats and civic institutions now getting only sporadic attention or no coverage at all. Given the diminished product that readers see every day, this narrative has the ring of truth.

But the economic logic of the media business suggests that cash-strapped news outlets might have taken a more strategic approach. Even in newspapers' highly profitable heyday, publishers authorized their staff to devote resources to the stories and coverage that would maximize their return on investment (That was why they were so profitable!). In a time of fiscal austerity, maximizing return on investment is even more critical, suggesting that newspaper executives would have been more deliberative about what local news content to keep and what to scrap.

Two key elements merit consideration. The first is cost. Coverage that is resource-intensive – for example, requiring significant reporting time or staff – is less attractive to publishers than content that can be produced cheaply. That's one reason investigative journalism has declined in recent years – because of the perception that it is too expensive to support.[25] The second element is demand: Content that will increase circulation, readership, or online traffic will be more valuable to publishers than coverage that produces a collective yawn from readers, regardless of how "important" it may be. Audience demand has become even more influential in an era in which web traffic and reader engagement produce real-time measures of the popularity of content. Indeed, critics argue that these metrics are so powerful that they can "drown out" other substantive evaluations of the quality of news reporting.[26] And since consumers express more interest in some types of local news than others,[27] we would expect newspapers to prioritize the coverage that is likely to produce a higher return on investment. After all, when someone's house is on fire, they don't grab an even selection of all of their possessions as they run for the door; they try to save the stuff that's most valuable.

School Board and County Government Coverage Are Cut Disproportionately

Our analysis finds indeed that the types of local government coverage that require significant reporting resources and aren't especially profitable were most likely to end up on the chopping block. We draw this conclusion by disaggregating our local politics measure into its component parts – stories mentioning the mayor, city government, county government, and local school boards.

[25] Hamilton 2016.
[26] Petre 2015.
[27] Pew 2019e.

Of course, coverage of these central aspects of local politics has never comprised a great deal of the news hole. Mayoral coverage is by far the most prominent, but even at its peak in our time series, it never constituted more than 4% of everything newspapers published (see Figure 3.3). That is paltry compared to the attention the newspapers in our sample devoted to topics not connected to local politics. For instance, in 2003, stories mentioning the president accounted for 15% of the news hole – nearly four times the coverage of mayors. Coverage of the four major sports accounted for 15% as well.

Relative to other local government stories, though, the prominence of mayoral coverage isn't surprising. In most cities, mayors are involved with most aspects of local politics, so coverage of local politics often means coverage of mayors. But it is also consistent with the media's tendency to personalize political news. Just as national political media frame most of their coverage around the actions of the president – even before Trump – local news outlets place city leaders front and center. Stories about elections, scandals, controversial decisions, and mayors' efforts to command the spotlight in their city often mean that mayors become the focal point of local political coverage.

Perhaps owing to its news value, mayoral coverage has experienced less severe reductions than the other parts of local government. For instance, between 2003 and 2017, the share of the news hole devoted to mayors fell 8%. Although the comparison is not easy to see in the figure, that was less than one-quarter of the 36% reduction in school board coverage. Put another way, one out of every three stories written about school boards in 2003 had disappeared by 2017. County government coverage, meanwhile, declined 24%. Coverage of city government also saw a substantial, though less extreme, reduction of 19%.

This was generally the case across the board, regardless of circulation size (see Figure 3.4). Even though we might expect smaller papers to have preserved more coverage of essential community institutions, such as schools and county commissions, the evidence says otherwise. In fact, consistent with our earlier findings, the reductions were largest when we look at the smallest papers in our sample. Among those with less than 15,000 circulation, the average reduction in schools coverage was 56%.

These patterns aren't just the product of especially severe cuts at a handful of outlets. When we consider the share of newspapers in each circulation category that cut coverage of their local school boards, the reductions are remarkably widespread. Eighty-three percent of papers

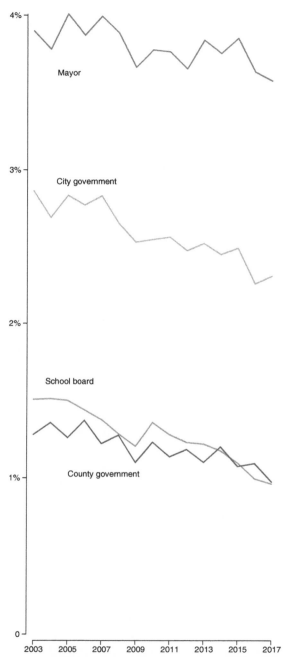

FIGURE 3.3. Types of local politics coverage as a share of the news hole
Note: Lines reflect the share of news coverage (the number of stories on a topic divided by the news hole) devoted to each of our four topics.

smaller than 25,000 circulation cut the share of their news hole devoted to schools between 2003 and 2017. That number was 90% among the outlets with circulations between 25,000 and 45,000. Those figures were just slightly bigger than the share of newspapers in the largest two circulation categories cutting school board coverage. The cuts to county coverage were similarly widespread, with roughly 7 in 10 newspapers in our data set devoting a decreasing share of the news hole to stories about county government.

With newspapers of different sizes in different markets in different states making such similar editorial judgments, the question is, Why? The dozens of interviews we conducted with editors and reporters suggest school board and county government coverage suffered because of a mix of both supply and demand factors. In an era of financial stress and changing business models, stories about school administrations and county government were viewed as producing a smaller return on investment. As a result, they ended up doomed to be deprioritized.

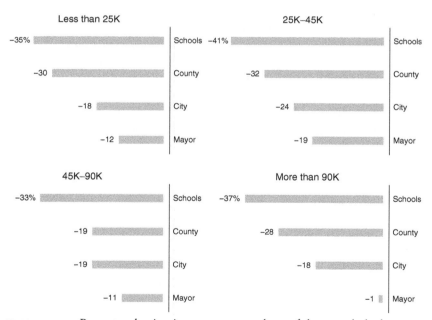

FIGURE 3.4. Percent reduction in coverage as a share of the news hole, by circulation size
Note: Bars represent the reduction in each type of coverage in 202 daily newspapers from 2003 to 2017.

Fewer Reporters Means Less Schools Coverage

Consistent with our quantitative content analysis, numerous journalists told us that the education beat suffered especially significant cuts at their papers. In part, this was a matter of simple mathematics – with many papers trimming (or eliminating) their education staffs, schools coverage had to go. One journalist at a large paper in the Midwest, for example, told us that the paper once had eight people covering education. With a "very complicated system and something like 20 school districts," that was a sensible level of staffing. But by 2019, the education beat – private schools, public schools, colleges, and universities – had been whittled down to a single reporter. Not only can't the paper cover the many school board meetings it could years ago, but the depth of the coverage has also suffered. "We definitely can't follow up on anything that happens at those meetings," the journalist said. "There's no opportunity to dig deeper to be enterprising."

At the *Honolulu Star-Advertiser*, another big-city paper, education coverage also "took a hit," said Kevin Dayton, a veteran reporter who has worked as a journalist in Hawaii for more than two decades. Even as late as 2015 or 2016, the paper had one full-time and one part-time reporter covering primary, secondary, and higher education. But by 2019, a single part-timer remained. How might one part-time employee cover a statewide school board and a university system with 16 campuses? "Can't be done," Dayton told us.

Journalists at smaller newspapers offered similar accounts. Schools coverage at the *South Bend Tribune* "just isn't what it used to be," said reporter Jeff Parrott. "We used to have a specific reporter for each school corporation. Now we have one person who has to cover everything – inner city schools, affluent schools, schools way out in rural areas." That lone reporter "just doesn't have the luxury to attend all the meetings or have the detailed knowledge base we used to have." Consequently, Parrott said, the paper is "missing a lot of important things happening in the schools."

With shrinking newsrooms, the decision to scale back education coverage is partly about resource allocation. Publishers have become more reticent to commit reporters to a single beat – especially ones that often involve lengthy meetings, such as school boards – because that leaves them unavailable to cover other stories. "When you have fewer bodies, you can't send someone to every single meeting," said John Martin, an editor at the *Philadelphia Inquirer*. At the *Lexington Herald-Leader*,

Linda Blackford specialized in higher education for more than two decades as a reporter, becoming "one of the most respected journalists in Kentucky."[28] Now a political columnist, she explained that as the newsroom went through a period of "utter decimation" – going from about 120 people to 30 – she "came to cover more topics, and that's true of everyone." Instead of just higher education, Blackford also began writing about taxes, allegations of government corruption, and other stories. Covering fewer education-related meetings didn't reduce the quality of the paper's coverage, she said, since at those meetings "lots of the time, nothing happens." But the upshot of the changes is that the paper is decidedly "doing less."

Education reporting also took a hit because schools coverage is just not very popular. In a massive 2019 survey, the Pew Research Center found that the share of Americans describing local news about schools as "important" was lower than the percentage who said the same thing about weather, crime, traffic and transportation, and government and politics. Citizens also deemed school news as less "interesting" than stories about restaurants, arts and culture, and sports. Education reporting appears to reside in a consumer demand dead zone, less important than other hard news topics and less interesting than entertainment coverage.[29]

These twin forces – costly supply and weak demand – help explain why newspaper management has de-emphasized coverage of school boards, which often feature time-consuming meetings that rarely produce grabby headlines. When Jennifer Napier-Pearce became the editor of the *Salt Lake Tribune* in 2016, the newsroom had just been through four rounds of layoffs, and she was intent on avoiding another one. Her solution was to be more "selective," to choose "stories with scale," and to focus on what readers cared about most, stories that "are broader and have more impact." That meant a reduction in the number of reporters at local government meetings, including the school boards. But Napier, who has since left the *Tribune*, told us the trade-off was necessary to ensure that the paper is getting "the most bang for the buck." Blackford, the *Herald-Leader* columnist, said her coverage of higher education became more limited as the paper's website grew more important, "because those

[28] Peter Baniak, "Welcoming a New (but Familiar) Voice to the Herald's Opinion Pages," *Lexington Herald-Leader*, June 13, 2019. www.kentucky.com/opinion/article231474568 .html (January 26, 2020).
[29] Pew 2019d.

stories don't get the clicks." The analytics-driven decision-making of modern newsrooms is a far cry from an earlier era, when Martin, the *Philadelphia Inquirer* editor, could make $500 a week writing up dispatches from community meetings. "We didn't know who was reading the stories," he said, "but we had bodies to do it." With reporters' time and readers' attention now at a measurable premium, school board coverage hardly appears worth it.

As Circulation Drops, County Coverage Loses Value

The demise of county government coverage stems from a similar, but slightly different, form of economic discrimination tied to newspapers' changing business models. For much of the twentieth century, newspapers benefited from geographically large circulation areas. Having a subscription base in counties outside the cities where newspapers were headquartered not only boosted circulation revenue, but also made the paper attractive to advertisers in those communities. Business owners wanted to reach consumers who lived near their businesses, and the local newspaper was a natural vehicle. To keep hold of those readers – and more importantly, the advertising revenue – publishers had an incentive to cover the county governments that served these often far-flung communities. Sometimes that meant establishing county bureaus, sometimes it meant simply assigning a staff reporter or freelancer to a county beat.

As advertising dollars moved elsewhere beginning in the early 2000s, the value of a print subscriber base in outlying counties declined. Because businesses could increasingly reach consumers in other ways, advertising in the printed paper became less of a priority. Consequently, newspapers had fewer financial incentives to maintain those readers, which often meant de-emphasizing coverage of county governments. As media scholars Jay Jennings and Meghan Rubado note, many newsrooms adopted a strategy of "refocusing of news content on the central or main city of the newspaper and a handful of more populous or high-readership neighboring communities."[30]

The *Toledo Blade* is a perfect illustration of this strategy because in many ways, it has defied the trends in local government coverage we've described up to this point. While most papers through the early 2000s slashed coverage of municipal government, the *Blade's* mayoral and city

---

[30] Jennings and Rubado 2019.

hall coverage generally held steady. In 2017, 5% of its stories mentioned city government, which was more than in any year in the last two decades, according to our content analysis. Kurt Franck, the *Blade*'s general manager and executive editor, told us that the paper had done better than many others because its independent owners, the Block family, were "committed to our journalism."

But even with supportive ownership, the *Blade* hasn't avoided significant cuts to its coverage of county government outside Toledo. Compared to the paper's peak in 2004, the share of the news hole devoted to county government in 2017 was down 17%. Much of this is about staff cuts, which have shrunk the newsroom by about half from the 170 who worked there in 2000. Beyond Lucas County, the largest in the paper's coverage area, the *Blade* can't devote much attention to counties where the paper has traditionally circulated, Franck told us. "We don't cover some of the outlying areas like we used to," he said. "I'm not proud that we've had to cut back. But it's about dollars and cents."

The retrenchment in coverage of county governments was a theme we heard repeatedly in our interviews with reporters and editors, from New England to the Midwest to the Gulf Coast. "Even in my small beat, I have towns where I have no idea what's happening," said Kim Haas, a correspondent for the *New Hampshire Union Leader*. "There's just not enough manpower." Newsroom cuts at the *Bloomington Herald-Times* have meant that "reporters have more beats, but still only 40 hours a week," Rick Jackson, the paper's managing editor, told us. "So if there's a decent story out of Brown County, which is far, it's unlikely we can do it." Mike Burbach, the editor of the *Pioneer Press* in St. Paul, explained that he has "had to condense to the core" and is "more concentrated now in our three core Minnesota counties." He compared these lean times to the "fat and happy days," when the paper's coverage was "far flung." For John Sharp, at AL.com, a story outside the site's metro coverage areas – Mobile, Birmingham, and Huntsville – has to be big to justify writing about it. Most mundane bureaucratic activities don't qualify. "If it's the city of Daphne [across the Mobile Bay], which is about 30,000 people, I don't go cover the budget there," he said. Others noted that they "miss a lot of news, especially in smaller townships" and that places they used to cover on the outskirts are "total news deserts now."

As is the case with education reporting, it's especially unattractive to devote resources to county government when it doesn't interest many readers. Several of the journalists we interviewed alluded to this point. Blackford, of the *Lexington Herald-Leader*, said the paper had only recently returned a reporter to Eastern Kentucky – and that was only feasible because his salary was being paid by the nonprofit Report for America. "We didn't have someone there for years," she said. "Fewer people are affected by anything that happens." John Hamilton, one of two political reporters for the *Wilmington News Journal*, was blunt about the cost-benefit calculation in covering politics outside the paper's core market: "We're not going to drive out to the middle of nowhere to talk about five candidates who are competing to win a handful of votes. We don't have time and no one cares," he told us. Spread thin already, the paper has to focus on "what draws interest in the community."

Quality over Quantity?

The story thus far is one of dark clouds for local journalism. But our analysis doesn't eliminate the possibility of a silver lining. Since our data rely on story counts, we can speak only to quantity, not quality. And many of the reporters and editors we interviewed voiced a surprising degree of optimism about the work they are doing, even in difficult circumstances. Forced to focus only on the top-priority stories, news-papers can no longer be "everything to everyone," as one reporter put it. That shift, some said, has led to journalism that better serves their communities than the wider array of coverage common in an earlier era.

Some reporters said one way in which that is true is that they now focus on finding areas of their communities that are underreported and bring them to readers' attention. At the *Boston Globe*, a small group of staffers is covering politics in Rhode Island, where a hollowed out *Providence Journal* can no longer cover significant parts of the state government as it once did. The *Globe*'s Ed Fitzpatrick, a former *Journal* reporter, gave as an example a story he wrote in 2019 about high rates of absenteeism among teachers in the Warwick public school system. Despite the fact that nearly half the system's teachers had been absent more than 10 days during the previous school year, other news outlets weren't covering it. "People need to know that," he said.

Numerous journalists also told us that while they can no longer provide the breadth of coverage they once did, there is a renewed focus on depth. At the *Bloomington Herald-Times*, Jackson said one of the paper's goals is to tell in-depth stories "better than everyone else." Although the paper doesn't have reporters for the specialized beats it once did – business, health care – the remaining staff is encouraged to focus on "bigger, broader projects, rather than covering all things all the time." In Tucson, the *Arizona Daily Star* has tried to provide their readers a unique lens on immigration, "understanding border issues in a different way," said Spitz, the paper's editor. For Napier-Pearce, formerly of the *Salt Lake Tribune*, the paper's comparative advantage is watchdog reporting. With a reputation for holding government accountable, she decided to make that type of coverage "a core value and high in our mission." A journalist at a small mid-Atlantic daily described a similar approach. "We're trying to position ourselves as a more in-depth news source," the reporter said. "We're going to provide background and interviews, not just the write up." In theory, that approach might yield more informative coverage for readers – prioritizing wheat, dispensing with chaff. The gamble is that readers care more about thorough reporting of major stories than more limited coverage of a wide array of topics.

The hope that journalists express about the work that they're doing is understandable. But it remains very much an open question whether the financial crisis of the 2000s has led to "better" coverage. Some newsrooms may want to tell the most important stories in a more compelling way, de-emphasizing their traditional roles as stenographers at boring meetings and humdrum press conferences. But whether the journalism being produced in America's newsrooms in fact better serves the democratic needs of communities will have to wait on a study that can systematically assess the quality of coverage of local governments and compare it over time. What we can say unequivocally is that when it comes to the amount of local political coverage, newspapers – and citizens – are far worse off today than they were two decades ago.

CONCLUSION

The last 20 years of local journalism have been grim, a narrative told in verbs such as demise, decimate, devastate, and decline. No part of the business has gone unaffected, with some newspapers disappearing altogether and others reduced to such shells that it just seems like they've disappeared. Our analysis in this chapter tells a consistent and worrisome story: Papers of all sizes across the country have dramatically reduced their coverage of local politics, and the cuts to schools and county government reporting have been especially severe. Despite some structural advantages, small outlets have done no better – and the smallest ones have fared worse – than their big-city counterparts in preserving coverage of local government. The data are bleak.

The implications of our findings are troubling. They underscore how the ability of the media to serve their most important democratic account-ability function is tied precariously to their economic fortunes. As covering school boards and county governments has grown more costly over the years, and as the demand for coverage of those institutions has waned, newspapers have responded by pulling back. Nothing in our interviews suggests that journalists see these parts of government as objectively less important than mayors or city hall; most lament the retrenchment. But as more than one told us, the cuts are simply a matter of economics. Reporting on schools and county government is less profit-able than other parts of the government, so it had to go. In the new normal for local media, government institutions that are time-consuming to cover or that don't generate online clicks are more likely to escape public scrutiny.

These effects will be felt more severely in some communities. As our analysis shows, reductions in local politics coverage have been the most severe – measured as a share of the news hole – in small newspapers. With relatively small budgets to begin with, small-market newspapers have been squeezed nearly to death. This is not to say that the reductions in large papers are not alarming; they are. But for residents of cities such as New York, Philadelphia, Los Angeles, or Atlanta, there is some comfort in the fact that local television stations and a handful of online outlets provide at least a modicum of information about what those cities' government officials do on a day-to-day basis. In the small communities where the cuts to local coverage have declined most sharply, newspapers constitute virtually the only substantive source of news about local gov-ernments. There's no place else for residents to turn.

Ultimately, our findings amplify and expand on the concerns raised by numerous scholars, journalists, and analysts. The economic logic of the news business has reduced citizens' ability to keep tabs on various parts of their local institutions. What remains to be seen is how coverage of local government matters for citizens' political engagement. That's the focus of the next two chapters.

4

As Local News Goes, So Goes Political Engagement

The profound withering of the local media environment in recent decades has left residents of communities across the United States with access to less and less reporting about their local governments. Throughout the same period, surveys have shown Americans paying less and less attention to local politics. Many cannot identify or even recognize the names of their local elected officials. And turnout in local elections has continued its downward slide.

To the journalists who have watched their newsrooms shrink, their colleagues depart, and column inches disappear from the newspaper, the connection between these developments is obvious. "People don't know what's going on," one editor at a mid-size Southern daily told us. "They can't be informed even if they want to be." With newspapers forced to focus only on the biggest stories, coverage of, and endorsements in, lower level races are scarce. Residents "don't know about the candidates for mining inspector or magistrate," said Jill Spitz, editor of the *Arizona Daily Star*. Uninformed and unmotivated, voters stay home.

The many public reports about the demise of local journalism conclude the same. "With the loss of local news, citizens are: less likely to vote, less politically informed, and less likely to run for office," read a sweeping 2019 report by PEN America.[1] "Voting and consuming news – these things go hand in hand," one editor told the report's authors. Media critic Margaret Sullivan observes that at many newspapers, "staff and ambitions are so diminished that they can no longer do the day-to-day

---

[1] PEN America 2019.

reporting that allows citizens to make good decisions at the polls about their governmental representatives."[2]

Compelling and intuitive as these accounts are, the link between the decline of local newspapers and citizen engagement is no slam-dunk. To some observers, the very technological forces that ushered in the local news crisis – the Internet and social media – may also blunt its effects by allowing voters to remain informed without a need for legacy gatekeepers in the traditional media. In addition, some academic research suggests the decline in local engagement may be a product of consumers abandoning local news, not reductions in newspapers' reporting capacity. If that is true, then journalists and philanthropic organizations may have the causal relationship exactly backward.

This chapter provides a thorough empirical account of the connection between local news and political engagement during the last two decades. Drawing on a variety of data sources, we go beyond the existing research to demonstrate that the demise of local newspapers we documented in Chapters 2 and 3 indeed contributes to reductions in political engagement in America's cities and towns. The concerns expressed by journalists and local news advocates are very real, and we offer persuasive evidence to back them up.

WHY NOT EVERYONE BLAMES LOCAL NEWS FOR THE DECLINE IN ENGAGEMENT

Because newspapers have long been the primary source of political information in communities across the United States, it would hardly seem controversial to assert that Americans' knowledge of and participation in local politics would have fallen. Indeed, a long line of research has shown that the mass media have a big effect on political engagement. When voters have access to large amounts of public affairs reporting, they know more about what their elected officials are doing.[3] Exposure to political news also stimulates participation.[4] Logically, a weaker local news environment should mean less engagement. But the claim that the erosion of

---

[2] Margaret Sullivan, "The Constitution Doesn't Work without Local News," *The Atlantic*, July 14, 2020. www.theatlantic.com/ideas/archive/2020/07/constitution-doesnt-work-without-local-news/614056/ (October 1, 2020).

[3] Delli Carpini and Keeter 1996; de Vreese and Boomgaarden 2006; Jerit, Barabas, and Bolsen 2006.

[4] Eveland and Scheufele 2000; Tolbert and McNeal 2003.

political coverage in local newspapers has led to a decline in citizens' engagement with local politics is not universally accepted.

Some critics argue that citizen engagement no longer depends on mainstream local news because the Internet has made it so easy to become informed. In this view, technology has "democratized" information, and the massive reduction of local government coverage in newspapers should have only a limited effect. After all, city council meetings are streamed online,[5] and local governments make huge amounts of information directly available to citizens.[6] Mayors use their own websites and email newsletters to communicate with constituents.[7] Candidates for county commissions and school boards create campaign websites, open to anyone with an internet connection. With information just a click away, traditional media outlets such as newspapers should be less important for promoting citizen engagement.[8]

These same sentiments have accompanied the meteoric rise of social media. They've perhaps been even more pronounced, with some imagining that Facebook, Twitter, and other forums could promote political engagement in two ways. First, with news feeds serving as the new "front page" Americans read over their morning coffee or on their way to work, keeping up with local government is quick, easy, convenient, and free. Mayors and other local elected officials can communicate directly and authentically with their constituents, provide updates on their cities and towns, and air grievances against other politicians.[9] And with the ability to personalize content, social media can serve up the information consumers are most interested in, further enhancing engagement. Second, the explicitly social nature of social media makes it easy for individuals and groups who want to organize protests, petitions, and letter-writing campaigns to solicit support and participation through their networks. Far better than individuals sitting at home alone reading the newspaper, the networks at the center of social media – actual friends and acquaintances,

---

[5] Type into any search engine the name of a city in the United States along with the phrase "live stream city council" and you'll find numerous results that allow you to click on a link and watch public meetings, either in real time or through many cities' public meeting archives.

[6] Scott 2006.

[7] "Meet the Mayors," United States Conference of Mayors. www.usmayors.org/mayors/meet-the-mayors/ (April 30, 2020).

[8] Kang and Gearhart 2010.

[9] Zack Quaintance, "Twitter, Facebook Offer Local Gov Tips at Mayors Conference," *Government Technology*, January 24, 2020. www.govtech.com/social/Twitter-Facebook-Offer-Local-Gov-Tips-at-Mayors-Conference.html (April 30, 2020).

as well as "friends" who live in the same geographic communities – can inform and mobilize, boosting engagement at the local level.

The obvious difficulty for the internet-as-savior account is that Americans' knowledge of local government and participation in local elections have been declining as the Internet has become a ubiquitous feature of modern life. One reason is the paucity of internet start-ups that cover local politics, as we discussed in Chapter 2. Another is that the nature of the Internet – and the dominance of web traffic by Google, Facebook, and Amazon – has served to reduce Americans' exposure to local information, not increase it.[10] Anyone on social media knows that most political news isn't about county commissions or city councils; it's about the latest political triumph or outrage in Washington, DC.[11]

The fact that the Internet hasn't saved political engagement, however, isn't evidence that its decline has been caused by local newspapers' retrenchment. One alternative argument is that changes in Americans' media habits are responsible. With a growing number of choices for news and entertainment, US consumers have gravitated away from local news sources to national ones. As people's media diets have become increasingly saturated with entertainment or national news via cable TV or the Internet, their connection to local politics has weakened.[12] By this account, declining coverage of local government is a lagging indicator of lower political engagement, not a cause.

Empirically sorting through these arguments has been difficult, as previous research has not thoroughly connected newspaper coverage over time to comprehensive measures of citizen engagement with local politics. To do so, we rely on a diverse collection of evidence to establish the relationship between local news and citizen engagement. Our analyses – which we describe in more detail throughout the chapter – are based on a combination of individual-level and aggregate-level data, self-reports and real-world behavior, and cross-sectional and panel surveys. More specifically, we draw on polling data to estimate the relationship between citizens' news consumption habits and their knowledge of local politics. We use election returns to connect news coverage of city politics to

---

[10] Hindman 2018. See also Hindman 2009 on the failure of the Internet to enhance democratic engagement.

[11] Matthew Weber, Peter Andringa, and Philip M. Napoli, "Researchers Analyzed More than 300,000 Local News Stories on Facebook. Here's What They Found," *NiemanLab*, September 12, 2019. www.niemanlab.org/2019/09/researchers-analyzed-more-than-300000-local-news-stories-on-facebook-heres-what-they-found/ (April 30, 2020).

[12] Darr, Hitt, and Dunaway 2018; Hopkins 2018; Trussler 2020.

patterns of voter turnout. We study online search behavior to examine how local news coverage affects Americans' interest in local government. And we take advantage of panel surveys to document an individual-level causal connection between changes in local news coverage and changes in local engagement. No single piece of our analysis is iron-clad on its own, but the accumulation of evidence produces a collectively persuasive account.

LOCAL NEWSPAPER READING AND LOCAL POLITICAL ENGAGEMENT

As an initial step, we first consider the relationship between local news consumption and local political engagement – do they in fact go "hand in hand"? If citizens no longer need traditional news outlets because they can interact with local government directly through city websites or social media, then newspapers' demise may be minimally important. But if people who read newspapers, whether in print or online, know more about local government and are more likely to participate in local politics than people who don't, that suggests newspapers' decline may have deleterious consequences for engagement. And if newspapers are more important for political engagement than other kinds of local media, such as TV news, that would be evidence that newspapers remain a powerful source of political information.[13]

To begin our examination of that relationship, we draw on multiple waves of the Cooperative Congressional Election Study (CCES). In 2016, 2017, 2018, and 2019, we developed survey modules that were administered to samples of 1,000 respondents each fall.[14] In 2016 and 2018, the surveys were conducted in the lead-up to the presidential and midterm elections. In 2017 and 2019, they took place in a nonelection year (in all but a handful of states). These are not panel surveys, so each year's sample includes a separate cross section of respondents.

In each survey, we asked two sets of questions. One queried respondents about their local news consumption habits. Although we asked about a range of media sources, our primary measure is based on a question about whether respondents had in the previous 24 hours read a local newspaper (either online or in print). The wording of this question –

---

[13] See also Peterson 2019.
[14] See Appendix H for information about the CCES and our measures of political engagement.

asking about consumption in the previous day – is useful for gauging whether respondents regularly consume a particular media source.

In a second set of questions, we asked respondents about their knowledge of and recent participation in local politics. Among them:

- the name of the mayor of their city or town (if they lived in a place with a mayor)
- the name of the superintendent or head of the local school district
- whether they had recently engaged in five types of local political participation[15]

We did not ask the same questions in every survey, but we did ask each item at least twice, so we have observations for each measure in multiple years.

The data demonstrate an unequivocal connection between newspaper reading and local engagement. Regular newspaper readers are more likely than nonreaders to know basic information about their local government and to participate in local politics. Even controlling for college education, gender, age, race, partisanship, and general political interest – all of which might affect people's engagement separate and apart from their news consumption habits – reading a local newspaper is a consistent and statistically significant predictor of whether respondents know the name of their mayor and local school superintendent.[16] For instance, in our 2019 survey, the probability that a respondent who read the newspaper knew his or her mayor's name was 55%. For a non-newspaper reader, it was 42% (see Figure 4.1). Similarly, newspaper readers in 2019 were 12 percentage points more likely than nonreaders to name their school superintendent.

Newspaper readers are also more likely to vote in local elections, reach out to elected officials, and attend local meetings. In 2017, for example,

---

[15] The activities are (1) voted in a local election; (2) attended a local political meeting; (3) signed a letter or petition about an issue in your community; (4) used social media to communicate about politics in your community; and (5) contacted a member of your local government. See Table H.1 for participation in each activity.

[16] We coded responses as correct if they included a name (i.e., something other than "I don't know" or leaving the answer blank). This is necessary because our surveys do not contain information about respondents' city of residence, which means we don't know for sure the name of their mayor and superintendent. Our choice to code as correct any substantive answer means that we are likely overestimating local knowledge and underestimating the effect of news consumption, since offering an answer is easier than knowing the right one. In that sense, the approach constitutes a conservative test of our argument. Appendix H includes additional discussion of this measurement strategy.

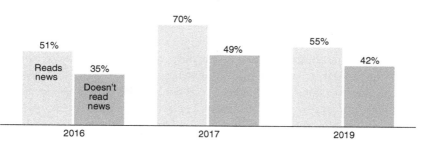

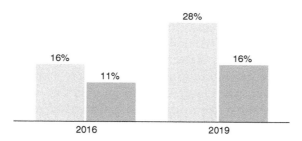

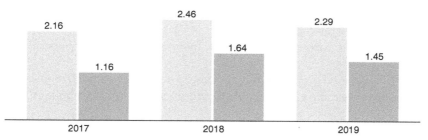

FIGURE 4.1. Local newspaper consumption and local political engagement
Note: Results are predictions from regression models controlling for numerous demographic and political variables (see Table H.2). The mayor and superintendent graphs display the probability that a respondent knows the relevant item, broken down by whether a respondent reads the local newspaper or does not. The participation graph presents the average number of acts of local participation (out of five) the respondent engaged in. Data are from 2016–2019 modules of the Cooperative Congressional Election Study.

newspaper readers engaged in an average of 2.16 acts of local participation. For respondents who said they didn't read local news, the average was just 1.16. In other words, local participation among newspaper readers was between 15% and 20% higher than among nonreaders.[17]

It is also newspaper reading specifically, rather than exposure to local news in general, that spurs political engagement. We know that because in addition to asking respondents about reading the paper, we also asked whether they watched local TV news. Figure 4.2 compares the knowledge and participation increase newspaper readers get to the boost that comes from watching local TV news. For simplicity, we rely just on our 2019 survey.

Across the three measures, the increase in knowledge among newspaper readers, compared to nonreaders, is generally larger than the comparable differences between TV watchers and non-TV watchers. Consider the odds that a respondent will name her school superintendent. It's 11 percentage points higher if she reads the newspaper than if she doesn't, but there is essentially no difference between a respondent who does and does not watch local TV news. In fact, TV watchers do about 1 point worse. Newspaper reading also boosts participation more than does watching TV news.[18] Our question about the mayor shows a similar pattern, although the difference is not quite statistically significant.[19] The more pronounced effect of newspaper exposure is perhaps not surprising given the paucity of substantive public affairs coverage on local TV news. Whereas television news may help residents stay informed about statewide and federal elected officials, as prior studies have shown,[20] newspapers appear particularly important for engagement with politics at the truly local level.

Still, these relationships remain suggestive, since we don't know that newspaper reading *causes* people to engage more with local politics. Our

[17] In 2019, we also asked respondents whether they approved or disapproved of their county governments. Once again, reading a local newspaper was a strong and significant predictor of whether someone could offer a response. Controlling for other factors, the probability that a newspaper reader could evaluate the county government was 85%. For nonreaders it was just 71%.

[18] We display percent changes to keep the participation effects on a comparable scale to the mayor and superintendent measures. In raw numbers, the newspaper effect is 0.66 (on the 6-point scale) and the TV effect is 0.21.

[19] Wald tests show that the newspaper coefficient is significantly larger than the local TV coefficient in the superintendent and political participation models ($p < 0.05$), but not in the mayor model.

[20] Hopkins 2018; Moskowitz 2021.

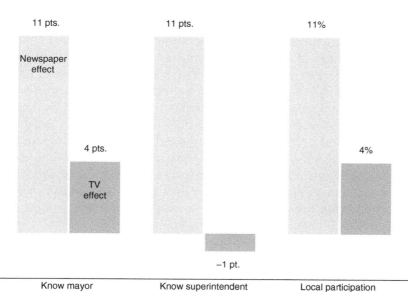

FIGURE 4.2. Newspaper reading versus local TV viewing and local political engagement
Note: Results are predictions from regression models controlling for numerous demographic and political variables (see Table H.3). The mayor and superintendent bars display the change in probability that a respondent knows the relevant item if he/she reads a local newspaper or not, and if he/she watches local TV news or not. The participation bars present the percent change in the average number of acts of local participation. Data are from a module of the 2019 Cooperative Congressional Election Study.

findings could result from the fact that the politically engaged are more likely to read the newspaper because they enjoy it. Controlling for a variety of factors helps mitigate this concern, as does the finding that newspaper readership is a stronger predictor of engagement than TV viewing. But we can't dismiss the possibility that the relationship is spurious. In addition, these analyses don't allow us to say anything about variation in the volume of actual newspaper coverage, either across communities or over time, to which respondents have access.

TURNOUT IN MAYORAL ELECTIONS

To demonstrate that variation in news coverage itself is related to political engagement in the real world, we draw on a data set of voter turnout in mayoral elections from 1993 to 2011. Compiled by Thomas

M. Holbrook and Aaron C. Weinschenk, these data are based on publicly available election returns from localities throughout the United States.[21] A key advantage of analyzing election data is that they represent actual political participation, not just survey respondents' self-reported behavior. For our analysis, we focus on the 217 elections in 73 cities for which we have both a measure of voter turnout and a measure of local newspaper mayoral coverage, drawn from the content analysis we detailed in Chapters 2 and 3.[22] For instance, in Boise, Idaho, we have turnout data from four mayoral elections – 2001, 2003, 2007, and 2011 – and coverage in those years from the local newspaper, the *Idaho Statesman*. With similar data in six dozen cities all over the United States, we can examine the relationship between local news coverage and turnout in local elections in a wide variety of contexts.

Although 1993 is the earliest election in the data set, most took place later, amid the local news crisis. In all, 76% of the elections we analyze occurred between 2003 and 2011, during which time the decline of local news accelerated. For every city, we have at least two elections, and for more than 60% of them, we have at least three. In 22 cities, we have 4 or more observations. Thus, we can consider not only how variation in news coverage may explain differences in voter turnout across cities, but also how changes in coverage can affect turnout from election to election within the same city.[23]

The basic trends confirm that over the course of this 18-year period, both news coverage and mayoral turnout declined. Turnout in the elections between 1993 and 1999, for instance, averaged 31.8%. In that same period, the average mayoral coverage share of the news hole was 4.8%. Fast forward to the last four years of our data set, 2008 through 2011, and turnout was just 21.9%. Meanwhile, mayoral coverage had fallen to 4.1% of the news hole, a 15% decline. This is a somewhat arbitrary division of time periods, but slicing the data in other ways yields the same conclusion: Between the end of the 1990s and through the first decade of

[21] We are grateful to Holbrook and Weinschenk for sharing their data.
[22] We exclude runoff elections. See Appendix I for a detailed description of the mayoral election data.
[23] The turnout measure is calculated by dividing the votes cast in the mayoral election by the city's citizen voting age population. As Holbrook and Weinschenk (2014) note, their estimates are similar to figures from other studies of mayoral turnout. On average, turnout in the 217 elections in our data set is 24.4%.

the 2000s, local mayoral coverage and mayoral turnout were on a twin downward trajectory.[24]

These rough comparisons don't account for a number of explanations for these trends, including the characteristics of the cities holding elections in particular years. But examining just the 22 cities for which we have data in at least 4 years allows us to focus on changes within the same localities. This approach has the advantage of holding constant many other variables that affect turnout, such as demographics, whether elections are partisan or nonpartisan, governmental structure, and population size. And when we do, the same pattern persists. In 15 of these 22 cities, the turnout rate in the most recent mayoral election was lower than in the earliest one. Likewise, the percentage of the news hole devoted to mayoral coverage fell in 16 of 22 cities. In Boise, Idaho, for example, as mayoral coverage in the *Idaho Statesman* fell from 7.7% (2001) to 3.5% (2011) of the news hole, mayoral turnout declined from 24.8% to 11.4%. Remarkably, that's a virtually identical 54% drop in both. At a purely descriptive level, local newspaper coverage and voter turnout have moved in tandem over time.

Figure 4.3 presents a more detailed look at the strength of the relationship. Each dot represents one of the 217 elections in our data set. Its placement on the graph reflects the percentage of the news hole devoted to mayoral coverage in that year (horizontal axis) and the level of voter turnout in the mayoral election (vertical axis).

The wide spread of the dots indicates substantial variation in the relationship. In some elections, both turnout and news coverage are relatively high (Philadelphia in 1999). In others, both are low (Wichita in 2007). And in some, the two do not appear strongly related (Louisville in 2006). But the downward sloping line – representing the average relationship between turnout and coverage – indicates a tendency for the two to move together. In statistical terms, the correlation between the two measures is 0.25, which represents a significant, albeit not intensely strong, relationship. The decline in newspaper coverage clearly

---

[24] For example, the turnout rate up through 2002 was 27.8%. But starting in 2003 – as the local news crisis began in earnest – turnout was just 23.4%. In those two periods, mayoral coverage dropped from 5.2% to 4.2% of the news hole. Alternatively, if we compare the first 50% of our observations (up through 2005) to the second half (2006 through 2011), we find that turnout and mayoral coverage were higher in the earlier period (26.3% and 4.7%) than in the later one (22.5% and 4.2%). Finally, when we divide the data into seven time periods spanning 1993–2011, the correlation between turnout and news coverage is 0.41.

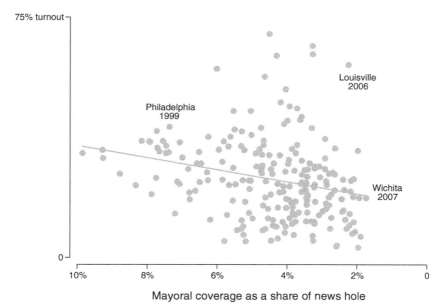

FIGURE 4.3. The relationship between mayoral turnout and local newspaper coverage
Note: Each dot represents one of 217 mayoral elections. The share of the news hole is based on our content analysis, and the mayoral turnout data were compiled by Thomas Holbrook and Aaron Weinshenck.

helps us understand variation in turnout, but it is also just one of many forces explaining why people vote.

Of course, to produce a persuasive estimate of the relationship, we can't just compare turnout and news coverage in one city to another, or from year to year within the same city. After all, turnout in a given election in a city is likely related to turnout in that city in earlier elections. Demographic factors, such as a city's ethnic makeup, population size, and education level, all affect turnout. And timing matters, too; when mayoral contests are held in presidential or midterm years, turnout will be much higher than in off-year elections.[25] When we employ fixed-effects and random-effects models to address these realities, we consistently confirm a relationship between local mayoral coverage and turnout.[26] Depending

---

[25] Hajnal and Lewis 2003; Holbrook and Weinschenk 2014; Marschall and Lappie 2018.
[26] See Table I.1.

on the model, a 1 percentage point decrease in coverage is associated with a 1–2 percentage point drop in voter turnout. In a place like Boise, that implies that the 4-percentage point drop in mayoral coverage between 2001 and 2011 may have accounted for up to 8 points of the 13-point turnout decline over that time. The precise relationship varies from city to city and election to election, but there is no doubt a connection.

A final set of analyses, in which we consider the possibility that reductions in local government reporting in general – not mayoral coverage specifically – contributed to the decline in mayoral turnout, bolster that conclusion.[27] We find that reductions in coverage of city government, school boards, and county government bear no relationship to turnout levels in mayoral elections. Instead, mayoral coverage in particular – the very information that voters would find most helpful – is significantly connected to turnout.

This finding has at least two important implications. First, it supports our contention that a loss of relevant reporting reduces citizens' engagement in local politics. When the cost of acquiring information about an upcoming mayoral election goes up, participation goes down. Second, when newspapers eliminate beats or reduce coverage of specific parts of government, political engagement connected to those institutions falls. That presumably does not bode well for future participation in elections for school boards or county government, where newspapers have made drastic cuts in recent years.

To be sure, our interpretation of these data – that news coverage is a *cause* of voter turnout – relies on some key assumptions. Perhaps most notably, we assume that a reduction in news coverage and not a change in other factors, such as campaign activity, is responsible for the decline in voter turnout. Although there are both theoretical and empirical justifications for that account, there are necessarily limitations on how strong our causal interpretation can be.

INTEREST IN LOCAL GOVERNMENT AND AMERICANS' ONLINE SEARCHES

People who read newspapers are more engaged with local politics, and reductions in local news coverage over the last 20 years are tied to the downward slide in turnout in local elections. But measures of people's

---

[27] See Table I.2.

actual behavior that we can more confidently tie to news coverage itself would provide further evidence for our causal argument. Here, we turn to Americans' online search behavior to study how local news reporting affects interest in local government.

Online searches are a valuable measure of local engagement for at least three reasons. First, searches are clear indicators of people's interest in a topic – in our case, local government. Although interest itself is not the same thing as knowledge or participation, it is a critical antecedent of both.[28] If people aren't interested in local politics, we can hardly expect them to know much about it or get themselves to the polls. Second, online searches represent real behavior. And because they happen in private, they're not subject to social desirability biases or social pressure that might lead people to exaggerate their true interest in politics. More so than answers in surveys, searches reflect genuine interest. Third, news coverage theoretically should lead to changes in the frequency of searches about local politics. That's because local politics represents a low-salience topic that most people don't think about in the absence of news coverage. This is different than searches that are driven by personal experience – for instance, when people suffer from allergies ("allergy medicine for sneezing") or need to buy new running shoes ("best deal Asics GEL"). Thus, to the extent that news coverage and online local politics searches move in tandem, it is almost certainly the case that the relationship is causal.[29]

Our analysis draws on Google Trends data from 2004 through 2016 in 50 metropolitan areas around the country, one in each state. For each metro area, we collected data on the popularity of Google searches related to the mayor, city government, and school boards.[30] Google Trends measures search popularity on a scale from 0 to 100, with higher scores indicating greater popularity. The score is relative to the popularity of searches for all other terms. We combine the search data with our content analysis of coverage of the same topics in the local newspaper serving

---

[28] Prior 2019.

[29] Some may wonder about reverse causality – the possibility that increases in citizen interest in local government might produce more news coverage. But that is highly unlikely, because it's hard to imagine how citizens en masse would become interested in, say, their local city council without having been alerted to some important development by the news media. In addition, prior empirical work has found that news coverage affects politics-related internet searches, but searches do not drive coverage. See Southwell et al. 2016 and Weeks and Southwell 2010.

[30] See Hopkins 2018 for a similar approach that examines interest in state governors.

each metro area in each year.[31] For example, we match the search data from Denver for each year to the news coverage data we collected from the *Denver Post*.

Consistent with our expectations, local politics searches have declined along with reductions in news coverage about local government. Consider the top panel of Figure 4.4. The solid line represents the average popularity of searches for "mayor" in the 50 metro areas for which we have data. Mayor searches were most popular in 2005, with an average score of 37, and least popular in 2012, with a score of 27. The dotted line plots the percentage of the news hole devoted to mayoral coverage each year, on average, for the 50 papers in these cities (and shows the familiar downward trend). Over the course of 13 years, as local newspapers devoted less coverage to the mayor, Americans were less inclined to Google the mayor. Statistically, the strength of the relationship is about the same as we found between news coverage and turnout in mayoral elections.[32]

Like with mayoral election turnout, national politics has a direct bearing on Americans' interest in mayors. Notice that mayor searches are less popular in presidential years, by an average of about two points. This suggests that interest in national elections takes relative attention away from local politics. But it is not the explanation for why news coverage and online searches of the mayor are related. In fact, when we exclude the presidential years, the correlation between news coverage and mayor searches is even stronger, further evidence that coverage itself is a key influence on interest in local government.[33]

The connection for city government is even more consistent.[34] As coverage of city and town councils has gone down, so has public interest. We can also glean insights from data missing from the city government analysis, which is based on just 40 cities. The other 10 had an insufficient number of searches for "city council" or "town council" to be included in the Google Trends data. That could very well be because those 10 cities also had particularly low levels of city government coverage. In the 40 cities with measurable online searches, the average percentage of the news hole devoted to city government across the time series was 2.8%. In

---

[31] See Appendix J for more details about the search data.

[32] The correlation is 0.28.

[33] The correlation for presidential years is 0.15 and 0.30 for non-presidential years.

[34] Despite the divergence in 2009, the correlation between the two is very strong (0.76). Excluding 2009, it is 0.88.

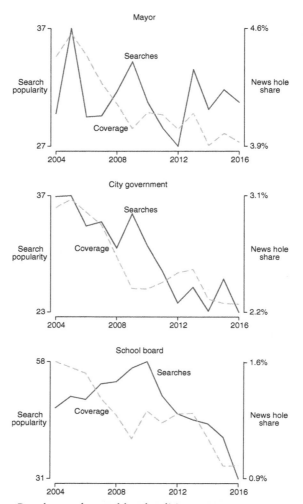

FIGURE 4.4. Google searches and local politics coverage
Note: Search popularity is based on Google Trends data; the share of the news hole is based on our content analysis.

the other 10, it was just 1.7% – roughly a 40% difference. When local residents don't see coverage of city government, their interest falls – to a degree that makes it impossible to gauge their Google searches.

The local school board results are more uncertain. While online searches and news coverage diverged between 2004 and 2009, the two measures were highly correlated in the second half of the time series.[35] It may be the case that parents' interest in their local school districts are driven more by personal experience – concern about their children's education – than by news coverage. Nonetheless, the strong downward trajectory of both school board searches and news between 2010 and 2016 at least suggests that recent cuts to education coverage at newspapers across the country may play a role.

The lines displayed in Figure 4.4 are averages, and, not surprisingly, the relationship between search behavior and news coverage varies from city to city.[36] Sometimes it is stronger, and sometimes it is weaker. But overall, the evidence points to the same conclusion – reductions in local government coverage lead to lower levels of interest in local government. Of course, this aggregate-level data has limitations of its own, since it cannot speak to the degree to which an individual citizen's exposure to local news affects his or her engagement.

KNOWLEDGE AND PARTICIPATION IN US HOUSE ELECTIONS

A skeptic could reasonably claim that many of the findings we've presented thus far are consistent with the argument that consumer behavior – and not news coverage itself – is responsible for decreases in local political knowledge and participation. The two-decade declines in mayoral turnout and interest in local government, for instance, could simply stem from people gravitating away from local news sources to national ones. Their behavior could have little to do with the fact that local newspapers have drastically cut their coverage. One way to address this concern is to hold time constant. If local engagement in different communities at the same point in time corresponds to the amount of local political coverage in those communities, then that relationship can't be explained by long-term changes in consumer behavior. Instead, it would provide further evidence that local engagement rises and falls – and in recent years, mostly falls – in response to newspaper coverage.

For that type of evidence, we turn our attention from municipal politics to US House elections. This has two virtues. First, congressional campaigns represent a somewhat different local political context. Although House elections involve local events and debates focused on the particular concerns of district residents, they also take place against the backdrop of

---

[35] The overall correlation is 0.46, which is driven by the 2010–2016 correlation of 0.79.
[36] See Appendix J.

national politics. In an increasingly nationalized political environment, citizen involvement in these hybrid elections – part local, part federal – might have more to do with how voters feel about leaders in Washington than what their local newspapers have to say. That makes this a hard test for our argument. To the extent that newspapers still matter in contemporary House elections, that is strong evidence of their importance for local engagement more generally.

The second is a matter of data and analytical leverage. Studying mayoral elections or local school boards often requires cobbling together data from numerous sources, and offers few opportunities for individual-level analysis. But because 435 House elections take place at the same time every two years, we have access to high-quality national surveys with both district- and individual-level data. Moreover, there are big differences in the nature and competitiveness of House campaigns. That means some races receive a lot of news attention, while others get little to none. The resulting variation provides an opportunity to examine how citizen engagement responds to differences in newspaper coverage in localities across the entire country.

The first step in our analysis requires creating a measure of local House campaign coverage. We conducted a detailed content analysis of general election coverage in all 435 House districts during the 2010 midterm elections. In each district, we identified the largest circulation local newspaper we could access through one of several electronic databases or the newspaper's online archives. (Many are the same papers we introduced in Chapter 2 and have used throughout the book.) We collected every newspaper article that mentioned at least one of the two major-party candidates for the House seat in the month leading up to Election Day (October 2–November 2, 2010). In all, we collected and coded 6,003 news stories, editorials, and op-ed columns.[37]

We assume that more coverage provides voters with more useful information about their electoral choices, and promotes knowledge and participation. So for the purposes of this analysis, we focus on the total number of articles published about each House race. As we'd expect, the volume of coverage varied widely – from no stories at all (in 7% of districts) to as many as 81 articles about a particular race. Overall, the average number of stories per race was 14.4 – roughly one every other

---

[37] See Appendix K.

day in the month leading up to the election. Not surprisingly, the more competitive a contest was, the more coverage it received.[38]

Because our content analysis reveals significant differences in coverage across House districts, we can leverage that spatial variation to determine whether the volume of coverage affects voters' congressional election knowledge and participation. To do so, we analyze data from the 2010 Cooperative Congressional Election Study. The CCES is an ideal survey because of its unusually large sample size (more than 50,000), enough to study the behavior of respondents within individual congressional districts.[39] Additionally, it includes several measures of political knowledge and participation relevant to understanding local political engagement: whether respondents could (1) place the Democratic and Republican House candidates in their district on an ideological scale, (2) offer a rating of their incumbent House member, and (3) say in the preelection survey who they planned to vote for.[40] If our argument holds, then individuals living in districts with more news coverage will be more informed about and more likely to participate in the congressional election than will people living in districts with less news coverage.

Beginning at the district level, that's exactly what we find. Consider the leftmost panel in Figure 4.5. It plots the relationship between the number of news stories in a congressional district and the percentage of respondents in that district who placed the Democratic candidate to the left of the Republican on an ideological scale (something just 37% could do).[41] The less coverage of a House campaign in a district, the smaller the share of district residents who accurately assessed their candidates' ideologies. And while most respondents successfully answered the other questions – 81% rated their incumbent and 79% expressed a vote intention – the

---

[38] For more on the variation in campaign coverage across districts, see Hayes and Lawless 2015.

[39] Our earlier analyses of the 2016–2019 CCES drew on data from modules we designed and that were administered as part of the larger survey. In this analysis, we rely on the CCES "Common Content," which the survey's principal investigators designed.

[40] We use intended vote in the House race because it allows us to tie participation directly to the congressional contest. A broader behavioral measure such as validated turnout would not be specific to the House election.

[41] Based on where respondents placed the Republican and Democratic House candidates in their districts on the ideological scale, we constructed a measure to indicate whether they (correctly) placed the Democrat to the left of the Republican. We follow previous work in using this as a measure of political knowledge (e.g., Adams et al. 2017).

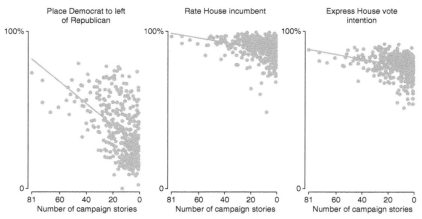

FIGURE 4.5. The relationship between news coverage and citizen engagement in US House elections

Note: The figure plots the number of campaign stories in a congressional district against the percentage of CCES respondents in each district who could array the candidates correctly on the ideological spectrum, rate the incumbent, and indicate for whom they planned to vote. We restrict the analysis to the 381 congressional districts with both a Democratic and Republican candidate and in which the local newspaper ran at least one story. The number of campaign stories is based on our content analysis of congressional elections in 2010.

districts where the fewest residents could do so were the ones with the least news coverage.[42]

A simplified analysis such as this, of course, doesn't account for a variety of factors that affect citizen engagement – an individual's socio-economic status, political interest, and partisanship, as well as features of the congressional campaign in the district, such as competitiveness and campaign activity. The potential confounding influence of campaign activity is especially important, since it could increase both news coverage and political engagement. To be sure that the relationship between coverage and engagement isn't just masking the influence of, say, candidate spending on TV ads or voter mobilization, we need to conduct a statistical analysis that accounts for those factors. But even after doing so, we find

[42] The correlations between the number of stories and each measure is 0.51 for placing the Democrat to the left of the Republican; 0.28 for placing the incumbent; and 0.29 for expressing a vote intention. These relationships are not sensitive to outliers; they are virtually identical when we drop the handful of districts with a very large number of stories (i.e., more than 60).

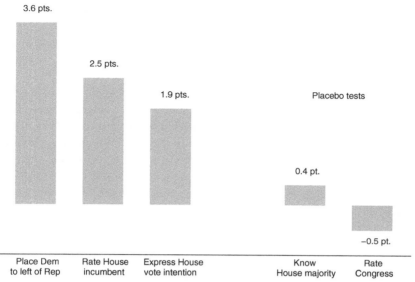

FIGURE 4.6. The effects of news coverage on citizen engagement in US House elections

Note: Results are predictions from regression models controlling for numerous demographic, political, and contextual variables (see Table K.1). Bars indicate the percentage point increase in the odds of respondents arraying the candidates correctly on the ideological spectrum, rating the incumbent, and indicating for whom they planned to vote based on a shift from one standard deviation below to one standard deviation above the mean story count. Data are from our congressional elections content analysis and the 2010 CCES Common Content.

that the volume of coverage devoted to a race continues to affect engagement. All else equal, a shift of two standard deviations in coverage (about 26 stories) changes the likelihood that a respondent accurately assessed the candidates' issue positions by about 3.6 points (see Figure 4.6). Larger shifts in news coverage produce larger increases. It's not surprising that we find the biggest effects on the ideological placement measure; news coverage is most influential when voters' knowledge is lowest. Plus, respondents were interviewed late in the campaign cycle, at a time when we would expect relatively less variation in political engagement. Yet, as the graph shows, the news effects persist even for rating the current incumbent and expressing a vote choice. Although the figure portrays these changes as increases to reflect the positive statistical relationship, the implication of this finding is that districts with less local news coverage had less engaged citizens.

The magnitude of these effects – modest, but significant – is in line with our earlier analyses of voter turnout and interest in local government. But because these results are based on individual-level data from models that account for both demographic factors and campaign activity, the newspaper effects are particularly credible.

Moreover, our analysis casts doubt on a plausible alternative explanation: That our findings simply reflect newspapers catering to their audience. In that telling, it could be that newspapers in districts where people are politically engaged devote more coverage to House elections because their readers are more interested in politics. If that were true, then the correlation between coverage and engagement would not mean that coverage is causing engagement to rise; it would be the opposite. But in two "placebo tests," we find no relationship between local coverage of the congressional election and two indicators of general political knowledge: whether a respondent knows which party controls the House of Representatives, and whether he or she can offer a rating of Congress.[43] In the right side of Figure 4.6, the number of stories about the House race fails to predict correct answers to those questions, suggesting that campaign news coverage is not simply a product of district-level political engagement.[44] That result bolsters our interpretation that when coverage of local House races declines, knowledge and participation do indeed go with it.

Our analysis of the 2010 midterms suggests that the demise of local newspapers has affected not only Americans' engagement with their mayors and city officials, but also the candidates in their House districts. Even in a period of growing nationalization, local newspapers still matter. Moreover, these effects cannot be explained by voters gravitating toward national news sources. Because our analysis took place at a single point in time, the trends in news consumption are held constant.

---

[43] Of course, exposure to news coverage of the campaign could in theory increase a respondent's ability to rate Congress and correctly identify the Democrats as holding the House, especially in an election year that is somewhat nationalized, as was 2010. But it seems plausible that the placebo test variables are likely to arise principally from general attentiveness to politics, whereas campaign-specific engagement – which our main dependent variables tap – is likely to depend much more heavily on an election's information environment. We think it is thus reasonable to expect that the placebo variables will not correlate with election news.

[44] Neither coefficient is statistically significant. See Table K.1 for the regression results.

TRACKING THE DECLINE IN CITIZEN ENGAGEMENT IN US HOUSE ELECTIONS

Still, we haven't put our argument to the toughest test – whether the *same* individuals' levels of engagement have fallen as their local newspapers have pulled back local political reporting. For that, we turn to the 2010–2014 panel component of the Cooperative Congressional Election Study. The 2014 wave of the CCES includes more than 9,000 respondents who also participated in the 2010 survey.[45] In the lead-up to the 2014 midterm elections, they answered the same questions they did in 2010 about the House election in their district – candidate ideology, incumbent ratings, and vote intention. Because these are the same people interviewed multiple times, we know that characteristics such as their education level or general political interest are unlikely to change very much. That eliminates a major threat to causal inference and allows us to measure the effect of local news on citizen engagement with greater precision and confidence.

In order to identify any news effects, we added to our content analysis from 2010 an identical measure of news coverage in 2014 for each House district. We followed the same procedures we did in 2010 – first identifying the largest circulation local newspaper we could access, and then collecting every article that mentioned the Democratic or Republican House candidate in the month leading up to Election Day. All told, we coded 4,524 stories.[46]

The 2010 and 2014 midterms in some ways represent a microcosm of the trends that have animated this entire book. First, local news consumers had access to less information about their House candidates in 2014 than four years earlier. In 2014, the typical House race saw 2.5 fewer stories in the month leading up to the election than in 2010. On average, this means that campaigns were covered roughly every other day in 2010, but only every third day in 2014. In addition, a slightly smaller share of stories about contested races in 2014 discussed both the Democratic and Republican candidates, suggesting that even the remaining coverage was less substantive. During this four-year time span, voter turnout declined as well. As typical for midterm elections, participation in both years was relatively low, with less than half the eligible electorate casting a ballot. But between 2010 and 2014, turnout fell from

---

[45] See Appendix K for details on the CCES 2010–2014 Panel Study.
[46] See Appendix K.

41.8% to 36.7%, an illustration of growing voter disengagement in local elections.[47]

Some of the decline in both coverage and turnout is due to differences in the political environment. In 2010, the prospect of Republicans flipping the House (which they did) generated a more competitive landscape than in 2014. Indeed, *The Cook Political Report* rated as "safe" 372 districts in 2014, compared to 316 in 2010, and less competitive races received less coverage. But even holding competitiveness constant, coverage of House races declined, almost surely as a function of the reduction in reporting resources at local newspapers. For example, in safe districts, local newspapers in 2010 published on average 9.6 stories about the House race, but just 8.9 in 2014. In more competitive districts, papers in 2010 published 23.5 stories on average, compared to 22.9 in 2014. These changes are by no means dramatic, but a 3–6% decline over just a four-year span underscores the extent to which newspapers were scaling back.

In order to estimate the precise effect of this decline on Americans' engagement, we first measured the change in the number of news stories about the House race in each survey respondent's district between 2010 and 2014. Then, we looked at how each CCES respondent answered the knowledge and participation questions in 2014 as compared to 2010. If, for example, a respondent correctly placed the Democratic candidate to the left of the Republican in 2010, but not in 2014, we coded that as a decline in knowledge. If a respondent failed to rate the House incumbent in 2010, but then did so in 2014, that reflects an increase in knowledge. We coded wrong answers in both years, or correct answers in both years, as no change.

Statistically, we expect a positive relationship between changes in news coverage and engagement: As coverage increases in a district from one election to the next, so should knowledge and participation. But substantively, that means that the reverse – and more common – scenario is also true: When coverage declines between 2010 and 2014, we expect engagement to follow.

The data in Figure 4.7 show that when we track the same respondents over time, their levels of engagement indeed rise and fall in response to their local newspapers' coverage. For instance, a two standard deviation increase in coverage (about 28 stories) between the two elections leads to a 3.7 percentage point increase in the odds that a respondent who could

---

[47] See Michael McDonald's turnout estimates at the United States Elections Project (www.electproject.org/).

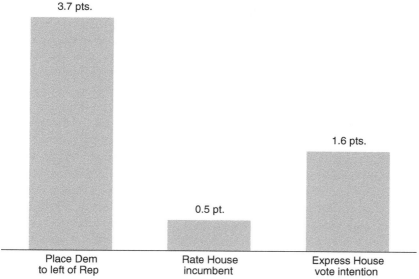

FIGURE 4.7. Effect of a change in US House campaign coverage on engagement
Note: Results are predictions from difference-in-difference regression models that control for changes in candidate spending (see Table K.2). Bars indicate the percentage point increase in the odds of respondents correctly arraying the candidates on the ideological spectrum, rating the incumbent, and indicating a vote choice in 2014 after not having been able to do so in 2010. The point estimates are based on a two standard deviation increase in the number of campaign stories between 2010 and 2014. Data are from our congressional elections content analysis and the 2010–2014 CCES Panel Study.

not accurately place the Democrat and Republican on an ideological scale in 2010 could do so in 2014. The key implication of that result is that in most districts in 2014 – where coverage was lower compared to 2010 – respondents were *less* likely to be able to do this. The same is true, to a smaller degree, for rating the incumbent and stating a vote choice.[48] Critically, these analyses account for changes in candidate spending, which means we can be confident that the effects we attribute to news coverage aren't the result of other types of campaign activity.[49]

---

[48] A cross-sectional analysis in 2014 controlling for lagged dependent variable values in 2010 produces comparable results. See Appendix K.

[49] Although redistricting took place in most states following the 2010 midterms, it should not compromise our analysis because we are estimating individual-level, not district-level, effects. Our coding ensures that we know what the information environment was like in the district that each respondent lived in in 2010 and 2014, regardless of whether that

Still, it's important to rule out the possibility that these findings are the product of a parallel trend – the increasing number of Americans getting their news from national, rather than local, news sources. Since the decline in newspaper coverage happened at the same time as national news consumption was rising, even our panel analyses might misattribute to *coverage* what is really caused by decreasing *attention* to local news.

To investigate that possibility, we rely on a CCES question that asked respondents whether they watched both local and national broadcast news. Although we would prefer a richer measure of respondents' news habits, this indicator at least allows us to track whether changes in one aspect of media consumption correspond to changes in political engagement. The data suggest that getting more national news – at least on TV – is not responsible for the declines in engagement we identify. For instance, among respondents who increased their national news viewing, 12.4% accurately placed their House candidates in 2010 but failed to do so in 2014 – an indicator of a decline in engagement. For people whose national news attention did not increase, that number was actually higher, at 15%. The pattern was similar for our other measures of engagement. These are merely descriptive comparisons, but when we model this relationship more rigorously, we find that changes in local newspaper coverage continue to predict respondents' knowledge and participation in House elections.[50] Changing news habits have no doubt contributed to voters' lower levels of local engagement, but the hollowing out of America's local newspapers is a major culprit of its own.

CONCLUSION

This chapter has presented a wide array of data demonstrating a consistent link between local newspaper coverage and Americans' engagement with local politics. Surveys reveal that local newspaper readers know more about their city and school officials and are more likely to vote, attend meetings, and participate in other forms of local activism than nonreaders. They're even more engaged than their neighbors who watch local TV news. Trends in local elections provide more evidence. As

district was the same in both years. In addition, controlling for changes in candidate spending captures the key source of district-level variation that would influence knowledge and participation. For more details, see Hayes and Lawless 2018.

[50] See Table K.3 for the regression models, which show that while national news habits contribute to Americans' declining engagement with local politics, the decline of local news has a separate and independent effect. See Peterson (2019) for a similar conclusion.

mayoral coverage in local newspapers has declined, so has turnout in elections for mayor. Less newspaper coverage of local politics has also contributed to Americans' declining interest in local government, as evidenced by their Google searches. And in House elections, voters living in districts with less coverage are less likely to know basic information about their congressional candidates, even accounting for a wide variety of other factors. This is true whether we compare residents in different districts to each other, or follow the same individuals over time.

No single piece of our analysis proves that the demise of newspapers is responsible for the decline in local engagement. But collectively, the accumulated evidence – from surveys, election returns, internet searches, and measures of news coverage itself – is impossible to ignore. The Internet has not boosted Americans' engagement with local politics, and the popularity of cable news and websites dominated by national politics does not solely account for its decline. The diminishment of newspapers – the core institution of civic life in local communities – has significantly eroded Americans' connection to the officials and governments who represent them.

This chapter has been about generalities – in knowledge, interest, and turnout in local politics. A key question in the contemporary era, however, is whether the damaging effects of newspapers' decline have been larger in some places, and for some people. That's the focus of the next chapter.

5

Everyone Loses When Local News Declines

Two of the voters we interviewed as part of a nationwide survey in the fall of 2019 could not have seemed more different. One, a 59-year-old California resident living in the Central Valley, identified as a Democrat. Calling himself liberal, he held predictable policy positions: expanding access to Medicare, bolstering the Environmental Protection Agency's regulatory powers, and opposing military intervention in Iran. Recently, he had fallen on hard times. Having never graduated from high school, he was unemployed and his financial circumstances were deteriorating.[1]

Three thousand miles across the country lived a woman whose profile could hardly have been more distinct. Making her home in Lackawanna County, Pennsylvania, she described herself as a conservative Republican. She supported President Trump's efforts to withhold funding from sanctuary cities, repeal the Affordable Care Act, and ban transgender people from military service. Born in 1947 amid the postwar baby boom, she had gone to college, earned a bachelor's degree, and now worked full-time in the education field.

The standard story of modern American politics is that voters like these are mirror images, sharing nothing but antipathy for each other's political values. But on one count, the liberal California high school dropout and the conservative Pennsylvania college graduate were in lockstep: Neither had any idea about what was going on in their respective local governments. When we asked who their mayor was, neither knew. School

[1] These interviews were conducted as part of a module of the 2019 CCES. Other personally identifying information is not available.

superintendent? Same answer. Asked if they thought their county government was doing a good job, neither could say. Nor could they identify the
most important political issue facing the community where they lived;
when prompted, the Pennsylvania Republican demurred, and the
California Democrat, stretching the definition of local issues, said "the
President we have now." In the previous year, neither had attended a local
meeting, signed a local petition, voted in a local election, or participated
in local politics in any fashion.

These voters' total and identical disconnection from local politics is
surprising not only because they have such different partisan and ideological profiles. It also defies a pattern identified in recent research – that
changes to the media environment have led people like our college-
educated Pennsylvania Republican to become more politically engaged,
while at the same time made it easier for less educated citizens like our
California Democrat to opt out of politics altogether. Indeed, in the
2016 presidential election, the Pennsylvania conservative voted for
Trump, whereas the California liberal stayed home. But the story of this
chapter is that when it comes to local engagement, the dynamic is very
different: The decline of local news affects the political behavior of
citizens across the spectrum very similarly. The growing scarcity of
reporting about local government has led to growing disengagement
among Americans of all stripes.

WHOSE ENGAGEMENT DECLINES WHEN LOCAL NEWS DISAPPEARS?

The notion that the dramatic upheaval in the local news environment
might not affect everyone the same way emerges from an important line of
research about changes to the national media landscape. In an influential
book and article, political scientist Markus Prior argues that the explosion of media options in recent decades has increased some Americans'
political engagement and reduced others'.[2] These disparate effects help
resolve what appeared to be a strange contradiction: Despite the "spec-
tacular rise" in political information available on cable TV and the
Internet, Americans' levels of political involvement did not appreciably
increase in the latter years of the twentieth century.[3]

[2] Prior 2005, 2007.
[3] Prior 2005, p. 578.

Prior's explanation hinges on the differences between people he calls "news fans" and "entertainment fans." News fans are interested in politics, follow it closely, and enjoy consuming political media – think people who watch CNN all day and follow journalists and pundits on Twitter. With nonstop access to coverage of national politics, news fans can indulge their political interest to a degree never before possible. And for them, more exposure to news has meant increases in political knowledge and participation.[4]

Meanwhile, the opposite dynamic has played out for entertainment fans. More interested in the Kardashians than Congress, entertainment fans can now avoid politics almost entirely if they so choose. Instead of spending free time with the news – as many did during the era of broadcast TV dominance – they can now binge sitcoms on Netflix or watch ceaseless sports on ESPN. With less "accidental" exposure to politics, entertainment fans have become less knowledgeable and less likely to turn out to vote. The flat-lining of Americans' political engagement, according to Prior, is because declining engagement among entertainment fans has canceled out increasing engagement among news fans. With the rise of social media and digital political advertising amplifying the trend,[5] the information-rich get richer while the information-poor get poorer.

At first glance, it seems possible that a similar dynamic could be at play at the local level. Newspapers have long been a source of incidental exposure to the news – people glanced at the front-page story about the mayor's election on their way to the sports section or the classified ads. Local papers' demise has thus reduced the kind of casual exposure to local politics that can boost engagement for people who aren't otherwise motivated to seek out the news. Citizens who are more politically interested, however, may be insulated from the decline because they can get information from other sources, such as social media. In that telling, the patterns of declining local engagement we documented in Chapter 4 would be due to a downward trend only among people who are less politically interested to begin with.

But the unique nature of the local news environment suggests a different reality: that local engagement is falling for everyone – news and entertainment fans alike. As the national media landscape has expanded, many local news markets have contracted. Newspapers have dramatically

---

4 See also Hersh 2020.
5 Kim 2016; Lee 2019; Sung and Gil-de-Zúñiga 2014.

cut their coverage of local government. Local news start-ups haven't gotten off the ground in most cities and have mostly failed in the markets where they have emerged. And online local political information is scarce, whether from interest groups, "citizen journalists," or social media. While Americans live in a "high choice" environment when it comes to national politics, media choice for local politics remains distinctly low.

As a result, the erosion of the best source of local political information – newspapers – has likely affected the most and least politically interested citizens similarly. With few sources for information, even very motivated residents have limited alternatives to replace their dying newspapers. Our expectations are consistent with Prior's fundamental contention – the structure of the information environment has a profound effect on the distribution of political engagement. In the case of local communities across the United States, however, we expect that a falling tide is sinking all boats.

POLITICAL INTEREST AND LOCAL NEWS CONSUMPTION

As an initial test of our argument, we examine whether political interest is a weaker predictor of Americans' attention to local news than national news. This is a critical question because the growing inequality in national political engagement has occurred precisely because political interest so strongly shapes people's news habits. If the relationship between interest and local news consumption is relatively weak, that provides further justification for our expectation that the decline of newspapers will have uniform effects on local engagement.

First, we must classify respondents according to political interest – those who tend to be more interested in politics and those who tend to be less interested. Although political interest is a ubiquitous concept in studies of political engagement, scholars haven't coalesced around a single way to operationalize it.[6] Much work relies on self-reports of interest or attentiveness to politics.[7] Some research uses measures of news habits or preferences, such as Prior's designation of news and entertainment fans.[8] Still other studies employ factual political knowledge.[9] We rely on education – specifically, college education – as a proxy for political interest. Two basic factors guide this decision. First, education serves as a

[6] See Prior 2019 for a review.
[7] Bennett and Bennett 1989; Dubois and Blank 2018; Fiske, Lau, and Smith 1990.
[8] Prior 2005; 2007; Hayes and Lawless 2015.
[9] Price and Zaller 1993; Zaller 1992.

substantively good substitute; college graduates are consistently more politically interested than people without higher education.[10] Second, education gives us a consistent measure across the numerous aggregate- and individual-level data sources we analyze in this chapter. Although surveys provide a variety of ways to account for political interest, fewer options exist when using data on, say, cities. College education can be reliably and accurately measured across all of our analyses, allowing us to treat the concept consistently.

With college education as a consistent and serviceable measure of political interest, we use data from our 2017, 2018, and 2019 Cooperative Congressional Election Study surveys to examine the relationship between interest and news consumption at both the local and national levels. Controlling for other factors, education and local news consumption are not significantly correlated in any of the three years.[11] College graduates are no more likely than their less educated neighbors to pay attention to local news. Education is, however, a strong and consist- ent predictor of whether a respondent follows national news.[12] In short, political interest does not influence Americans' local news consumption the way it shapes their attention to national news.[13]

Respondents' own accounts of how their local news consumption has changed over time bolster that conclusion. We included in our 2019 CCES survey a series of questions about whether respondents' local news consumption increased, decreased, or stayed the same over time. If it changed, we asked for the reasons.[14] The survey results suggest that

---

[10] For a similar use of education as a proxy for political interest, see Gillion, Ladd, and Meredith 2020; Hayes and Guardino 2013; Zaller 1994.

[11] See Table H.4.

[12] In each year, the effect of education in the national news attention model is significantly larger than in the local news attention model.

[13] A supplemental analysis supports our decision to use college education as a proxy for political interest. When we run our models with a measure of political interest based on how often respondents say they "follow what's going on in government and public affairs," the results are the same: Political interest is a significantly stronger predictor of attention to national news than local news.

[14] Although asking respondents to report changes in news habits has its perils, doing so should not pose a significant problem for our purposes. Even if people cannot character- ize their news consumption with a great deal of precision, there is no reason to think that any errors would differ in direction or magnitude for college graduates and nongraduates. Prior (2009) does find that college graduates are more likely to inflate their media exposure, likely as a consequence of social desirability – people with more education likely feel more pressure to exaggerate their interest in public affairs. But it is not clear how this would affect answers to a question about *changes* in news consumption. To our

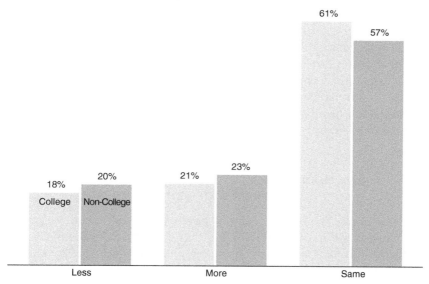

FIGURE 5.1. Changes in following local news over time, by college education
Note: Results are based on the 994 respondents to our 2019 CCES survey. None of the differences between college and non-college-educated respondents is statistically significant.

college-educated and non-college-educated Americans have responded to changes to the local news environment in similar ways and for similar reasons. Roughly one-fifth of respondents follow local news less than in the past, one-fifth follow it more, and the rest report no change. This is the case for respondents with and without a college education (see Figure 5.1).[15]

Homing in on people's reasons for gravitating away from local news, no significant differences emerge between college and non-college-educated citizens either. Regardless of education, the most common reason, given by 37% of respondents, was that there are so many other options

knowledge, no prevailing social norm would lead more educated respondents to inflate (or deflate) changes in their news habits.

[15] The fact that people have gravitated toward and away from local news in roughly equal proportions stands in contrast to patterns for national news. Nearly 37% of CCES respondents reported following national news more now than in the past, and only 16% reported following it less.

for news now.[16] A close second (35%) – again for both groups – was that coverage of the local community isn't as good or thorough as it used to be. Fewer people (17%) indicated that they consume less local news now because it's not convenient to access. But here too, a college education had no bearing on selecting that reason. The survey data are consistent with the argument that education, and thus political interest, may play a more limited role when it comes to local news habits than what we often see at the national level.

DIFFERENT COMMUNITIES, SIMILAR DECLINES IN ENGAGEMENT

Citizens' political interest appears to have only a weak relationship with their consumption of local news. But that doesn't necessarily mean that reductions in local newspaper coverage similarly affect people who are politically interested and those who aren't. To assess that claim directly, we begin with aggregate data and focus on the relationship between news coverage and engagement across communities with varying levels of political interest among residents.

We first return to the mayoral election data we introduced in Chapter 4. As a reminder, we have voter turnout data and local newspaper coverage for 217 mayoral elections in 73 cities from 1993 to 2011. For each city, we also collected US Census data on the percentage of residents with a bachelor's degree, which we again use as a proxy for political interest.[17] If the reduction of local political reporting exacerbates inequality in local political participation, then the resulting declines in voter turnout should be larger in less educated cities. Those are the communities with a larger portion of residents who lack the interest to look elsewhere for information their local paper may no longer provide. But if, as we expect, reductions in local coverage have similar effects regardless of citizens' political interest – largely because there simply is no place else to look for information – then we should see little difference across cities.

---

[16] We presented respondents who reported consuming less local news than they used to with a series of possible reasons for the change. We then asked them to select all the reasons that contributed to their declining local news consumption.

[17] The education data come from the 2000 Census, roughly the midpoint of the time period covered by our elections.

The basic connection between education and turnout is consistent with our argument. When we divide the cities into quartiles based on the percentage of residents with a bachelor's degree, we find no clear differences in turnout. In the first quartile – the least educated cities – the average turnout rate in mayoral elections is 25.8%. This is virtually the same as in the third (25.9%) and fourth (26.5%) quartiles, where a much larger share of the population is college-educated.[18] Indeed, in Newark, New Jersey – the least educated city in the data set – average turnout in four mayoral elections was 28.0%. In San Francisco, where the college graduation rate was five times higher, turnout in two elections averaged just 26.7%. In contrast to national elections, the percentage of college-educated residents in a city does not explain variation in voter turnout at the local level.[19]

Most importantly, the results are similar when we plot the relationship between mayoral turnout and news coverage, broken down by a city's level of college education (see Figure 5.2). If declines in local news coverage exert their strongest effect in places where political interest is lowest, then the slope of the lines should be steepest in the first quartile, become less steep in the second, and so on. That would indicate that as political interest in a community grows, the news effect weakens.

But that's not what we find. The similarity in slope across each of the graph's four panels is striking. No matter how educated a city's population is, turnout and news coverage decline at more or less the same rate.[20] When we model the relationship more rigorously, we find no statistically significant interaction between mayoral coverage and education. At least in the aggregate, the effect of declining local news coverage on municipal turnout does not depend on residents' political interest.

We draw the same conclusion when we revisit our data on Google searches. Recall that we collected information about the popularity of local government-related web searches in 50 metropolitan areas from 2004 through 2016. We then matched those data to our newspaper content analysis of each city's local political coverage over the same

---

[18] The second quartile turnout rate is 21.0%.
[19] See also Tables I.1 and I.2, where college education is not significantly associated with turnout.
[20] The correlations between turnout and mayoral coverage are: first quartile, 0.26; second quartile, 0.27; third quartile, 0.35; fourth quartile, 0.16.

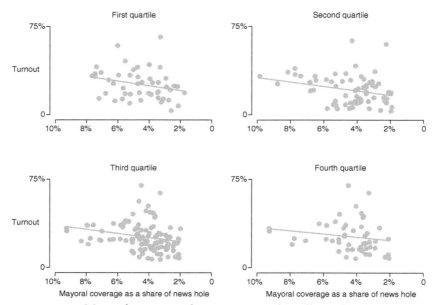

FIGURE 5.2. Mayoral turnout and news coverage, by college education
Notes: Each dot represents one of 217 mayoral elections in 73 cities. The share of the news hole is based on our content analysis, and the mayoral turnout data were compiled by Holbrook and Weinshenck. Quartiles are based on US Census data of the percentage of residents in each city with a college degree.

period. Here, we divide the cities based on their level of education and compare the relationship between coverage and searches.[21]

Once again, we find little evidence that the trends depend on a city's level of education. As an illustration, city government news coverage and city government searches move similarly in low and high education metro areas (see Figure 5.3). In both cases, the over-time trend is downward; the most coverage and highest search popularity occur in the earliest years. Even the period in which coverage and searches show their biggest divergence – 2009 through 2013 – is the same in both graphs. The forces driving Americans' interest in their city governments do not appear to differ significantly in more and less educated communities.

---

[21] With just 50 cities, we cannot separate the data into quartiles; there are too few observations to produce sensible divisions. Thus, we divide the cities into "low" and "high" education categories based on the median percentage of residents with a four-year bachelor's degree. The data come from US Census estimates for 2014–2018.

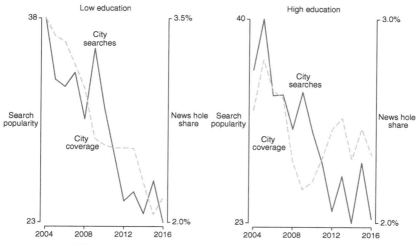

FIGURE 5.3. City government searches and news coverage, by college education
Note: Search popularity is based on Google Trend data; the share of the news hole is based
on our content analysis. The division between low and high education cities is based on the
median percentage of each city's residents with a bachelor's degree, based on US
Census estimates.

The popularity of mayoral and school board searches show a similar
pattern. Although the correlations between searches and news coverage
are lower than for city government (see Chapter 4), differences in the
trends for low and high education cities are generally modest. In addition,
there is no clear pattern in terms of whether the relationship is stronger in
high or low education cities. In the cases of city government and schools,
the correlation between searches and coverage is stronger in the low
education cities. But for mayoral coverage, it's stronger in the high
education cities.[22] All of this suggests that education – a proxy for
political interest – plays only an inconsistent role in moderating the effect
of news coverage at the local level.

As a final way to look at the relationship between local news and
political engagement across communities, we return to our data from
the 2010 US House elections. We draw once again on the 2010 CCES

[22] The correlation between city government searches and coverage is 0.80 in low education
cities, and 0.50 in high education cities. For school searches, it is 0.64 for low education
and 0.17 for high education cities. And for mayor searches, it is 0.17 for low education
and 0.25 for high education cities.

and the content analysis we introduced in Chapter 4, in which we coded the total number of stories about the House candidates in each congressional district's largest newspaper in the month leading up to the election. As with mayoral turnout and online searches, we consider whether the effects of news coverage are different in communities with higher and lower levels of education. In this case, we focus on congressional districts, which we divide into quartiles based on the percentage of college graduates in the district.[23] And we find the same homogenous pattern.

Regardless of how educated are a district's residents, the relationship between the volume of news coverage about the House campaign and various levels of political engagement in the district is virtually identical. Figure 5.4 provides one illustration. Each panel of the figure plots the percentage of residents who could correctly place the Democratic candidate to the left of the Republican on an ideological scale against the number of campaign stories published by the local newspaper. Irrespective of whether a district has a relatively low or high percentage of college graduates, the slope of the line – a measure of the strength of the relationship between the two variables – is quite similar.[24] In the two lowest education quartiles, a decrease of 10 campaign stories leads to a 7.1% reduction in the share of residents who could accurately place the candidates on the ideological scale. That is statistically indistinguishable from the 6.6% reduction in the upper two education quartiles.[25] The pattern is similar for respondents' ability to rate the House incumbent or express a preelection vote intention.[26]

At the aggregate level, these data – encompassing mayoral turnout, online searches about local government, and engagement in congressional campaigns – paint a consistent picture: Local newspaper coverage has similar effects in cities and towns with different levels of education. Thus far, relatively high levels of political interest do not seem to have insulated communities from the effects of the decline in local news.

[23] We use data from the 2010 CCES survey to calculate district-level educational attainment.
[24] The correlations are as follows: first quartile, 0.60; second quartile, 0.48; third quartile, 0.43; fourth quartile, 0.57.
[25] These figures are based on regression models in which the share of district residents accurately placing the candidates is regressed on the number of campaign stories, the education measure, and an interaction between the two.
[26] The correlations for rating the House incumbent are as follows: first quartile, 0.29; second quartile, 0.30; third quartile, 0.21; fourth quartile, 0.37. For expressing a vote intention, they are: first quartile, 0.35; second quartile, 0.36; third quartile, 0.23; fourth quartile, 0.28.

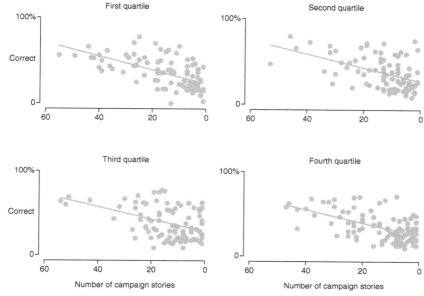

FIGURE 5.4. Correct placement of the Democratic US House candidate to the left of the Republican, by college education

Note: The figure plots the number of campaign stories in a congressional district against the percentage of CCES respondents in each district who could array the candidates correctly on the ideological spectrum, divided into quartiles of college education at the district level. We restrict the analysis to the 381 congressional districts with both a Democratic and Republican candidate and in which the local newspaper ran at least one news story. The number of campaign stories is based on our content analysis of congressional elections in 2010.

WITHOUT NEWS, CITIZENS OF ALL KINDS DISENGAGE

The aggregate data tell a uniform story about the effects of local news: As it declines, so does engagement for everyone. But these analyses can't speak to whether the influence of local coverage might differ among *individuals* with varying levels of political interest. For that, we need to take further advantage of our individual-level surveys of Americans' local knowledge and participation.

As a starting point, we consider whether the effect of news consumption on local political engagement differs among citizens who are college-educated and those who aren't. To conduct this analysis, we model the effect of reading local news and education on the knowledge and

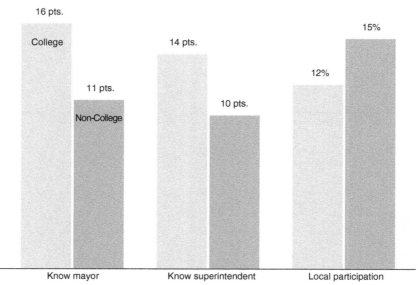

16 pts.

FIGURE 5.5. Effects of reading a local newspaper on engagement, by college education

Note: Results are predictions from regression models controlling for numerous demographic and political variables (see Table H.5). The mayor and superintendent bars display the change in probability that a respondent knows the relevant item if he/she reads local news. The participation bars present the predicted percentage point boost in the number of acts of local participation (out of five possible) the respondent engaged in if he/she reads local news. None of the comparisons between college- and non-college-educated respondents is statistically significant. Data are from the 2019 module of the Cooperative Congressional Election Study.

participation measures we included in the 2019 CCES survey. This allows us to determine whether the effects of reading the paper are statistically different among people with a college education versus those without one.

As we showed in Chapter 4, citizens who read local news are more likely than those who don't to know their mayor and school superintendent, and to participate in various local political activities. But the comparisons in Figure 5.5 illustrate that political interest does not consistently moderate the local news effect on citizen engagement. When we compare college-educated and non-college-educated respondents, in no case can we be confident that the magnitude of the news effect is statistically bigger for one group than the other. But even if we set aside statistical significance and assume these are "true" differences, the direction of the effects isn't consistent. In the case of knowing the mayor and school superintendent, college-educated respondents learn more from reading the local newspaper. When it comes to local participation, however, the local news effect is bigger for non-college-educated respondents. Exposure to local news has substantial effects on Americans' local engagement, but it doesn't reliably depend on their level of political interest.

This analysis, of course, relies on respondents' self-reported news consumption. But the 2010 CCES and our House campaign content analysis allows us to assess whether the pattern holds when we use on a direct measure of the local news environment. If the volume of news coverage affects political engagement of college and non-college-educated respondents similarly, then that's one more piece of evidence that the decline in local news leads to deleterious consequences for all citizens.

And it does. The lines in each panel of Figure 5.6 plot the probability that a respondent can place the Democratic House candidate to the left of the Republican on the ideological scale, rate the district incumbent, and express a vote intention as the number of campaign news stories decreases. Notice that education (or political interest) matters for citizen engagement; the darker lines in the figure are always above the lighter lines, indicating that a college degree exerts a positive effect on political knowledge and participation. The negative slope for all six lines is a reminder that news coverage matters, too – when there are fewer campaign stories, respondents are less engaged.[27]

The most important takeaway from the figure, however, is that regardless of whether a respondent has a college education, the effect of news coverage on each measure is virtually identical, as indicated by the parallel lines. As coverage declines, engagement for both groups falls at the same rate. A comparison of the minimum-maximum effects underscores this point. In the model that predicts whether a respondent can express a vote intention, a shift from the most news coverage (60 stories) to the least (no stories) results in a nearly identical decline for both groups – 2.8 percentage points for college-educated and 3.1 points for non-college-educated respondents. When local newspaper coverage declines, everyone gets information-poorer, not just the people least attentive to politics.

---

[27] To ease the presentation, we drop outlying districts – those with more than 60 campaign stories – from the graphs. The findings are identical if we include them.

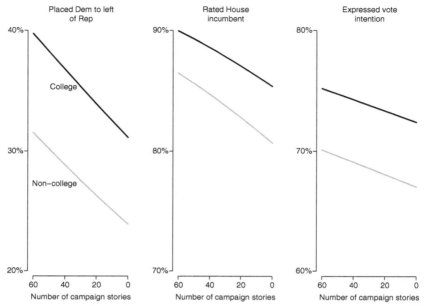

FIGURE 5.6. Effects of news coverage on engagement in US House elections, by college education
Note: Results are predictions from regression models controlling for numerous demographic, political, and contextual variables (see Table K.4). None of the interactions between the number of campaign stories and college education is statistically significant. Data are from the 2010 Cooperative Congressional Election Study's "Common Content," and our content analysis of the 2010 House elections.

As a final way to assess whether politically interested citizens are insulated from the effects of the decline in local news, we return to the 2010–2014 panel component of the Cooperative Congressional Election Study. We demonstrated in Chapter 4 that when we track the same respondents over time, their local political knowledge and participation rise and fall in response to their local newspapers' coverage. Here, we examine whether the rise and fall differs in magnitude based on level of education.

Once again, we find little systematic evidence that education moderates the effects of news consumption on local engagement. Figure 5.7 compares respondents with and without a college degree. The bars represent the effect of a two standard deviation increase in campaign coverage

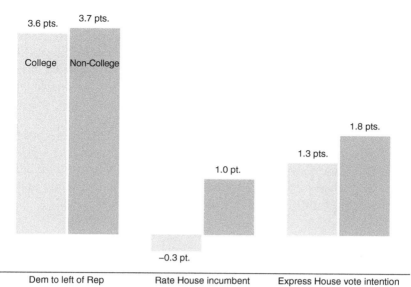

FIGURE 5.7. Effect of shifts in US House campaign coverage, by college education

Note: For the complete regression models, see Table K.5. Bars indicate the percentage point increase in the odds of respondents correctly arraying the candidates on the ideological spectrum, rating the incumbent, and indicating a vote choice in 2014 after not having been able to do so in 2010. The point estimates are based on a two standard deviation increase in the number of campaign stories between 2010 and 2014. Data are from our congressional elections content analysis and the 2010–2014 CCES Panel Study.

(about 28 stories) between the two elections on our measures of local knowledge and participation. An increase in coverage leads, for example, to a 3.6 percentage point increase in the odds that a college-educated respondent who could not accurately place the Democrat and Republican on an ideological scale in 2010 could do so in 2014. The magnitude of the effect is almost exactly the same – one-tenth of a percentage point larger – for a non-college-educated respondent. We also find no difference in the effect of changes in coverage on the likelihood of expressing a preelection vote choice for respondents with a college degree as compared to those without one. The half-point gap is not statistically significant.

Changes in news coverage do exert a statistically stronger effect on non-college-educated respondents' likelihood of rating their House incumbent. For this one measure of engagement, a decline in local coverage may be more consequential for less politically interested individuals. But even that is uncertain. In a series of alternative analyses, we cannot reproduce the finding, suggesting that the result appears to be sensitive to modeling choices.[28] Given the generally uniform findings across education levels in the rest of our analyses, it seems unlikely that local news effects are consistently stronger among less politically interested citizens.

Collectively, the individual-level findings look a lot like the results from the aggregate data: When local news declines, everyone pays a price in knowledge and participation. Politically interested citizens have little in the way of alternative sources of information, so even if they want to seek out local news, their options are limited.

CONCLUSION

Over the course of the last 20 years, the expansion of the US media environment opened up a gap in political participation in national politics – political junkies became even more active, while those with middling interest in politics stayed home. But our analyses in this chapter tell a very different story about citizen engagement in America's cities and towns. As newspaper coverage of local government has declined, engagement has fallen for everyone. With few alternatives for substantive news about local politics, even the politically interested know less and vote less than they did two decades ago. That is as true for college-educated Pennsylvania Republicans as it is for California Democrats who didn't finish high school.

This is not to say, however, that the decline in local engagement is the same in all communities across the country, or will continue to be. In places where local newspapers have managed to survive the rise of the Internet, the drying up of advertising revenue, and the effects of the coronavirus pandemic, local engagement may stabilize or decline only moderately. But in the many cities where newspapers have folded or been so hollowed out as to become civically irrelevant, residents – news and entertainment fans alike – may find themselves increasingly unmoored from the actions of their local governments. Current trends in citizen engagement, in short, depend less on the composition of the community than on the severity of its journalistic crisis.

---

[28] In cross-sectional models employing a lagged dependent variable from 2010, we find no significant interactions between campaign coverage and education. See Table K.6.

As a practical matter, nonmetropolitan areas are most likely to suffer the consequences of the erosion of local news. As we demonstrated in Chapter 3, newspapers in smaller communities have cut coverage to the same degree as big city papers, if not more. Because many small-market papers constitute the only available source of local government reporting, though, the effects of their demise may be especially profound. To the ills heaped upon smaller, rural communities by the decades-long increase in economic inequality, now add greater damage from the crisis in local journalism.

Although the magnitude of the effects of declining coverage are most acute in places with an already severely diminished information environment, the basic problems arising from the demise of local newspapers are more or less the same in every US community. As local journalism goes, so go the prospects for democratic accountability. Those prospects, then, hinge on reinvigorating local news in the United States, and Americans' exposure to it. How to do that is the focus of the next chapter.

6

Saving Local News

The turmoil in the local news business is not just about journalism – it is about the democratic health of American communities. As we have shown in the previous chapters, the internet-induced financial upheaval in the newspaper industry is nothing short of a crisis. Coverage of local public affairs across the United States has declined severely since just the turn of the century. And as Americans' exposure to local political news has waned, they have grown less knowledgeable about local government and less likely to participate in local elections. The question is no longer whether local news is dying or whether citizen engagement is withering along with it. The question now is how to save it.

For even many journalists, that ship has sailed. "I can't even imagine what the first step would be to turn things around," Josh Ellerbrook of the *Lima News* in Northwest Ohio told us. With readers and advertisers migrating away from print journalism and digital revenue failing to make up the difference, a veteran reporter at a Southern daily put his paper's timeline for survival at "about five years." The industry is "just limping toward the finish line," said Alex Rose, a longtime journalist at Pennsylvania's *Delaware County Daily Times*. Indeed, the overwhelming majority of reporters and editors we interviewed shared a fatalistic view. "We can't save local news," a reporter from a midsized paper in the Midwest told us. "The best we can do is stop it from dying a fast death."

At the root of this pessimism is a generational reality – newspapers' most loyal readers won't be around for much longer. "When the Baby Boomers die, it's over for local papers," said Jeff Parrott, of Indiana's *South Bend Tribune*. "Everyone who reads the print edition will be dead." Local news is no longer the centerpiece of Americans' daily routine the way that it once was. "If you love to read the paper with your coffee and your Cheerios in the morning, then there's a good chance you're dying," said Jim Camden, a reporter at the *Spokesman-Review* in Washington. Even though the paper "costs less than a latte – and way less than an extra hot latte with a hazelnut shot," younger consumers expect to get the news without paying for it, he told us. A newly minted reporter who turned 24 the week we interviewed her validated her more senior colleagues' fears: "In my demographic, we read all of our information online and we want it all for free." Local news faces an existential threat – plain and simple – because there's an ever-diminishing demand for the product.

Is there any hope? Despite the industry's challenges, we think there is. Here, we shift our focus away from newsroom layoffs and shrinking news holes to the other side of the equation: consumer interest in local news, among young and old Americans alike. We focus on growing the audience because the reality is that local news – whether in the form of newspaper companies or nimbler digital start-ups – will not be able to serve its core democratic functions in the absence of consumer demand. If citizens are uninterested in coverage of their local representatives and government institutions, news organizations will have little incentive to provide it. Thus, one essential element of a campaign to save local journalism is boosting Americans' interest in knowing what their local elected officials are doing.

Although changing consumer preferences is not easy, we show in this chapter that informing citizens about the importance of local government and reminding them of its relevance can go a long way toward increasing local news consumption. In a wide-ranging series of surveys and experiments, we are able to increase Americans' willingness to click on local news headlines and sign up for local news digests. That is true even for young people, where consumer demand for local news is the weakest. The newspaper industry of the twentieth century is a thing of the past, but growing consumer interest in local news – from both traditional outlets as well as emerging digital sources – can create incentives for news organizations to provide the coverage of local government that democracy needs.

THE PRESSING PROBLEM OF WEAK CONSUMER DEMAND

Saving the local news industry has become something of an industry itself. Hundreds of organizations – from newspapers to local start-ups to philanthropic foundations to teams of academics – have generated a seemingly endless list of ideas to pull local journalism back from the brink. The vast majority of reformers' energy has been on the supply side, seeking ways to improve news organizations' finances or expand their reporting capacity. Those initiatives have called for structural changes to the for-profit business model;[1] the emergence of a new class of civic-minded, wealthy benefactors; and government subsidies for the local news industry.[2] In the meantime, to save money newspapers have eliminated print production, gotten rid of their physical newsrooms, or cut salaries and staff, as we detailed in earlier chapters.[3] But as traditional cost cutting has managed only to soften the blow, some outlets have adopted new strategies to maintain their reporting: collaborating on investigative projects with their competitors;[4] seeking grant money to fund enterprise projects;[5] and welcoming to their newsrooms reporting fellows from organizations like Report for America.[6]

The emphasis on the supply side is essential, given what we've described throughout this book. If the reporting capacity of local news organizations continues to erode, local political engagement is likely to go with it. But the other side of the economic equation – consumers' demand

---

[1] Peter Kafka, "Here's an Idea to Save Local News: Stop Trying to Make a Profit from Local News," *Vox*, February 13, 2020. www.vox.com/recode/2020/2/13/21135166/local-news-nonprofit-plan-john-thornton-american-journalism-texas-tribune-recode-media-peter-kafka (July 18, 2020).

[2] Kerry Flynn, "The Call for Federal Support of Local News Is Getting Louder," *CNN.com*, April 20, 2020. www.cnn.com/2020/04/20/media/government-funding-local-news/index .html (July 18, 2020); and Christine Schmidt, "How Free Press Convinced New Jersey to Allocate $2 Million for Rehabilitating Local News," *Nieman Lab*, July 15, 2019. www .niemanlab.org/2019/07/how-free-press-convinced-new-jersey-to-allocate-2-million-for-re habilitating-local-news/ (July 18, 2020).

[3] David Ho, "Cutting Print: Making It Work When Publishing Days Must Go," *American Press Institute*, August 26, 2019. www.americanpressinstitute.org/publications/reports/ strategy-studies/cutting-print/ (July 18, 2020); Elahe Izadi, "The Newsroom Was the Beating Heart of the Local Newspaper. What's Lost When the Owner Shuts It Down?" *Washington Post*, August 18, 2020. www.washingtonpost.com/lifestyle/media/the-news room-was-the-beating-heart-of-a-local-newspaper-whats-lost-when-the-owner-shuts-it-do wn/2020/08/17/6e9840e4-dcd8-11ea-8051-d5f887d73381_story.html (August 19, 2020).

[4] Caroline Porter, "Adapting to a Changing Climate: How Collaboration Addresses Unique Challenges in Climate-Change and Environmental Reporting," *Center for Cooperative Media*, July 2020. https://medium.com/centerforcooperativemedia/climate-specific-reasons-help-propel-growth-in-journalism-collaborations-4696dc2f672c (July 18, 2020).

[5] Kristen Hare, "How the Times Picayune Is Rebuilding Its Environment Team in a Critical Time," *Poynter*, January 18, 2017. www.poynter.org/tech-tools/2017/how-the-times-pic ayune-is-rebuilding-its-environmental-team-in-a-critical-time/ (July 18, 2020).

[6] "Get Involved," *Report for America*. www.reportforamerica.org/get-involved/ (July 18, 2020).

for local news – is just as worthy of attention. Even if structural reform or an infusion of philanthropic or government funding can steady the industry's financial footing, its ability to sustain coverage of local government in the long run depends on an audience.

Attracting such an audience, however, is a challenge, especially given the menu of national news options. Traffic to local newspaper websites is so miniscule that it constitutes "just a rounding error" on the entire landscape of the Internet.[7] Even within the market for news, national news sites dominate local ones, soaking up more than 85% of consumers' visits.[8] This disparity is also evident in the 2019 Cooperative Congressional Election Study, where we asked a nationally representative sample of Americans several questions about their media habits.[9]

Even though surveys tend to inflate the overall size of the news audience, comparisons between local and national news attention highlight the problem.[10] A majority of Americans described themselves as local news consumers, but the share who said they follow local news "very closely" was 13 points lower than the percentage who said the same about national news (see the top of Table 6.1). Meanwhile, more consumers said they follow local news "not very closely" or "not closely at all" than said the same about national news. When respondents described their media habits in the previous day, they also reported significantly lower levels of attention to local than national news (see the bottom of Table 6.1). And although most Americans are media omnivores – consuming at least some national and local news – 19% of respondents reported exposure to only national news, while just 10% reported reading or seeing only local news. Put another way, the share of Americans who consume exclusively national news is twice as big as the share who consume only local news.

One key reason for the disparity is that to many Americans, the kind of news that might appear on the front page of the local paper – mayoral

---

[7] Hindman 2015.
[8] Hindman 2018.
[9] None of our findings appears peculiar to 2019. From surveys in 2017 and 2018, we identified the same patterns.
[10] Asking about both national and local news helps deal with the fact that survey measures of news consumption can be unreliable. People have a hard time accurately reporting their own behavior, and sometimes they may exaggerate their news consumption habits because they know that following the news is the socially desirable thing to do (Prior 2009). Although we have to be circumspect in characterizing absolute levels of local news consumption, this comparative approach demonstrates clearly that among people who express interest in following news of some sort, demand for local news is relatively weak.

TABLE 6.1. *Consumption of local and national news*

	Local News	National News
How closely do you follow ... ?		
Very closely	27%	40%
Somewhat closely	45	38
Not very closely	20	13
Not at all closely	8	9
In the past 24 hours, have you ... ?		
Read a newspaper, magazine, blog, or other outlet	41	45
Watched TV news (including cable)	45	55
Read or watched any news	65	74

Note: Sample sizes for each question range from 995 to 1,000.
Source: 2019 Cooperative Congressional Election Study.

elections or city council actions – is just not as interesting as what national politics offers. In our survey, we asked respondents whether the words "entertaining" and "boring" describe national and local politics. Compared to national politics, respondents were 11 points more likely to agree that local politics was boring and 9 points less likely to describe it as entertaining.[11]

And these figures actually underestimate the long-term problem for local journalism. That's because the most loyal group of local news consumers by far is the senior set. Consistent with the impressions of the journalists we interviewed, the survey data show that whereas 82% of Americans 65 or older reported paying either "very" or "somewhat" close attention to local news, just 69% of non-seniors did the same (If we consider only respondents younger than 45, that number falls to 63%). While American politics in recent years has been riven by divisions involving education, race, partisanship, and gender, age is by far the biggest cleavage when it comes to local news consumption (see

---

[11] In the era of Donald Trump, the fact that people are drawn more to national than local news for entertainment purposes is perhaps no surprise. Few Americans have a mayor who has ever done or said anything half as arresting as even the median Trump tweetstorm. But this is not entirely a Trump effect. Our findings – which we replicated in 2017 and 2018 – are consistent with evidence from the Obama era, during which time consumers in one experimental study were more likely to read a news story with a headline about the president than a story with a headline about their mayor (see Hopkins 2018).

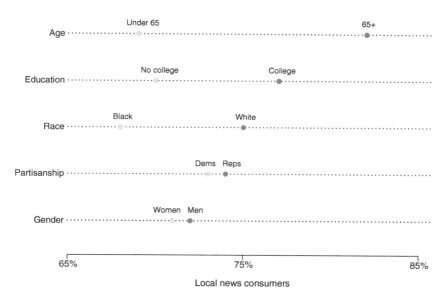

FIGURE 6.1. Demographic gaps in following local news
Notes: Dots indicate the percentage of respondents in each demographic category who report following local news "somewhat" or "very closely." Data come from the 2019 Cooperative Congressional Election Study.

Figure 6.1). As the population ages and increasingly is made up of generations whose interest in local news is more tepid, the consumer demand problem for the industry will only grow.

This reality has led to dour assessments, shared by the journalists we interviewed, about the prospects of growing the local news audience. The proliferation of media outlets devoted to national politics, after all, has made coverage about Congress and the president ubiquitous and inescapable to consumers who have even a passing interest in public affairs. The same can hardly be said about news from county commission meetings. Moreover, large national news organizations have a huge resource advantage over local outlets, plowing millions of dollars into maximizing their websites' "stickiness," an industry term describing audience engagement. And algorithms tend to surface national news coverage in search engine results and social media feeds, reducing consumers' chances of encountering local news during casual scrolling.[12] For many of these reasons,

---

[12] Fischer, Jaidka, and Lelkes 2020.

consumers view online local news as an "inferior good," which means
that it holds relatively little value and also makes it unlikely that people
will pay for it.[13] In 2019, industry analyst Ken Doctor concluded, "The
old world is over, and the new one – one of ghost newspapers, news
deserts, and under-informed communities – is headed straight for us."[14]
In other words, good luck bringing the audience back.

A NEW APPROACH TO INCREASING CONSUMER DEMAND FOR LOCAL NEWS

Although improving the abysmal state of local news websites[15] and capital-
izing on the relatively high trust among local outlets' audiences may help,[16]
the most common refrain when it comes to consumer demand is that
something more must be done. But no one knows quite what. The closest
thing to a strategy has been to emphasize what consumers would lose if local
news disappeared. In a 2020 editorial, the *Los Angeles Times* warned that
residents would "lose not just a crucial source of the information needed to
navigate the travails of daily life, but also in many cases the only local
organization working to hold government, businesses, and powerful individuals accountable."[17] Following layoffs at the *New York Daily News* in
2018, Kyle Pope, editor-in-chief and publisher of the *Columbia Journalism
Review*, wrote that journalists were running out of time to make the case to
America for "why the country should care if local news goes away":

> What does it mean not to have local news in your town? Would it change where
> you live, how you raise your kids, where they go to school? It would if a local coach
> were abusing kids, and would have kept doing so if a newspaper hadn't reported it.
> It would if money that was supposed to be going to city services was instead going
> to higher financing costs for government bonds, since no one was paying attention
> to the deals the city was cutting. It would if there were a spike in health viruses,
> because there wasn't the news infrastructure to warn people to be safe.[18]

---

[13] Hsiang and Ng 2020.
[14] Ken Doctor, "Newsonomics: By Selling to America's Worst Newspaper Owners, Michael
Ferro Ushers the Vultures into Tribune," *Nieman Lab*, November 20, 2019. www
.niemanlab.org/2019/11/newsonomics-by-selling-to-americas-worst-newspaper-owners-
michael-ferro-ushers-the-vultures-into-tribune/ (July 20, 2020).
[15] Hindman 2018.
[16] Knight Foundation 2019.
[17] "Editorial: Local Newspapers Are Dying. Here's How to Save Them," *Los Angeles
Times*, May 24, 2020. www.latimes.com/opinion/story/2020-05-24/local-newspapers-
dying-ways-to-save-them (July 28, 2020).
[18] Kyle Pope, "Who Suffers When Local News Disappears?" *Columbia Journalism Review*,
July 23, 2018. www.cjr.org/business_of_news/new-york-daily-news.php (August 5,
2018). See also, Denise Dick, "When a Newspaper Folds, We All Lose. That's

Compelling as these hypothetical scenarios are (and as prescient as Pope was about the emergence of a new virus), there are at least two difficulties with selling consumers on local news by asking them to envision how bad things might get if it didn't exist. First, it requires a complex cognitive task. Consumers would need to envision a future without local news, imagine its consequences, and then behave in some way – either by visiting a local news site or supporting it financially – to help sustain local news. Second, arguments framed in terms of loss, while often persuasive, can reduce people's tendency to engage in costly activism.[19] Emphasizing the dangers of a world without local journalism may successfully engender worry, but it might not expand the market for local public affairs information. Rather, we need a new approach that doesn't rely on speculation or doomsday scenarios.

We contend that the route to reinvigorating demand for local news, among older and younger Americans alike, lies not in browbeating consumers about the necessity of local journalism itself. Instead, a better strategy is to boost interest in local news indirectly by reminding the public about the importance of its bread-and-butter content: local government. If more people see local politics as a critical part of their communities, the more likely they will be to seek out coverage of it.

Theoretically, we focus on two sets of attitudes that have been the focus of much research on social and political behavior. One set of beliefs should generate what scholars call "instrumental" motivations, which can lead people to take action because they expect to receive some kind of benefit. If citizens believe, for instance, that local governments make decisions that have consequences for their own lives – say, setting property tax rates – they may follow local news for the purposes of learning enough about the issues to cast an informed vote or influence elected officials in some way.

To measure the prevalence of these instrumental motivations, we asked respondents whether they'd use the terms "affects my life," "important," and "relevant" to describe local and national politics. Although not everyone sees local politics this way, most believe that local government is consequential and a majority view local government as just as relevant

---

Especially True in Youngstown, Ohio," *Washington Post*, July 5, 2019. www .washingtonpost.com/outlook/2019/07/05/when-newspaper-folds-we-all-lose-thats-espe cially-true-youngstown/?utm_term=.69068b4b6f92 (August 10, 2019).
[19] Levine and Kline 2019.

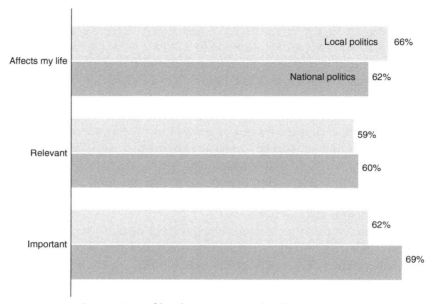

FIGURE 6.2. Impressions of local versus national politics
Notes: Bars represent the percentage of respondents who reported that each word or phrase described local and national politics. Data come from the 2019 CCES survey.

to their lives as national politics (see Figure 6.2). These sentiments cut across generations, with respondents under 65 just as likely to express them as senior citizens. Regardless of age, many Americans care about the actions of the institutions that local news outlets cover.

A second set of motivations are "expressive," which can lead people to take an action not because they expect a tangible benefit but because it provides them emotional or psychological satisfaction. For example, if people believe that keeping up with the news is an important part of being a good citizen or community member, then they may pay attention to local news as a way of adhering to community norms.[20] Such beliefs can strongly influence people's social and political behavior.[21]

---

[20] This is consistent with a body of work that views news consumption as a function of the "uses and gratifications" people want media to satisfy (e.g., Blumler and Katz 1974; Lee 2013). See also Hopkins (2018, 62–67) for a related review of the literature on political engagement.

[21] See Sinclair (2012) for an overview of social influence in politics.

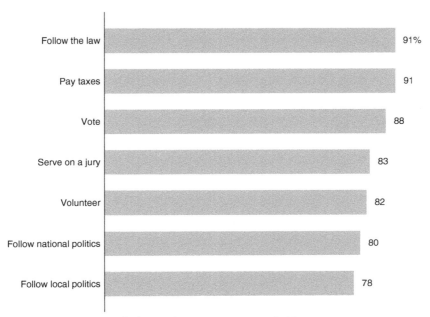

FIGURE 6.3. Views of what makes someone a good citizen
Note: Bars indicate the percentage of respondents who said that each activity was "pretty important" or "essential" for good citizenship. Data come from the 2019 CCES survey.

Indeed, the vast majority of Americans agree about the social importance of following local news. In our survey, we asked how important it is for people to engage in a variety of activities "in order to be a good citizen." The most widely embraced norms are following the law and paying taxes, but nearly 8 in 10 think following local politics is an important part of being a good citizen, too (see Figure 6.3).[22] Once again, younger and older respondents have similar attitudes, suggesting that a wide swath of Americans believe that keeping up with local government is a prevailing social norm worth adhering to.[23]

---

[22] For a set of similar findings, see John Gramlich, "What Makes a Good Citizen? Voting, Paying Taxes, Following the Law Top List," *Pew Research Center*, July 2, 2019. www .pewresearch.org/fact-tank/2019/07/02/what-makes-a-good-citizen-voting-paying-taxes-following-the-law-top-list/ (August 9, 2020).

[23] Seniors are somewhat more likely than non-seniors to say that following local politics is an important part of being a good citizen (87% compared to 75%). That difference, however, is due to seniors being more likely than non-seniors to view every responsibility we asked about as more important for being a good citizen. The divides are 10–12 percentage points across the board. In other words, controlling for differences in beliefs

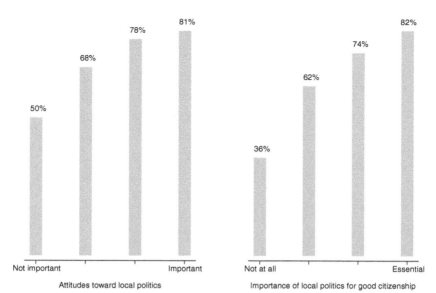

FIGURE 6.4. The relationship between local news consumption and attitudes about local politics

Notes: Bars represent the percentage of respondents who report following local politics "somewhat" or "very" closely. Data come from the 2019 CCES. N = 1,000.

The relevance of both instrumental and expressive attitudes for local news consumption is evident in Figure 6.4. In the left-hand panel, the x-axis represents a scale, ranging from 0 to 3, based on the number of terms – affects my life, relevant, and important – that respondents said described local politics. A respondent who thought all three terms described local politics, for example, received a score of 3. Someone who thought local politics was only relevant and important received a score of 2.[24] For each point on this "importance" scale, we calculated the percentage of local news consumers in the group – people who said they followed local news "somewhat" or "very" closely.

There is a clear relationship between the importance respondents ascribe to local politics and their consumption of local news. The over-

---

about citizenship in general, younger and older Americans have virtually identical views about the importance of following local politics.

[24] The mean was 1.86.

whelming majority of respondents (81%) with the most positive instrumental attitudes pays attention to local news. Only 50% of those who view local politics as unimportant do the same.[25] People's views of local government – especially in terms of how important they believe local politics is – appear to give them an instrumental motivation to keep up with the news. Indeed, in an open-ended question, 68% of local news consumers said that they follow local news because it's important to stay informed about what's happening in their neighborhood, community, or town.

Expressive motivations appear to affect local news consumption, too (see the right-hand panel of Figure 6.4). As we move across the categories of the importance of following local politics for good citizenship, the percentage of respondents in each who regularly consume local news steadily increases. Whereas less than half the people for whom following local politics is "not at all important" for being a good citizen are regular local news consumers, the number rises to more than 8 out of 10 among people who believe it is "essential."[26]

These findings point toward two potential ways to increase demand for local news. The first applies to the segment of the public – about one-third – that does not view local politics as relevant to their lives. For some, these sentiments may reflect general disenchantment with the political system. But for many – as evidence throughout the book has suggested – the source of these views is a lack of information: They don't know what their local government does and are unaware of the profound influence it has on their daily lives.

Research suggests that simply informing or reminding these individuals about the relevance of politics in their community might increase their motivation to follow local news. A variety of studies have shown that

---

[25] The results are similar when we replace attention to local politics with self-reported consumption of local news. The results also withstand standard demographic controls, as well as measures of a respondent's trust in local media.

[26] At the same time, the correlation between the instrumental and expressive value of local politics and actually keeping up with local government is not particularly strong. It is also weaker than the corresponding correlations with respect to national politics and consuming national news. For instance, the correlation between attitudes about the importance of local politics and local news attention is 0.31, but the same relationship at the national level is 0.49. Likewise, the correlation between thinking that following local politics is an important component of citizenship and local news attention is (again) 0.31, but 0.50 for the comparable questions about national politics and news attention.

information can significantly alter people's political beliefs or behavior. For instance, people who possess – or are provided with – knowledge about crime rates, foreign aid, or a wide variety of policy areas often have substantially different attitudes about those issues than people with less accurate information.[27] When people are better informed, they also vote differently and are more likely to participate in politics.[28] There is evidence this is true when it comes to local politics in particular. One set of studies found that when people received information about the effectiveness of their local governments, attitudes about their local elected officials changed.[29] These findings suggest that for Americans who are generally unaware of what local government does, receiving information that emphasizes its importance may serve to increase their interest in local politics and boost their motivation to follow local news.

The second way to increase demand applies to the substantial number of people who view local politics as important – either for instrumental or expressive reasons – but are not regular local news consumers. About one in five respondents who said in our surveys that following local politics is "essential" to being a good citizen, for instance, don't live up to that standard themselves. That represents a significant degree of slack between some Americans' instrumental and expressive attitudes and their media habits. For them, activating those attitudes – making them more salient – as they make news consumption decisions may motivate them to follow local news.

This logic draws on the large body of "priming" research in psychology, political science, and communication. The basic idea is that people's decision-making is influenced by the attitudes or "considerations" that are most cognitively accessible.[30] Cognitive accessibility is determined by how recently or frequently a consideration has been activated in a person's mind. In a standard example, voters exposed to heavy media coverage about the economy are more likely to evaluate the president on the basis of economic conditions than voters not exposed to the same coverage. Priming – or simply making more salient – a particular set of considerations may be enough to lead someone to a different decision

---

[27] Althaus 1998; Gilens 2001.
[28] Bartels 1996; Hayes and McKee 2009; Nicholson and Miller 1997.
[29] James 2011.
[30] Higgins and King 1981; Iyengar and Kinder 1987; Krosnick and Kinder 1990; Scheufele and Tewksbury 2007.

or behavior. In our case, that means exposure to messages about the importance of local politics could make those views more salient and boost interest in and consumption of local news.

Of course, informing and reminding people about the importance of local politics won't create wholesale changes in their consumption patterns. News habits are strongly influenced by the availability of content – for instance, in social media feeds – and the dominance of national news in the media ecosystem means that local news will always have a hard time breaking through. But informing people about the relevance of local government or priming existing attitudes about its importance may nudge them to seek out local news and to pay attention when they encounter it. Even a resulting modest boost in consumer demand could give news organizations the incentive to preserve the coverage of local government that is essential for democratic accountability.

TESTING THE ARGUMENT: AN EXPERIMENTAL APPROACH

We test these arguments with an experimental approach that draws on four studies we conducted between 2018 and 2020. The experiments involve different samples and contexts – a nationally representative survey conducted in the midst of a presidential impeachment debate; a multi-wave survey of Democrats during the 2020 presidential primaries; an exit poll during the 2018 midterms in the Washington, DC suburbs; and a second exit poll during the 2019 legislative elections in Virginia. The experiments rely on two messages to determine whether providing people information and activating attitudes about the importance of local politics can increase their consumption of local news. One message reminds voters that local governments make decisions that affect people's lives. A second emphasizes the social norm that following local politics is part of being a good citizen. Despite the variety of settings, we find consistent evidence that both messages can boost local news interest and consumption. Critically, these messages also significantly close the generation gap, bringing younger Americans' interest in local news close to the levels of their senior citizen counterparts.

George Washington University Politics Poll

In September 2019, we embedded in the nationally representative George Washington University Politics Poll an experiment designed to test our information and priming arguments.[31] In some ways, this was an inauspicious moment to try to activate interest in local news. The country was in the run-up to a wide open Democratic presidential primary and gripped by a debate over what would eventually become the first set of impeachment charges against Donald Trump. The majority of the survey of 1,200 US adults focused on national politics, but toward the end, respondents encountered the experiment.

The first part of the experiment involved showing respondents a series of three statements "that many Americans agree with." Two of the statements were the same for everyone: "People should vote for the best person for the job, not just their favored political party" and "It is important for students to learn about American politics and history in school." As a way of ensuring that respondents read the statements, we asked whether they had heard them before.[32]

The experimental treatment occurred in a third statement shown to each respondent. People randomly assigned to the control group saw "Money can help make people comfortable, but it can't buy happiness." Because the statement is unrelated to politics, it should not affect people's interest in local news. Respondents assigned to the two experimental treatments saw one of two other statements. The first, designed to give people information about the relevance of local government, read, "Local governments make many decisions that affect your life and the lives of your neighbors." We call this the Local Government treatment. The second, intended to prime the importance of local politics, read, "Following local politics and government is an important part of being an informed citizen." This is the Informed Citizen treatment.

After respondents saw these statements, we told them we wanted some information about the kind of news they liked to follow. For each of the following four headlines – which we told respondents they "might come across on a website or in social media" – we asked how likely they would be to click and read the full story:

- City Council passes bill to limit new housing permits despite vocal opposition
- President says he will defy Congress, issue executive order expanding transportation plans

---

[31] The survey was fielded by the firm YouGov.
[32] We were not actually interested in whether they had heard them, but this was a mechanism to ensure exposure.

- New restaurant opens in building that once was home to a movie theater
- Major league baseball ticket sales decline for the fourth straight year

Respondents could say they were "not at all," "not very," "somewhat," or "very" likely to click each. If the two treatments boost interest in local news, then respondents in the Local Government and Informed Citizen conditions should express a greater likelihood of clicking the City Council story – the one headline related to local politics – than respondents in the control group.[33]

And they do. The difference is driven primarily by the fact that respondents in the treatment groups were more likely to say they were "very likely" to click the City Council story (see Figure 6.5).[34] On the other end of the spectrum, treatment group respondents were also less likely to say they were "very unlikely" to click the City Council story, although those differences are somewhat smaller and less certain.[35] On the whole, both the Local Government and Informed Citizen treatments had similar effects, suggesting that both providing information and activating social norms about citizenship can work to increase demand for local news in the aggregate.[36]

We also find that increasing respondents' interest in local news does not drive down engagement with other news topics. When we compare interest in the stories about national politics, a restaurant opening, and baseball ticket sales, we uncover no significant differences between the control and treatment groups. This is important for two reasons. First, it suggests that the treatments effectively targeted attitudes associated with local news, rather than just news or public affairs in general. Second, it indicates that our strategy for increasing interest in local news does not threaten audiences for other types of content. Admittedly, the choice environment of our survey does not force respondents to make trade-offs – they can express high levels of interest in all stories if they so choose.

---

[33] We randomized the order in which each headline appeared.

[34] In a logit model, the *p*-value of the difference between the Local Government treatment and the control is 0.11 (one-tailed), and the *p*-value of the difference between the Informed Citizen treatment and the control is 0.05 (one-tailed).

[35] In the control group, 15.2% of respondents said they were "not at all" likely to click the City Council story, while the share was 12.3% in the Local Government treatment and 12.6% in the Informed Citizen treatment.

[36] If we convert responses from the "not at all" to "very" likely scale into numerical values (ranging from 1 to 4), interest in the City Council story was higher in the two treatment groups (a mean of 2.79 in each) compared to the control (2.70). The *p*-value of the difference between the control group mean and the treatment group means is 0.08 (one-tailed).

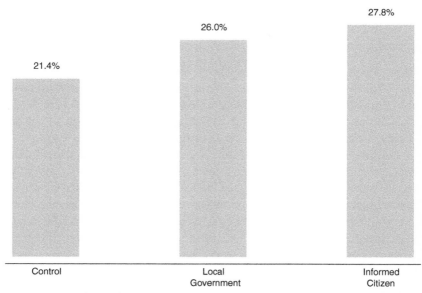

FIGURE 6.5. Share of respondents "very likely" to click City Council story, by experimental condition

Notes: Data come from 1,199 respondents in the 2019 GW Politics Poll. The sample size was 405 in the control group, 399 in the Local Government treatment, and 395 in the Informed Citizen treatment.

But at least in this context, increased engagement with local news does not appear to compromise interest in national politics, food, or sports.

The fact that these relatively mild experimental treatments produced differences in expressed interest in local news, particularly in the midst of a survey about a presidential campaign and impeachment inquiry, is encouraging. But because we did not have prior measures of respondents' attitudes about local politics, it is impossible to say whether the treatments work for the reasons we expect. That is, does the Local Government treatment provide information about local government's relevance, and the Informed Citizen treatment prime existing attitudes about the importance of local politics? For that kind of evidence, we turn to a second study.

Democratic Panel Survey

The second experiment took place in the final wave of a four-wave panel survey of a national sample of Democrats conducted from January

through August 2020. The experiment was virtually identical to the GW
Politics Poll experiment – respondents were randomly assigned to a
control, Local Government, or Informed Citizen condition.[37] But the
panel format, involving repeated interviews with 1,704 of the same
individuals, allows us to determine *how* the treatments work, and how
the two messages may boost local news interest among different groups of
people.[38]

In the second wave of the survey (March 2020), we asked respondents
about their views of local politics. These were the same questions we used
to tap into instrumental and expressive attitudes in the 2019 CCES:
whether local politics affects their lives and is relevant and important, as
well as how important following local politics is to being a good citizen.
We used the responses to create a scale that accounts for both sets of
beliefs.[39] Higher scores on the scale indicate that respondents viewed local
politics as more important.[40]

The key question is how these preexisting attitudes about local politics
moderate the effects of our experimental treatments. If the Local
Government treatment works by providing information about the
importance of local government – which some respondents may not be
aware of – then these preexisting attitudes should not moderate its effects.
Instead, the treatment should work simply by making people more aware
of the relevance of local politics. The effects of the Informed Citizen
treatment, however, should depend on people's prior views of local
politics. The people who already believe local politics is important should

[37] The only difference is that we modified the headline about Major League Baseball because
the coronavirus pandemic had delayed the season.
[38] The survey was run by researchers at George Washington University and fielded by
YouGov. Respondents were individuals who identified themselves as Democrats and
Democratic-leaning independents.
[39] We rescaled the variable to range from 0 to 1. The sample weighted mean is 0.54, with a
standard error of .01.
[40] Measuring these attitudes in March gives us an additional check on the argument that
attitudes about local politics influence interest in local news. Because respondents in the
2019 CCES were asked about both interest in local politics and local news in the same
survey, it is difficult to disentangle cause and effect. But here, since we measured attitudes
about local politics months before the experiment, we can be more confident that any
relationship we uncover is causal. And indeed, we find a significant relationship. Focusing
on control group respondents (who were not subject to an experimental treatment), we
find that individuals who scored higher on the importance of local politics scale in March
were more likely to say in August they would read the local news story. For instance,
among respondents who scored below the median on the scale, 46% said they were either
"somewhat" or "very" likely to click and read the full City Council article. For those
above the median, that number was 69%.

respond most strongly when reminded (primed) that following it is part of being a good citizen.

The experiment confirmed the general findings from the GW Politics Poll – 63% of respondents in the treatment groups said they were either "somewhat" or "very" likely to click the City Council story, compared to just 57% in the control group.[41] The Local Government treatment (64%) had a somewhat stronger effect than the Informed Citizen treatment (61%).[42] Critically, the experiment also provided support for the theoretical mechanisms we anticipated.

Turning first to the Local Government treatment, the magnitude of its effect does not depend on people's predispositions about local politics. Each bar in Figure 6.6 represents the percentage point increase in the likelihood, based on a shift from the 20th to the 80th percentile of the local politics importance scale, that a respondent said he or she would click the City Council story. In other words, the height of the bars indicates how strongly people who already viewed local politics as important reacted to the experimental treatments. The critical finding is that the increase among those assigned to the Local Government treatment was statistically indistinguishable from those assigned to the control. While respondents' interest in local news increased, their attitudes about local politics played no greater role in generating that increase than they did in the control group.

The reason is that the strongest effects of the Local Government treatment occurred among people who were the least likely to be informed about the activities of local government. Although we do not have direct measures of local political knowledge, we do know whether respondents at least occasionally read a local newspaper – something that we showed in Chapter 4 is strongly associated with possessing basic information about local politics.[43] Non-newspaper readers in the Local Government treatment were 12 points more likely to say they would click

---

[41] The *p*-value is 0.04. On the numerical scale (ranging from 1–4), the average "likely to click" score was 2.75 in the Local Government condition, 2.68 in the Informed Citizen condition, and 2.61 in the control group. The *p*-value of the difference between the control mean and the combined treatment means is 0.06 (one-tailed). The *p*-value of the difference between the Local Government treatment and control is 0.03, and 0.17 between the Informed Citizen and control.

[42] The Local Government treatment is significantly different from the control ($p = 0.03$), while the Informed Citizen treatment is not ($p = 0.14$).

[43] Fifty-three percent of respondents said they either "regularly" or "sometimes" read a local newspaper.

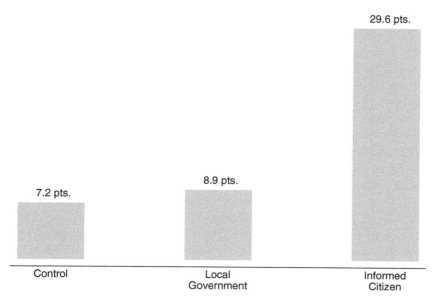

FIGURE 6.6. Differences in treatment effects based on respondent attitudes about local politics

Notes: Bars represent the percentage point increase in being "very likely" or "somewhat likely" to click on a City Council headline, moving from the 20th to 80th percentile on the importance of politics scale, within each experimental condition. Data come from 1,704 Democratic voters who participated in a four-wave panel survey from March to August 2020. The sample size for each condition was similar: 566 in the control group; 573 in the Local Government treatment; and 565 in the Informed Citizen treatment.

the City Council story than nonreaders in the control group. But among newspaper readers, the treatment effect was a nonsignificant 2 points. This is exactly what we would expect if the treatment is providing respondents information they didn't already have. Local newspaper readers presumably know that local government affects their lives and the lives of their neighbors – they see evidence of it every day. But because that is less apparent to people who don't read the newspaper, the Local Government treatment had a much more substantial effect.

On the other hand, the experimental effects in the Informed Citizen treatment are amplified among people who already think local politics is important. The percentage of respondents in the Informed Citizen treatment who said they were likely to click the City Council story was nearly 30 points higher for people at the 80th percentile of the local politics scale than for those at the 20th percentile.

Figure 6.6, however, should not be read to suggest that the Informed Citizen treatment is more effective than the Local Government condition. The Local Government treatment, remember, generated larger effects overall, including among people whose attitudes about local politics were not particularly favorable. Thus, reminding people that local governments have a substantial influence on their lives may boost interest in local news even among individuals who don't care much about local politics in the first place. Reminding people of the social norms associated with citizenship, however, appears to work because it primes existing attitudes about local politics. Among people who didn't already think local politics was important, the treatment had a negligible effect.

Of course, one limitation of the panel survey is that it includes only Democrats. We cannot say whether a different pattern would apply among Republicans, which is always a real possibility when considering attitudes toward the media. But two factors increase our confidence that our strategies for increasing local news consumption cross party lines. First, the survey evidence involves psychological processes that are not partisan in nature. Second, although partisan polarization shapes views of the media, that is much less true of local news organizations. Thus, a communication campaign that informs and reminds people of the importance of local politics may be able to increase interest in local public affairs across a broad segment of the public.

Still, for our strategy to be practically useful, we need to show that it can encourage people to do more than *say* they would click a City Council story. Survey responses are arguably cheap talk. In order to reinvigorate demand for local news, consumers must be motivated to engage in some kind of costly behavior, such as actively seeking it out on a regular basis.

Election Day Exit Poll Experiments

To determine whether these messages about local politics can encourage a more costly expression of interest in local news among actual voters in the real world, we embedded an experiment in two Election Day exit polls. We conducted the first in Arlington County, Virginia, just outside Washington, DC, on November 6, 2018.[44] The second took place in the City of Charlottesville, Virginia, on November 4, 2019. In both cases, when a voter agreed to participate, the exit pollster handed the voter a

---

[44] See Appendix L for details on the exit poll procedures, questionnaires, and samples.

pen and a one-page survey on a clipboard. The exit pollster then stepped away so that the respondent could privately complete the survey, which included questions about the federal and county races in Arlington and state legislative and city elections in Charlottesville. In all, we conducted surveys with 1,068 voters in Arlington and 2,999 in Charlottesville.[45]

The final question on each survey allowed us to test whether our information and priming arguments could generate for voters a more substantial commitment to local news than merely saying they would click on a made-up City Council story. In both experiments, we asked participants whether they wanted to sign up for an electronic digest of headlines from one of their community's local news outlets. Voters in Arlington saw a question that read, "Are you interested in signing up for a daily digest of local news from ARLNow.com so that you can keep up with what's going on in your community?" ARLNow is a local news start-up that covers politics, culture, and community events in Arlington County.[46] In addition to posting stories throughout the day, the site sends a summary of its coverage each afternoon to users who have signed up for its news digest. In Charlottesville, respondents were asked whether they would be interested in signing up for a daily digest of local news from the *Daily Progress*, the major local newspaper serving central Virginia. We invited respondents to provide their email address in a space provided on the survey.[47] Together, the studies allow us to examine whether we can increase demand for local news from both an online start-up and a traditional newspaper.

The experiment involved three versions of the wording of the ARLNow or *Daily Progress* question, to which we randomly assigned respondents. One group (the control) saw only the basic wording that asked respondents if they wanted to sign up. A second and third group randomly received the Local Government and Informed Citizen treatments immediately before being asked whether they wanted to sign up for the local news digest. The wording of the two treatments was identical to the GW Politics Poll and Democratic Panel Survey experiments. Support for our argument requires respondents in the treatment conditions to provide their email addresses at higher rates than those in the control group.

---

[45] See Appendix Table L.1.

[46] The site, which describes itself as a "local, independent online news and lifestyle publication," was founded in 2010. For more information, see: www.arlnow.com/about/.

[47] Respondents who provided their email addresses were later signed up for the digests.

Before turning to the results, it is important to emphasize that asking respondents to give their email address to a stranger for the purposes of signing up for an actual local news digest allows us to measure the kind of costly behavior that likely suggests a genuine interest in local news. Nothing prevented respondents from refusing, and they received no specifics about the kind of local news stories that would subsequently populate their in-boxes.[48] Thus, we interpret providing an email address as a strong signal of increased interest in local news.

Overall, 10.4% of respondents in Arlington provided their email addresses; in Charlottesville, 14.7% did so. But critically, Figure 6.7 illustrates that in both locations, the proportion was higher in the Local Government and Informed Citizen treatments than in the control condition. The experimental effects were somewhat stronger in Charlottesville, but the overall patterns are the same – respondents exposed to information about the importance of local politics were always more likely to sign up for the local news digest.[49] We also found that the two experimental treatments had similar effects, although the Informed Citizen treatment had a slightly larger effect than the Local Government condition in Arlington, while the reverse was true in Charlottesville.

The Arlington experimental results also suggest that some respondents who did not go so far as to provide their email addresses were still influenced by the treatments. In response to the question about the local news digest, voters could give their email address, simply answer "No," or check a box that read, "I already subscribe to ARLNow.com." Given randomization, the share of respondents in each condition who already subscribed should be the same. But we found that the percentage of voters in the treatment conditions who already subscribed was 4.6 percentage points higher than in the control group.[50] One interpretation is that the treatments reminded voters that they *should* consume local news. Giving

[48] Of course, respondents could provide a fake email address or one they only use for marketing purposes. But the design provides a superior measure of actual interest in the news than attitudinal measures typically used to gauge news consumption.

[49] In the Arlington experiment, the difference between the Local Government treatment and the control is not statistically significant, but the p-value of the difference between the Informed Citizen treatment and control is 0.09 (one-tailed). In Charlottesville, both treatments are significantly different from the control ($p < 0.05$). In neither study is the difference between the effect of the two treatments significant.

[50] In the control, 21.4% of respondents said they already subscribed. That figure was 28.4% in the Local Government treatment and 23.7% in the Informed Citizen treatment. The Local Government effect is significant ($p < 0.05$) while the Informed Citizen effect is not.

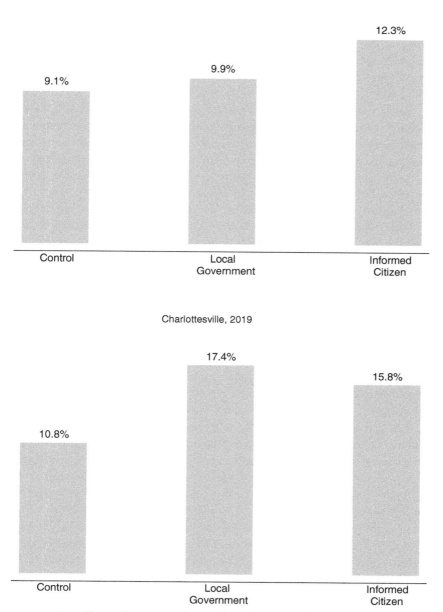

FIGURE 6.7. Share of voters signing up for a local news digest in exit polls
Note: See Appendix L for details about the Arlington and Charlottesville exit polls.

their email address to a stranger was more than they were willing to do, so in an effort to appear engaged with local news, they responded that they already subscribed. We can't know whether this is the case, and we did not find the same pattern in Charlottesville, but such behavior is consistent with the logic of our argument – that making these attitudes salient encourages people to engage with local news (or, as a first step, acknowledge that they should).

Because we do not have prior measures of people's attitudes about local politics, we cannot fully test the mechanisms by which the two treatments operate. But a question in the exit poll about people's attention to politics suggests that the information treatment had the strongest effects among people least likely to be knowledgeable about local politics. Among respondents in Charlottesville who said they follow politics "very closely," the Local Government treatment effect was 3.2 points. Among those less attentive to politics, however, it was twice as large: 6.4 points. Likewise, in Arlington, the Local Government treatment effect for those who follow politics very closely was not statistically distinguishable from the control group – the treatment had no effect. But among those who follow politics less closely, the Local Government treatment effect was 2.8 points. The exit polls did not include measures analogous to our local politics importance scale, so we can't test the priming argument. But the results all suggest that the mechanisms we have posited are clearly important for boosting interest in local news.

To be sure, we should be somewhat cautious when extrapolating from our study to the broader US population. Owing partly to location – across the Potomac River from the nation's capital and amid a college town, respectively – both Arlington County and Charlottesville are highly educated and politically engaged communities. Moreover, we sampled voters – people who had just minutes before demonstrated a high level of political engagement by casting a ballot in a midterm or off-year election. But the results, which are consistent with our findings from two national survey experiments, show that it is possible to boost interest in local news in exactly the kind of place where consumers hold beliefs that might make them amenable to the messages we tested. That we find effects in both types of elections, and for two types of local news outlets, offers promise for a demand-side solution to the local news crisis.

Closing the Generation Gap in Local News Interest

As promising as the experimental results are, the efficacy of a communication effort doesn't depend just on its ability to increase overall levels of interest or consumption. For the strategy to present any hope for the future of the industry, it must work among a wide swath of Americans – especially young people, who are significantly less interested in local news than their older counterparts. That's one of the most important features of our approach. Because seniors (those 65 and older) and non-seniors (those under 65) have similar attitudes about local politics, our experimental treatments should, theoretically, work across generations. But with non-seniors consuming less local news in the first place, their interest has more room to grow. The fact that roughly one-quarter of the respondents in each study was 65 or older allows us to make some consistent comparisons to determine whether our treatments can, in fact, close the generation gap in local news interest.[51]

In short, we find that they can. The left side of Figure 6.8 presents the average treatment effects in the GW Politics Poll and the Democratic Panel Survey for non-seniors (lighter bar) and seniors (darker bar). The right side of the figure does the same for the two exit polls. For simplicity, we combine the two experimental conditions and compare them to the control.

In the GW Politics Poll, the percentage of non-seniors who were "very likely" to click the City Council story was 5.2 percentage points higher among those who received either the Local Government or Informed Citizen treatment than in the control. For seniors, the comparable effect was 7.6 points. Although the average effects for seniors appear slightly larger in the survey experiments, in neither study are they significantly different from the effects for non-seniors. And in the exit polls, the pattern is reversed; the treatments boosted local news interest more among non-seniors – and significantly so in Arlington.

The upshot is that the treatments either closed the generation gap in local news consumption or flipped it in the favor of younger consumers. To illustrate, Figure 6.9 shows the effects of the Informed Citizen treatment among both sets of exit poll respondents. Among control group voters in Arlington, the percentage of seniors who signed up for the local news digest was nearly twice as large as the share of non-seniors who did the same. In Charlottesville, there was virtually no generation gap. But after being exposed to the Informed Citizen treatment, the gap between

---

[51] The share of respondents 65 or older was 22% in the GW Politics Poll, 20% in the Democratic Panel Survey, 22% in the Arlington exit poll, and 29% in Charlottesville exit poll.

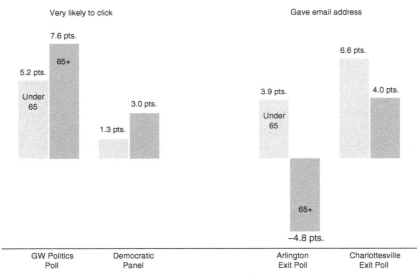

FIGURE 6.8. Average experimental treatment effects, by age group
Notes: Bars represent the average treatment effect in each experiment for seniors and non-seniors. In the GW Politics Poll and Democratic Panel, the bars indicate the change in the percentage of respondents who indicated that they'd be "very likely" to click on a City Council headline if they were exposed to the Local Government or Informed Citizen treatment as opposed to the control. For the exit polls, the bars indicate the difference in providing an email address for respondents exposed to a treatment versus the control.

seniors and non-seniors in Arlington shrunk to just 2.5 percentage points. In Charlottesville, non-seniors were nearly 3 percentage points *more* likely than seniors to provide their email address. Activating attitudes about local politics can not only increase the number of local news consumers, but perhaps lay the foundation for a future audience.

CONCLUSION

There is little optimism about the future of local news from journalists, industry observers, academics, and most anyone else paying attention. For good reason. Virtually any business facing uncertain revenue streams and relatively weak demand would find little comfort in the seemingly daily announcement of closures, layoffs, and hedge fund takeovers.

But the results of our experiments suggest a ray of hope. Reminding Americans about the importance of local government can increase interest

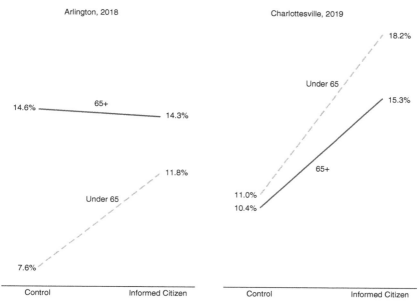

FIGURE 6.9. Share of voters signing up for a local news digest in exit polls, by age group
Note: Lines represent the change in the percentage of seniors and non-seniors who provided their email address after being exposed to the Informed Citizen treatment.

in local news. The right messages can boost interest among people who don't know much about what their local government does, as well as among those who know that local government is important but whose news habits don't always reflect that reality. These messages can also help close the generation gap and bring younger consumers to the local news market. A communication strategy like the one we've described will not create extensive changes in news consumption; the effects of our experimental treatments are generally modest. But they represent systematic evidence that the audience for local news can grow.

Increasing demand may be one effective way to increase the supply of local political reporting. As in most businesses, the consumer is king. If readers demonstrate that they want to know what their local elected officials are doing, local news outlets will devote resources to covering local government.

The strategy, however, can only prove practically feasible if newspapers, local news start-ups, and organizations working to promote local journalism remind the country about the importance of local politics. On one hand, this might seem unrealistic – whoever heard of a marketing campaign to boost a generic public good like local news? The fact that local newspapers have long been reticent to market themselves beyond what many journalists consider the self-evident worth of their reporting suggests that a new approach might succeed. And such an effort would be no different than public health campaigns seeking to improve people's lives by providing them information and behavioral guidance. The health of our democracy is at stake, and there is no reason that a communication campaign based on the principles we've articulated here is not worth trying.

7

Local News and American Democracy

In June 2018, voters in the District of Columbia approved a ballot initiative to raise the city's minimum wage for restaurant workers who rely on tips. Existing law allowed restaurant owners to pay servers and bartenders a little less than four dollars an hour as long as they made significant gratuities. Advocates of the initiative argued that the system was unfair, benefited employers at the expense of employees, and perpetuated income inequality. A majority of voters in six of the city's eight wards agreed, and the measure passed by 10 percentage points.[1]

Within a day of the election, there were rumblings that the City Council planned to overturn the victory. Some elected officials said they thought the public was confused about what the initiative meant. Others contended that voters simply got it wrong, pointing out that even many tipped workers didn't support the measure. Regardless of whether confusion or wrongheadedness accounted for the result, critics argued that low turnout – just 18% – diminished the legitimacy of the election. "Initiative 77 was passed by a small fraction of DC's eligible voters, but its impact will be felt like an earthquake," said one opponent in the restaurant business.[2] Another suggested that an election held "in the middle of the

---

[1] Rachel Sadon, "10 Things You Should Know about Initiative 77 and the 2018 D.C. Primary," *DCist.com*, June 20, 2018. https://dcist.com/story/18/06/20/x-things-to-know-about-the-2018-dc/ (accessed October 12, 2020).

[2] Martin Austermuhle, "D.C. Voters Approve Initiative 77, Ballot Measure that Eliminates Tipped Wage," *WAMU*, June 19, 2018. https://wamu.org/story/18/06/19/d-c-voters-approve-initiative-77-ballot-measure-eliminates-tipped-wage/ (October 12, 2020).

summer" somehow could not truly reflect the public's preferences.[3]
"Virtually everyone I know did not support it," said a council member
who represented the city's wealthiest neighborhoods. "We can change the
law."[4]

And they did. Four months after the election, the City Council, by a
margin of 8 to 5, scuttled the measure before it was enacted.[5] "If the law is
a bad law, it should be amended or repealed," the Council's chairman
told reporters. "It does not matter if the law was adopted by the council,
the voters or Congress."[6]

Setting aside the question of whether ballot initiatives constitute a
sound way to make public policy, the episode illustrates a fundamental
threat arising from Americans' growing disengagement from local politics. The smaller the number of voters who turn out in an election, the
easier it is to challenge the results. Politicians and groups who don't like
an outcome can plausibly cast doubt on whether a slim electorate's
decisions reflect the broader public will. Elections are democracy's mechanism to hold government officials accountable and ensure citizen representation, but participation by only the few weakens their effectiveness.

The demise of the newspaper industry in the last two decades has
exacerbated the problems of limited public engagement in local politics.
The downward slide of local government coverage has left the nation less
knowledgeable about its local elected officials and less likely to participate
in local elections. These trends are concerning enough as they have
already played out. But they are particularly worrisome given local journalism's precarious future. Without a revitalization of the local media
environment, democratic accountability and quality representation in
cities and towns across the United States will become increasingly elusive.

---

[3] Rachel Sadon, "10 Things You Should Know about Initiative 77 and the 2018 D.C.
Primary," *DCist.com*, June 20, 2018. https://dcist.com/story/18/06/20/x-things-to-know-
about-the-2018-dc/ (accessed October 12, 2020).

[4] Julia Airey, "Initiative 77's Fate to Be Decided by D.C. Council," *Washington Times*, June
20, 2018. www.washingtontimes.com/news/2018/jun/20/initiative-77s-fate-be-decided-
dc-council/ (October 12, 2020).

[5] Fenit Nirappil, "It's Official: D.C. Council Has Repealed Initiative 77, which Would Have
Raised Pay for Tipped Workers," *Washington Post*, October 16, 2018. www
.washingtonpost.com/local/dc-politics/its-official-dc-council-has-repealed-initiative-77/20
18/10/16/05323 41a-d0b5-11e8-b2d2-f397227b43f0_story.html (October 12, 2020).

[6] Fenit Nirappil, "D.C. Council Overturns Wage Hike for Bartenders, Servers – Four
Months after Voters Approved It," *Washington Post*, October 2, 2018. www
.washingtonpost.com/local/dc-politics/dc-council-takes-initial-vote-to-overturn-initiative-77-
four-months-after-voters-approved-it/2018/10/02/da906320-c651-11e8-b1ed-1d2d65b86d
oc_story.html (October 12, 2020).

LESS NEWS, LESS ACCOUNTABILITY

Throughout the first years of the twenty-first century, the struggles of the newspaper business happened mostly under the radar. While journalists and industry observers were well aware of the mounting financial challenges, the existential threat posed by declining advertising revenue and legacy print production costs remained for the most part hidden from public view. But as daily newspapers shrunk, cut their reporting staff, and sometimes withered into unrecognizable husks, the extent of the local news crisis became impossible to ignore.

Still, the scale of the devastation had been hard to quantify. But as we showed in Chapters 2 and 3 through our original content analysis of more than 200 newspapers across the country, the decline in coverage of local government can only be described as profound. Consider these core findings about local political reporting over the course of the last 20 years:

- Overall, coverage of local politics – mayors, city and county governments, and school boards – has fallen by 50%.
- Newspapers have cut local politics reporting more severely than other content, such as national politics and sports.
- Papers of all sizes have seen their news hole shrink, but local politics has taken the biggest hit at small papers.
- Reporting on school boards and county governments has fallen most dramatically, largely because it is costly and generates less reader engagement.

The great danger for local communities is obvious: With fewer, less capable watchdogs, there is often no one keeping tabs on government officials. "The next 10 or 15 years in this country are going to be a halcyon era for state and local political corruption," said David Simon, the creator of *The Wire* and a former *Baltimore Sun* reporter. "It is going to be one of the great times to be a corrupt politician. I really envy them. I really do."[7] This is no melodramatic exaggeration from a Hollywood producer. The journalists we interviewed emphasized how difficult it has already become for local papers to serve their traditional role as the Fourth Estate. *Bloomington Herald Times* reporter Rich Jackson told us that newspapers' financial hardship has allowed governments to keep

---

[7] Ryan Bort, "John Oliver Explains Why Local Newspapers Are So Important," *Newsweek*, August 8, 2016. www.newsweek.com/john-oliver-last-week-tonight-journalism-488321 (October 13, 2020).

secrets from the public. "Communities have never been that willing to open up records to reporters," he said. "They used to do it, though, because we were willing to spend $10,000 or $15,000 on lawyers to open records and for open meeting challenges." Once those resources dried up, so did access to information and a reminder to elected officials that someone was watching.

The media's collective watchdog capacity is even further compromised because newspapers have long been community agenda-setters, alerting other news outlets to important stories and generating follow-up coverage. In Utah, for example, Jordan Carroll of the *Standard-Examiner* told us that her paper's impact was typically magnified because local television stations are "basically using us as syndicated outlets ... copying and sharing our content with their statewide audiences." But with ever-shrinking newsrooms, that's increasingly rare, said Kim Haas, a correspondent at the *New Hampshire Union Leader*. "We can't serve that function anymore," she told us.

Some observers have hoped that other sources might step in and provide the local political coverage that has disappeared from newspapers. But our analysis of alternative venues for local news demonstrated that it has not happened in any measurable way, at least so far. Although a few local news start-ups have succeeded,[8] they are virtually nonexistent in smaller, nonmetropolitan communities – the very places where we found the share of local government coverage to have declined the most. Meanwhile, local television has remained committed to its main menu of crime, weather, and sports, not local public affairs. And a network of partisan sites – perhaps the most aggressive entrant into the local news market – masquerade as traditional outlets but have no interest in serving the broader public interest.[9] All of this comes against the backdrop of a long-term decline in the civic associations and organizations that historically helped provide local information and spur political engagement.[10] As a result, an increasingly anemic local newspaper industry further shifts the power dynamic so that journalists cannot provide the kind of

[8] Mark Jacob, "Are Digital Startups the Great Local News Hope or a Disappointment?" *Poynter*, July 27, 2020. www.poynter.org/locally/2020/are-digital-startups-the-great-local-news-hope-or-a-disappointment/ (October 19, 2020).
[9] Davey Alba and Jack Nicas, "As Local News Dies, a Pay-for-Play Network Rises in Its Place," *New York Times*, October 18, 2020. www.nytimes.com/2020/10/18/technology/timpone-local-news-metric-media.html?action=click&module=News&pgtype=Homepage (October 19, 2020).
[10] Skocpol 2003.

independent monitoring on which democratic governance depends. Smaller newsrooms, fewer reporting resources, and less coverage of local politics have placed America's cities and towns on a path toward less political accountability.

LESS NEWS, A LESS INFLUENTIAL PUBLIC

As concerning as the weakening of local newspapers' watchdog capacity is, its demise might be less worrisome if citizens could turn elsewhere to remain informed about local government and engaged with local politics. But as we showed through an array of data in Chapters 4 and 5 – national surveys, local election returns, and online search behavior – as local newspaper coverage diminishes, so does political engagement:

- Local newspaper readers are far more likely than nonreaders to know who their local elected officials are and to participate in local politics.
- As newspaper coverage of municipal politics has declined since the early 1990s, voter turnout in mayoral elections in cities across the country has fallen.
- Americans' online search behavior reveals that in the last 20 years, citizens have become less interested in local government. That trend tracks closely with the amount of local political reporting in their communities.
- When the volume of newspaper coverage of US House elections falls, so do citizens' knowledge of their congressional candidates and likelihood of voting.
- The decline in local newspaper coverage has reduced engagement for everyone, not just the least educated or least politically interested Americans.

These findings depict an environment in which citizens have a harder time constraining the actions of local officials. "If we're gone," said Linda Blackford, a longtime journalist at the *Lexington Herald-Leader*, "people won't have the information we provide. There's nowhere else to get it." And if voters don't know what's happening, officials have fewer incentives to hire capable staff, work in the public interest, and manage city finances prudently. As one example, after Jeff Parrott, of the *South Bend Tribune*, published an investigative series revealing that a local public bus company chief executive had verbally abused his staff and used a corporate credit card for personal travel, the company restructured and implemented new accountability measures. "Without this series of stories,"

Parrott told us, "the public never would have known that their tax dollars were being misused." For public servants, incompetence and corruption carry far less risk if their constituents are unlikely to find out.

Likewise, if political engagement is confined to a shrinking few, it becomes less likely that public policy will reflect the public will – as District of Columbia voters discovered when the City Council vacated their minimum wage vote. Another illustration came from a reporter in rural Pennsylvania, who described an episode involving a revision to a local zoning ordinance, the kind of mundane governmental action that many newspapers no longer cover. In an effort to expand development and ease conservation restrictions without opposition, town supervisors tried to skirt a law that required public hearings. But coverage from the local paper alerted community residents, who showed up and successfully demanded environmental safeguards. "If I hadn't written about that," the reporter told us, "there wouldn't have been the pushback that there was." The fact that engagement is declining across the board – everyone has suffered – is cold comfort. Even if the decline of local news does not exacerbate long-standing inequalities in local engagement, it serves to reinforce them by closing off one route to broader mobilization.

To be sure, we do not interpret our findings as an indication that local engagement will soon disappear, leaving government in the hands of elites free from scrutiny or unfettered by electoral pressure. From time to time, events create conditions that mobilize local citizens to action. In 2018, voter turnout in the midterm elections soared to its highest level in a century.[11] Tens of millions of Americans arrived at the polls to cast votes in races not only for Congress but for county supervisor, school board, city council, and others. In the summer of 2020, outrage over the deaths of black Americans at the hands of police generated protests directed at local law enforcement and city governments across the country. The groundswell of engagement led to local ballot initiatives intended to force reform and create more accountability for police.[12]

But these instances do not mean that we should not worry about local political engagement. In both cases, after all, citizens were spurred to local action primarily because of national politics. The 2018 elections –

[11] Ed Kilgore, "2018 Turnout Was the Highest of Any Midterm in More than a Century," *Intelligencer*, November 13, 2018. https://nymag.com/intelligencer/2018/11/2018-turnout-was-the-highest-of-any-midterm-since-1914.html (October 16, 2020).
[12] Ruairí Arrieta-Kenna, "6 Places where Police Reform Is Going Straight to the Voters," *Politico*, October 15, 2020. www.politico.com/news/magazine/2020/10/15/police-reform-ballot-initiatives-2020-420614 (October 16, 2020).

including down ballot races across the country – were largely viewed as a referendum on the first two years of the Trump Administration and unified Republican control in Washington, DC.[13] In a similar vein, the local protests led by Black Lives Matter and other groups drew unprecedented levels of participation in part because of the Trump Administration's belligerent response. Yet one critical element of the system of federalism built into the US Constitution is that voters see themselves both as Americans and as residents of their states and towns. This dual role is meant to create a sort of political competition that can help keep the national government in check. When local political behavior becomes increasingly linked to national politics, however, that separation of powers is compromised. It becomes harder to maintain the productive tension that allows Americans' community ties to serve "as a critical counterweight to the centralization of authority in Washington, DC."[14]

MORE DEMAND, MORE DEMOCRACY

The two decades since the turn of the century could hardly have been worse for local journalism. Newspapers' finances were in shambles, more journalists were laid off than were coal miners, and political engagement declined as news reporting about local governments evaporated.[15] But incredibly, the worst was yet to come.

When the coronavirus turned the world upside down in early 2020, these trends accelerated at a rate that – even for the reeling newspaper industry – seemed unfathomable. Within six months, 36,000 journalists had lost their jobs, seen their pay cut, or been furloughed.[16] Small and mid-size market papers were hit especially hard, with more than 60 newsrooms closing altogether and hundreds of others scaling back coverage

[13] Lee Drutman, "America Has Local Political Institutions, but Nationalized Politics. This Is a Problem," *Vox*, May 31, 2018. www.vox.com/polyarchy/2018/5/31/17406590/local-national-political-institutions-polarization-federalism (October 16, 2020).

[14] Hopkins 2018, p. 235.

[15] Erika Bolstad, "Covid-19 Is Crushing Newspapers, Worsening Hunger for Accurate Information," *Stateline*, September 8, 2020. www.pewtrusts.org/en/research-and-analysis/blogs/stateline/2020/09/08/covid-19-is-crushing-newspapers-worsening-hunger-for-accurate-information (October 17, 2020).

[16] Damian Radcliife, "Covid-19 Has Ravaged American Newsrooms – Here's Why That Matters," *The Conversation*, July 20, 2020. https://theconversation.com/covid-19-has-ravaged-american-newsrooms-heres-why-that-matters-141955 (October 17, 2020).

and production.[17] Revenue was already hard to come by, but the shuttering of restaurants and retail outlets reduced advertising dollars by another 50%.[18] At a time when local governments were making far-reaching decisions that are a matter of life and death – mask mandates, social distancing requirements, virtual learning, and economic reopening – newspapers found themselves increasingly unable to keep the public informed.

There could hardly be a more important time to reinvigorate the demand for local news – both as a way of reengaging Americans with local politics and giving local news outlets a financial incentive to cover local government in a way that enhances democracy. Despite the myriad challenges, the survey and exit poll experiments we described in Chapter 6 suggest a way forward:

- Tapping into Americans' underlying beliefs and knowledge about local politics is the way to bring them back to local news.
- For the majority of citizens who believe local government affects their lives and that following local politics is an important part of being a good citizen, activating these attitudes makes them more likely to consume local news.
- For the roughly one-third of the public who don't know what their local government does and are not aware of its relevance for their day-to-day lives, informing them about the importance of local politics increases their interest in local news stories.
- These strategies not only boost overall demand, but can also close the wide generation gap in local news consumption.

Increasing citizen demand for local news cannot, in and of itself, save the local news industry. But given that audiences have fallen away and that advertising dollars have followed, any viable strategy for reinvigorating local news – and thus the foundation of local democracy – must address the demand side of the equation. But time is short. As Parrott, the *South Bend Tribune* reporter, put it, "I'm worried that it's going to take us going away before people realize the importance of local journalism and the importance of accountability for local officials."

---

[17] Kristen Hare, "The Coronavirus Has Closed More than 60 Newsrooms across America. And Counting," *Poynter*, September 30, 2020. www.poynter.org/locally/2020/the-corona virus-has-closed-more-than-25-local-newsrooms-across-america-and-counting/ (October 17, 2020).

[18] Adam Gabbatt, "US Newspapers Face 'Extinction Level' Crisis as Covid-19 Hits Hard," *The Guardian*, April 9, 2020. www.theguardian.com/media/2020/apr/09/coronavirus-us-newspapers-impact (October 17, 2020).

Appendices

Appendix A
Interviews with Reporters and Editors
at Local Newspapers

Throughout the book, we draw on more than three dozen in-depth interviews with reporters and editors at local newspapers across the country. These interviews provide a valuable addition to our main empirical approach, giving us journalists' first-hand perspectives on the local news crisis, the changes they've observed in their newsrooms over time, and how their work has evolved as newspapers have struggled financially.

We compiled the sample of journalists from the 202 daily newspapers that serve as the basis of our local news analysis in Chapters 2 and 3 (see Appendices C and D). These papers represent the largest circulating daily newspaper in each congressional district whose archives provide consecutive coverage dating back at least to 2003. We visited each paper's website to identify the news editor and a reporter who writes regularly about local politics (the mayor, city or county government, school boards, etc.). When multiple reporters shared responsibility for local news coverage, we selected the reporter with the most recent story listed on the website. We then sought to locate email addresses for each. We acquired contact information for 370 journalists – one reporter and one editor at 185 of the 202 newspapers in our database.

In September 2019, we sent email requests to each reporter and editor asking if we could interview them for a book about local news. Two weeks after the initial request, we sent follow-up emails. All told, we heard from 61 journalists; taking into account undeliverable emails, this represents a 19%

response rate.[1] Although not unusually high, it was sufficient to generate interviews with journalists from 24 states at newspapers large and small.

From September through November 2019, we conducted semi-structured interviews with 22 local news reporters and 16 editors (27 spoke for attribution and 11 asked to remain anonymous). The following questions/topics guided the interviews, which ranged from 10 to 45 minutes in length (although not every respondent answered all of them):

- Length of time at paper and specific role/beat.
- Has your newsroom changed over the last decade or so?
- Over that same period, has your paper's coverage of local politics – the mayor's office, city hall, the local school board – changed? Would you say you do more reporting on those offices, less, or about the same?
- Are there specific areas of the community that you're no longer able to cover? Are there beats that the paper just doesn't staff anymore? Is the content of the coverage different?
- What would you say has been lost as a result of these reductions? How do you think this has affected the community?
- Do you have competitors? Who are they? Websites? Is there less competition now than there used to be? Has this changed anything about the paper's approach?
- Do you have any sense that papers of your size have had an easier or harder time dealing with turbulence in the industry?
- Do you ever hear from readers about changes to the paper?
- Can you tell us about how the paper has tried to maintain readers even as resources and staff have become increasingly scarce?
- What measures has your paper taken to try to make sure that you're able to give the public essential information about local government and politics?
- Do you think there are other ways to bring back readers who have gravitated to other forms of news?
- What's the future of the business?

We took detailed notes and transcribed the interviews in real time as we spoke to the reporters and editors on the phone.

---

[1] After sending the initial emails, we received bounce backs for 47 reporters and editors for whom we were unable to locate an alternative email address that didn't also bounce back. From the remaining 323 journalists, 50 told us they were willing to be interviewed, and 11 declined to participate. Of the 50 with whom we tried to schedule an interview, 38 scheduled a time and answered the phone.

Appendix B
Staffing Data at Regional Newspapers

In Chapter 2, we present data on newsroom employment between 2000 and 2009 from a selection of large regional newspapers for which we could acquire reliable staffing data. These 40 newspapers in most cases represent the largest-circulation paper in their state. In the cases in which electronic data from the largest paper were unavailable, we use the state's second-largest paper. In some cases, reliable staffing data for large newspapers in a state during this period were not available, which is why we do not include all 50.

The data in Figure 2.4 come from hard copies of the *Editor & Publisher International Yearbook*, which are archived at the Library of Congress. Between 2000 and 2009, *Editor & Publisher* reported the results of an annual survey they sent to all newspapers throughout the country. Part of the survey asked the papers to list their staff. The survey was conducted in prior years as well, but earlier data are less useful because newspaper consolidations and mergers make it difficult to compare staffing numbers.

The survey asked for the names and positions of people who occupied two categories of interest to us: (1) News Executives and (2) Editors and Managers. In some years, this latter category was called Editorial Management. The data in Figure 2.4 reflect changes in the total number of unique news executives and editors and managers at each newspaper during this period. Sometimes the same individual held multiple positions – for example, Editorial Page Editor and Columnist, or Gardening Editor and Homes Editor. We counted unique *individuals*, since eliminating an employee and giving his or her title and responsibilities to another employee represents a reduction in the number of staff available to cover the news. Had we simply tallied up the number of positions listed, we would have double-counted employees at some newspapers, leading to an underestimate of newsroom cuts.

In responding to the survey, newspapers had discretion to determine which positions they listed under these headings, which means there is some variability from paper to paper. But if we make a couple of plausible assumptions, these data offer a useful picture of staffing changes over time at the same newspaper. First, we assume consistency in the positions that a given newspaper deems appropriate for inclusion from year to year. For that reason, we don't include several large papers where the newspaper appears to have changed how it defined relevant staff. For instance, the *Minneapolis Star Tribune* had wildly different numbers in 2000 and 2009, suggesting changes to the way the paper reported staff figures, not actual changes to the size of the newsroom. Second, even though our measure does not focus on staff devoted to political coverage, we assume that as a newsroom's executive and editing staff shrinks, the paper's newsroom staff at large is probably also shrinking. Some of that would be manifest in coverage of politics, even if some areas might be hit more than others.

Even making these assumptions, the staff data look the way we would expect. Newsrooms are bigger at larger papers and smaller at smaller ones. For instance, in 2009, the last year in our time series, the correlation between staff size and circulation in our full data set of papers from all 50 states is 0.71. That relationship is similar for most years.[1]

---

[1] Moreover, our data are generally consistent with Peterson's (2021) analysis using newsroom staffing figures from other sources.

Appendix C
Newspaper Sampling for Local Politics Content Analysis

The content analyses of local politics coverage in Chapters 2 and 3 are based on a study of 202 newspapers for which we collected data from 2003 through 2017. For some of the analyses we present in Chapter 2, we restrict the sample to the 121 of those newspapers for which we have data stretching back to 1996.

Several considerations guided our sample selection. First, given our interest in the relationship between local news coverage and political engagement, we wanted to focus on outlets that likely play a role in shaping citizens' knowledge and participation in local politics. This meant that we focused on daily newspapers rather than weekly publications. Although weekly newspapers have been hard-hit by the local journalism crisis, they do not constitute a primary source of information about local government for most Americans. Second, we wanted our sample to be geographically diverse, which would allow us to determine whether any patterns are peculiar to particular regions of the country. Third, we needed a sample of newspapers whose full-text electronic archives were available.

To draw a sample that meets these criteria, we focused on selecting one newspaper from each of the nation's 435 US House districts. Congressional districts gave us a consistent geographic unit, each with a similar population size. This ensured that our sample would be geographically diverse and include newspapers from every region of the country. It would also include papers large enough to constitute a meaningful source of coverage of local politics. To choose a specific newspaper, we first consulted maps and located the largest city in each district. Then we identified the largest circulating daily newspaper in each.[1] In the vast majority of cases, this was a straightforward, though time-consuming, task.

From that list, we then narrowed our sample to daily newspapers whose full text was available in NewsBank; NewsBank's electronic archives for most papers go back further in time than other databases. Because our research question demands a longitudinal analysis, we further restricted our list of papers to those for which NewsBank contained consecutive full-text archives dating back at least to 2003, roughly the moment when the Internet began to disrupt newspapers' business model. That means that for every paper in our data set, we can analyze at least 15 years' worth of coverage. In 13 cases, the paper was not available in NewsBank, so we accessed the archives through ProQuest. In the handful of cases in which the paper was unavailable from either database, we included instead the paper in the district with the second-largest circulation. Our sample includes at least one paper from every state, and in most cases also includes the largest paper in each state. The full list appears in Appendix D.[2]

One of the challenges of studying local news in a period of industry upheaval and newspaper consolidation is that changes to the news outlets themselves can make longitudinal analysis difficult. Some papers in our data set in 2017, the final year of our content analysis, are consolidated versions of newspapers that had previously been two separate editions or two entirely different papers. *The Atlanta Journal-Constitution*'s first year of publication, for example, was 2001. Before that, the *Atlanta Constitution* was published in the morning, and the *Atlanta Journal* was published in the evening. The two papers shared a consolidated Sunday edition. To address this issue, for each of the papers in our sample, we began data collection the first full year the paper operated in its current form (i.e., 2002 for the *Atlanta Journal-Constitution*).

The resulting sample yields a collection of newspapers that is not only geographically diverse, but also varies in terms of size. Table C.1 presents the percentage of newspapers in our sample by circulation. In the 1996–2017 sample, which we rely on in Chapter 2, 44% of the papers

[1] The circulation data we cite in discussions of these data are from 2014. The relative sizes of these papers have not changed substantially since that time.
[2] Although we began our sampling with 435 congressional districts, our final sample includes just 202 newspapers because some papers' archives were not electronically available, some papers' electronic archives did not go back to 2003, and occasionally a single newspaper was the largest paper in multiple congressional districts.

TABLE C.I. *Distribution of newspaper circulation in samples for the local politics content analysis*

	1996–2017 Sample (Chapter 2)	2003–2017 Sample (Chapter 3)
Less than 25,000 circulation	9% (11)	20% (41)
25,000 to 45,000 circulation	13 (16)	20 (41)
45,000 to 90,000 circulation	34 (41)	30 (60)
More than 90,000 circulation	44 (53)	30 (60)

Notes: Entries indicate the percentage (and number) of papers whose 2014 circulation size falls into each category.

had a circulation larger than 90,000; the rest are mid-sized or smaller. That upward skew in the distribution reflects the fact that larger papers began making their content available to NewsBank earlier than did smaller newspapers. In the 2003–2017 sample, which forms the basis of our analysis in Chapter 3, smaller papers make up a larger proportion. Although our data do not include the smallest dailies in the country, we have enough variation in size to determine whether the decline in local news has been more severe at larger or smaller papers.

Appendix D
Newspapers Included in the Local Politics
Content Analysis

	State	Time Series	Circulation
Akron Beacon Journal	OH	1996–2017	45,000–90,000
Albany Times Union	NY	1996–2017	45,000–90,000
Albuquerque Journal	NM	1996–2017	45,000–90,000
Amarillo Globe News	TX	2003–2017	25,000–45,000
Anchorage Daily News/Alaska Dispatch News	AK	1996–2017	45,000–90,000
Anderson Independent Mail	SC	2003–2017	Less than 25,000
Anniston Star	AL	1996–2017	Less than 25,000
Argus Leader	SD	2003–2017	25,000–45,000
Arizona Daily Star	AZ	1996–2017	More than 90,000
Arizona Republic	AZ	2003–2017	More than 90,000
Arkansas Democrat-Gazette	AR	1996–2017	More than 90,000
Arlington Heights Daily Herald	IL	1996–2017	More than 90,000
Athens Banner Herald	GA	2003–2017	Less than 25,000
Atlanta Journal-Constitution	GA	2003–2017	More than 90,000
Augusta Chronicle	GA	2003–2017	45,000–90,000
Austin American-Statesman	TX	1996–2017	More than 90,000
Bakersfield Californian	CA	2003–2017	25,000–45,000
Baltimore Sun	MD	1996–2017	More than 90,000
Bangor Daily News	ME	1996–2017	45,000–90,000
Batavia Daily News	NY	2003–2017	Less than 25,000
Baton Rouge Advocate	LA	1996–2017	More than 90,000
Baytown Sun	TX	2003–2017	Less than 25,000
Beaumont Enterprise	TX	2003–2017	Less than 25,000
Beaver County Times	PA	2003–2017	25,000–45,000
Belleville News-Democrat	IL	2003–2017	45,000–90,000
Billings Gazette	MT	2003–2017	25,000–45,000

	State	Time Series	Circulation
Birmingham News	AL	1996–2017	More than 90,000
Bismarck Tribune	ND	2003–2017	Less than 25,000
Bloomington Herald Times	IN	1996–2017	Less than 25,000
Boston Globe	MA	1996–2017	More than 90,000
Brownsville Herald	TX	1996–2017	Less than 25,000
Bucks County Courier Times	PA	2003–2017	25,000–45,000
Buffalo News	NY	1996–2017	More than 90,000
Burlington County Times	NJ	2003–2017	Less than 25,000
Burlington Free Press	VT	2003–2017	Less than 25,000
Cape Cod Times	MA	2003–2017	25,000–45,000
Carroll County Times	MD	2003–2017	Less than 25,000
Casper Star-Tribune	WY	2003–2017	Less than 25,000
Cedar Rapids Gazette	IA	1996–2017	45,000–90,000
Centre Daily Times	PA	1996–2017	Less than 25,000
Charleston Gazette-Mail	SC	2003–2017	45,000–90,000
Charlotte Observer	NC	1996–2017	More than 90,000
Chattanooga Times Free Press	TN	1996–2017	45,000–90,000
Chicago Sun-Times	IL	1996–2017	More than 90,000
Chicago Tribune	IL	1996–2017	More than 90,000
Clarion-Ledger	MI	2003–2017	25,000–45,000
Cleveland Plain Dealer	OH	1996–2017	More than 90,000
Colorado Springs Gazette	CO	1996–2017	45,000–90,000
Columbia Daily Herald	TN	2003–2017	Less than 25,000
The Columbian	WA	1996–2017	45,000–90,000
Columbus Dispatch	OH	1996–2017	More than 90,000
Commercial Appeal	TN	1996–2017	More than 90,000
Concord Monitor	NH	2003–2017	Less than 25,000
Connecticut Post	CT	2003–2017	45,000–90,000
Cookeville Herald-Citizen	TN	2003–2017	Less than 25,000
Corpus Christi Caller-Times	TX	1996–2017	45,000–90,000
Daily Camera	CO	2003–2017	25,000–45,000
Daily Herald	UT	2003–2017	25,000–45,000
Dallas Morning News	TX	1996–2017	More than 90,000

(continued)

	State	Time Series	Circulation
Dayton Daily News	OH	1996–2017	More than 90,000
Daytona Beach News Journal	FL	2003–2017	45,000–90,000
Delaware County Daily Times	PA	1996–2017	25,000–45,000
Delaware State News	DE	1996–2017	25,000–45,000
Denver Post	CO	1996–2017	More than 90,000
Des Moines Register	IA	2003–2017	45,000–90,000
Detroit Free Press	MI	2003–2017	More than 90,000
Duluth News Tribune	MN	1996–2017	25,000–45,000
El Paso Times	TX	2003–2017	45,000–90,000
Erie Times-News	PA	1996–2017	45,000–90,000
Evansville Courier and Press	IN	1996–2017	45,000–90,000
Fayetteville Observer	AR	1996–2017	45,000–90,000
Flint Journal	MI	1996–2017	45,000–90,000
Florida Times Union	FL	1996–2017	45,000–90,000
Fort Wayne Journal Gazette	IN	1996–2017	45,000–90,000
Fort Worth Star Telegram	TX	1996–2017	More than 90,000
Frederick News-Post	MD	2003–2017	25,000–45,000
Fresno Bee	CA	1996–2017	More than 90,000
Gainesville Sun	FL	1996–2017	25,000–45,000
Grand Island Daily Independent	NE	2003–2017	Less than 25,000
Grand Rapids Press	MI	2003–2017	45,000–90,000
Greeley Tribune	CO	2003–2017	25,000–45,000
Greensboro News and Record	NC	1996–2017	45,000–90,000
Hartford Courant	CT	1996–2017	More than 90,000
The Herald News	MA	2003–2017	Less than 25,000
The Herald-Sun	NC	1996–2017	Less than 25,000
Honolulu Advertiser/Star-Advertiser	HI	2003–2017	More than 90,000
Houston Chronicle	TX	1996–2017	More than 90,000
Huntington Herald-Dispatch	WV	2003–2017	25,000–45,000
Huntsville Times	AL	1996–2017	25,000–45,000
Idaho Statesman	ID	2003–2017	25,000–45,000
Indianapolis Star	IN	2003–2017	More than 90,000
Inland Valley Daily Bulletin	CA	2003–2017	45,000–90,000
Jackson Citizen Patriot	MI	2003–2017	Less than 25,000
Jefferson City News Tribune	MO	2003–2017	Less than 25,000

	State	Time Series	Circulation
Jonesboro Sun	AR	2003–2017	Less than 25,000
Kansas City Star	MO	1996–2017	More than 90,000
Knoxville News Sentinel	TN	1996–2017	45,000–90,000
La Crosse Tribune	WI	1996–2017	25,000–45,000
Laredo Morning Times	TX	1996–2017	Less than 25,000
Las Vegas Review-Journal	NV	2003–2017	More than 90,000
The Ledger	FL	1996–2017	25,000–45,000
Lewiston Tribune	ME	1996–2017	Less than 25,000
Lexington Herald-Leader	KY	1996–2017	45,000–90,000
Lima News	OH	2003–2017	25,000–45,000
Lincoln Journal Star	NE	2003–2017	45,000–90,000
Long Beach Press Telegram	CA	1996–2017	45,000–90,000
Los Angeles Times	LA	1996–2017	More than 90,000
Louisville Courier-Journal	KY	2003–2017	More than 90,000
The Lowell Sun	MA	2003–2017	25,000–45,000
Marietta Daily Journal	GA	2003–2017	Less than 25,000
Marysville Appeal Democrat	CA	2003–2017	Less than 25,000
Miami Herald	FL	1996–2017	More than 90,000
Midland Daily News	MI	2003–2017	Less than 25,000
Milwaukee Journal Sentinel	WI	1996–2017	More than 90,000
Minneapolis Star Tribune	MN	1996–2017	More than 90,000
Modesto Bee	CA	1996–2017	45,000–90,000
The Morning Call	PA	1996–2017	45,000–90,000
Monterey County Herald	CA	2003–2017	25,000–45,000
Muskegon Chronicle	MI	2003–2017	Less than 25,000
Naples Daily News	FL	1996–2017	45,000–90,000
New Hampshire Union Leader	NH	1996–2017	25,000–45,000
New Haven Register	CT	1996–2017	45,000–90,000
New York Times	NY	1996–2017	More than 90,000
Newark Star-Ledger	NJ	1996–2017	More than 90,000
Newport News Daily Press	VA	1996–2017	45,000–90,000
News-Tribune	WA	1996–2017	45,000–90,000
Observer-Reporter	PA	2003–2017	25,000–45,000

(continued)

	State	Time Series	Circulation
Ocala Star-Banner	FL	1996–2017	25,000–45,000
The Oklahoman	OK	1996–2017	More than 90,000
The Olympian	WA	2003–2017	Less than 25,000
Omaha World-Herald	NE	1996–2017	More than 90,000
Orange County Register	CA	1996–2017	More than 90,000
The Oregonian	OR	1996–2017	More than 90,000
Orlando Sentinel	FL	1996–2017	More than 90,000
Owensboro Messenger-Inquirer	KY	1996–2017	25,000–45,000
Pasadena Star-News	CA	2003–2017	Less than 25,000
The Patriot-News	PA	1996–2017	45,000–90,000
Philadelphia Inquirer	PA	1996–2017	More than 90,000
Pine Bluff Commercial	AR	2003–2017	Less than 25,000
Pioneer Press	MN	1996–2017	More than 90,000
Pittsburgh Post-Gazette	PA	1996–2017	More than 90,000
Portland Press-Herald	ME	2003–2017	25,000–45,000
Post and Courier	SC	1996–2017	45,000–90,000
Press of Atlantic City	NJ	1996–2017	45,000–90,000
Press-Register	AL	1996–2017	45,000–90,000
Providence Journal	RI	1996–2017	45,000–90,000
Raleigh News and Observer	NC	1996–2017	More than 90,000
Redding Record Searchlight	CA	1996–2017	Less than 25,000
The Register-Guard	OR	2003–2017	45,000–90,000
The Republican	MA	1996–2017	45,000–90,000
Richmond Times-Dispatch	VA	1996–2017	More than 90,000
Riverside Press Enterprise	CA	1996–2017	More than 90,000
Roanoke Times	VA	1996–2017	45,000–90,000
Rockford Register-Star	IL	2003–2017	45,000–90,000
Sacramento Bee	CA	1996–2017	More than 90,000
Salina Journal	KS	2003–2017	Less than 25,000
Salt Lake Tribune	UT	1996–2017	More than 90,000
San Antonio Express-News	TX	1996–2017	More than 90,000
San Bernardino Sun	CA	2003–2017	45,000–90,000
San Diego Union-Tribune	CA	1996–2017	More than 90,000
San Francisco Chronicle	CA	1996–2017	More than 90,000
San Gabriel Valley Tribune	CA	2003–2017	45,000–90,000

	State	Time Series	Circulation
San Jose Mercury News	CA	1996–2017	More than 90,000
Santa Fe New Mexican	NM	1996–2017	Less than 25,000
Santa Rosa Press Democrat	CA	1996–2017	45,000–90,000
Sarasota Herald Tribune	FL	1996–2017	45,000–90,000
Savannah Morning News	GA	2003–2017	25,000–45,000
Seattle Times	WA	1996–2017	More than 90,000
Sioux City Journal	IA	1996–2017	25,000–45,000
South Bend Tribune	IN	1996–2017	45,000–90,000
Southwest Times Record	AR	2003–2017	25,000–45,000
Spokesman-Review	WA	1996–2017	45,000–90,000
St. Louis Post-Dispatch	MO	1996–2017	More than 90,000
Standard-Examiner	UT	2003–2017	45,000–90,000
Star-News	NC	1996–2017	25,000–45,000
The State	SC	1996–2017	45,000–90,000
State Journal Register	IL	1996–2017	25,000–45,000
Sun Herald	MS	1996–2017	25,000–45,000
The Sun News	SC	2003–2017	25,000–45,000
Sun Sentinel	FL	1996–2017	More than 90,000
Syracuse Post-Standard	NY	1996–2017	45,000–90,000
Tampa Bay Times/St. Pete Times	FL	1996–2017	More than 90,000
Telegraph	GA	1996–2017	25,000–45,000
The Times-Tribune	PA	2003–2017	45,000–90,000
Times Picayune	LA	1996–2017	More than 90,000
Toledo Blade	OH	2003–2017	45,000–90,000
Topeka Capital Journal	KS	2003–2017	25,000–45,000
Trenton Times	NJ	1996–2017	25,000–45,000
The Tribune	CA	2003–2017	25,000–45,000
Tulsa World	OK	1996–2017	More than 90,000
Ventura County Star	VA	2003–2017	45,000–90,000
The Virginian-Pilot	VA	1996–2017	More than 90,000
Waco Tribune Herald	TX	2003–2017	25,000–45,000
Watertown Daily Times	NY	1996–2017	Less than 25,000
Waukesha Freeman	WI	2003–2017	Less than 25,000
Wenatchee World	WA	1996–2017	Less than 25,000

(*continued*)

	State	Time Series	Circulation
Whittier Daily News	CA	2003–2017	Less than 25,000
Wichita Eagle	KS	1996–2017	45,000–90,000
Winchester Star	VA	2003–2017	Less than 25,000
Winston-Salem Journal	NC	2003–2017	45,000–90,000
Wisconsin State Journal	WI	1996–2017	45,000–90,000
Wyoming Tribune-Eagle	WY	2003–2017	Less than 25,000

Appendix E
Content Analysis of Local News Coverage

To track the amount of coverage of local politics in each paper, we performed a series of keyword searches within NewsBank (and ProQuest) for each newspaper for each year of our time series. Our search terms focused on several major topics pertaining to local public affairs: mayors, city government, county government, and school boards. Although these four categories don't exhaust every possible topic, they capture stories about the core local governmental institutions in most communities. Other research that relies on topic models to identify the focus of local news coverage validates our approach.[1]

LOCAL POLITICS COVERAGE

The data collection was straightforward. For each specific topic of coverage, we identified relevant search terms and trained a group of research assistants to collect data on the number of news stories that included each term. Our searches for stories about the mayor simply involved searches of the word "mayor." To identify stories about city government, we searched for "city council," "town council," "city commission," or "town commission." These terms reflect the legislative bodies that make decisions in most cities. Because states use a wide variety of forms of county government – or provide only limited power to counties – county government-related searches required more variation than the other topic areas. To identify stories about county government, we searched for

---

[1] See Martin and McCrain 2019; Peterson 2021.

stories mentioning "county commission," "county legislature," "county board," "county council," "county executive," and several other permutations. For instance, in Louisiana, we searched for "parish council" and in Alaska, we tracked mentions of "borough assembly," which are those states' versions of county governments. In Arkansas, our searches included "quorum court," and in Texas "commissioners court." Because our searches were fairly exhaustive, we are confident that our data contain an accurate portrayal of coverage of these different topics. Finally, we searched for "school board" to identify stories about local school district governance.

OTHER TOPICS

In addition to our analysis of local political coverage, we also tracked news stories published in our local papers about national politics, state politics, and sports. We searched for stories with the word "president" as well as stories with the word "Congress."[2] We tracked attention to state politics with searches of the word "governor." And to track coverage of non-hard news topics, we measured the number of stories mentioning one of the four major professional team sports in the United States: "basketball," "baseball," "football," and "hockey."

NEWS HOLE

The final piece of our content analysis involved measuring the size of a newspaper's "news hole." This is an industry term to describe the amount of space available for editorial content once all advertising has been placed. Although industry professionals typically discuss the news hole in terms of column inches or the percentage of editorial space, our measure is the total number of items the paper published each year, according to the NewsBank (or ProQuest) archive.

Our measure offers several benefits. Most importantly, it allows us to discern the extent to which reductions in coverage of local government stem from cuts to overall editorial space or business decisions by newspaper publishers. The measure also helps address the fact that newspaper content in NewsBank or ProQuest is occasionally missing. This usually stems from transmission problems between newspapers and the database

[2] These two terms capture local newspapers' attention to national politics, an approach similar to the one used by Hopkins (2018).

firms. Although the number of missing days is typically not large, it does vary from paper to paper. That could potentially lead to inaccurate comparisons between papers. But since any missing days in the archives would also affect our news hole measure, we can be more confident that the *proportion* of coverage devoted to a topic – say, mayoral coverage – is consistent across papers.

RELIABILITY AND ACCURACY OF MEASURES

We did not conduct formal reliability tests because our content analysis did not require any subjective judgment, only keyword searches. But to ensure that research assistants searched the electronic databases properly and recorded the number of stories about each topic accurately, we spot-checked their work. In only a handful of cases did we find discrepancies, most of which involved minor differences or simple clerical errors, and all of which we corrected.

The broader question is whether our fairly blunt method of analysis – keyword searches – accurately picks up stories specific to the individuals or institutions we assume it does. For instance, searching for the word "mayor" would likely turn up stories beyond those that focus solely on the mayors in the cities or towns included in a given newspaper's circulation area. In the wake of September 11, 2001, for example, local newspapers across the country ran numerous stories that referred to New York City Mayor Rudolph Giuliani. Similarly, keyword searches for "president" or "governor" will capture stories that might be about the president of a local chamber of commerce or references to a governor on an automobile engine. To be sure, this means that the annual counts might sometimes overstate the absolute amount of certain kinds of news content.

But two factors mitigate against this over-counting as a threat to the validity of our conclusions. First, there is no theoretical reason to think that the prevalence of these "false positives" will be systematically higher in any particular paper (or category of papers). Second, it is unlikely that the rate of false positives will change significantly over time. Since our argument is about the decline of local news over time, our conclusions about longitudinal change should not be affected substantively.

Nonetheless, we conducted a series of analyses to determine whether our approach was leading us to different conclusions than if we had tried to search for specific names (e.g., "Mayor Will Wynn"). First, in one-quarter of our papers (49 total) we conducted a series of supplemental

analyses in which we ran our database searches using both general terms
(e.g., "governor") and permutations of the elected official's name (e.g.,
"Governor Jennifer Granholm," "Gov. Jennifer Granholm," "Governor
Granholm," "Gov. Granholm"). The average correlation between those
searches was 0.60. That indicates that the two searches do not produce
identical results, but that the results are strongly related. Critically, when
we examine trends over time, they generally move similarly, with both
types of searches showing reductions in news coverage over time.

Second, we investigated an issue peculiar to NewsBank, which involves
the duplication of some news stories. From our conversations with pro-
grammers at the company, we learned that multiple versions of the same
story occasionally appear in the archives. This happens because each
newspaper's HTML file and software system determine how it transmits
content to NewsBank and thus the way search results appear. In some
cases, the software captures and sends only the final web version of a
story to NewsBank. In others, multiple versions of the story are sent
because some software packages have default settings that capture every
single version of an article as a separate entry. Moreover, each newspaper's contract with NewsBank determines whether the paper transmits
online content. In the rare cases when a newspaper does not send web
content, NewsBank scrapes the full HTML from the paper's website,
thereby capturing each headline and corresponding article. But they have
no method for getting rid of duplicates in cases where the newspaper
sends its print coverage and NewsBank captures the online content.
Variation in content transmission can certainly have implications for
our measures. But as long as each paper has used a consistent method
to send content to NewsBank over time – and we have no reason to
believe that is not the case – then the patterns we uncover are meaningful,
even if the raw counts are not perfectly precise.

To validate this assumption, we conducted a series of robustness
checks in which we "de-duplicated" a sample of newspapers' coverage.
This involved clicking on articles with similar titles to determine whether
the content was identical. After doing this for thousands of articles in
more than a dozen papers, we found nothing to suggest that the issue of
duplicated content would affect the conclusions we draw from our analysis. And as far as we can tell, ProQuest's system is not fundamentally
different, which suggests there should be few comparability issues in using
both databases. Indeed, the correlations between our content measures in
the newspapers that are available in both NewsBank and ProQuest are
high. As one example, the correlations are around 0.90 for the local news

searches we ran in both databases for the *Post and Courier* in Charleston, South Carolina.

We also conducted an analysis to validate our news hole measure, which is the total number of stories published each year by each newspaper, as archived by NewsBank. If newspapers over time shorten (or lengthen) the stories they publish, changes in our news hole measure could reflect changes in the newspaper's format or style rather than available editorial space. As a way of validating that our measure accurately captures the true news hole, we conducted an analysis using microfilm archives of newspapers at the Library of Congress in Washington, DC.

More specifically, we selected 10 papers in our data set for which the Library of Congress had full microfilm archives during the course of our time series. We trained a group of research assistants to carry out the analysis and supervised their work at the Library of Congress. For each paper, we randomly selected a single week in each year and counted the number of pages in the paper for that week. We included only the main editorial sections of the paper, not special advertising inserts, coupons, *Parade Magazine* (which local newspapers don't produce themselves), or other sections that did not carry news of some sort. We then multiplied the total number of pages for each sampled week by 52 to generate an estimate of the number of pages available for editorial content in a given year. This method produced a measure of the space for editorial content strongly related to the news hole measure we use in the book. On average, the correlation between the page counts and the NewsBank (or ProQuest) story counts was 0.78, indicating strong validity for our measure. Of the papers we analyzed, only the *Idaho Statesman* had a correlation lower than 0.30, which likely resulted from the challenges of counting special inserts that were difficult to categorize as containing news or merely advertising.

A second concern is that the news hole could be less relevant in an era of online publishing. Because newspaper websites do not face space constraints, the ability to publish will not be affected by the shrinking surface area of the paper. But given the current newspaper landscape, our measure of the news hole is a good proxy of the overall volume of coverage. Perhaps most importantly, the shrinking of the news hole can't be divorced from the shrinking of general newsroom resources (including staff). Its decline reflects less of an ability to cover the news. Even if space constraints don't apply to online publishing, reductions in newsroom staff do. There might be unlimited space to post stories, but there is a decidedly limited number of people to write them.

Moreover, our interviews with editors and reporters made it clear that the print newspaper is still the prize for most publishers because advertising rates are so high. Thus, a newspaper is likely to emphasize filling up the available printed paper with its most high-value content. One reporter at a small daily in the South told us, for example, that her paper's goal is to get people to buy the paper, which means "generating as much exclusive content … and keeping it offline." Although most papers don't go that far – the reporters we spoke to mentioned they often do "quick hits" for the web, put up "breaking news" headlines throughout the day, and provide updates to stories as more information becomes available – the overwhelming majority (about 75%) also conveyed that they spend their time thinking about and writing for the print edition.

Finally, the way NewsBank and ProQuest archive content means that our measure should reflect much of what appears on newspapers' websites. Newspapers aren't in the habit of producing a lot of website-only content. James Brooks, who has covered Alaska politics for more than a decade, is one of those reporters who writes "quick hits." He then builds on those 50 or 100 words pieces throughout the day. "People like breaking news, so this gives them that," he explained. But he also noted that "the endpoint is the same." The online story at the end of the day is exactly what will appear in the *Alaska Dispatch* the next morning. Jennifer Napier-Pearce, the (now former) editor of the *Salt Lake Tribune*, squeezes as much as she can into print each day. If something is dated, even by a few hours, then it probably won't make it into the print edition. This is rarely the case with anything important, though. As Napier-Pearce puts it, "Core news is core news, and appears in both places."

Appendix F
Content Analysis of TV News Coverage

In Chapter 2, we collected data on coverage of local politics from transcripts of local TV stations' electronic archives in NewsBank. The sample includes 31 stations with coverage going back to at least 2007 and over at least 3 consecutive years. The stations cover nine different markets in six states.

For each of the 31 stations – for example, the local ABC, CBS, Fox, and NBC affiliates – we tracked coverage that included discussion of local government (mayors, city government, and school boards). We did not collect data on county government because it was exceedingly infrequent. We followed the same search protocol we used to identify relevant stories in the newspaper analysis (see Appendix E).

We also generated a measure of local politics coverage similar to the news hole measure we generated for the newspaper content analysis. More specifically, we calculated the percentage of transcripts for a given station in a given year that included discussion of local politics. This measure is not exactly the same as our newspaper measure, where stories, rather than newscasts, are the unit of analysis. But since we are most interested in the over-time trend – Did the level of attention to local politics on TV increase as newspapers cut their own coverage? – this does not significantly compromise our ability to compare the two.

It's important to note that different stations have differing numbers of days with missing transcripts – and some years have more coverage than others – so any effort to characterize the overall amount of local politics coverage would surely produce an underestimate. But as long as the days that are missing do not correlate systematically with higher or lower levels of local politics coverage – and there's no reason to think they would – then we can characterize the share of local TV broadcast news that covered local politics. And because the news hole for local TV newscasts has not changed much – typically still 22 minutes for information of any kind on a half-hour broadcast – the meaning of the denominator is consistent across our time series.

We then aggregated the stations within the nine markets where we can analyze coverage. For some markets, like Honolulu, we have many years of coverage. For others, like Denver, we have just a handful.

Appendix G
Analysis of Internet Start-Ups

The internet start-up analysis in Chapter 2 draws on the most comprehensive data set available of local news start-ups. Compiled by media scholar Michele McLellan, "Michele's List" has been used in previous academic research.[1] To be included on the list, a news start-up must be "devoted primarily to local news," update news reports "regularly," and meet a series of other standards common to news organizations, such as a commitment to accuracy.[2]

The list does not include every local internet site that occasionally posts news articles. Most notably, Michele's List does not include Patch Media, the network of news outlets that operates in about 1,000 communities across the country. But the list does account for exactly the type of site that – if the Internet can step in where newspapers have stepped away – would inherit the mantle of local news providers. And even though Patch is the largest hyperlocal news site, it accounts for an extremely small amount of internet traffic.[3] Thus, its omission from Michele's List would not affect any conclusions about whether online-only sources are a major source of information for citizens.

We started by examining the 462 sites based in the United States with a working URL. We do not include six sites whose founding date was listed as prior to 1999. These sites are primarily print publications that have since transitioned to the web. For the purposes of identifying the emergence of news online, their early founding dates as print publications are

---

[1] For examples, see Harlow and Chadha 2018; Chadha and Harlow 2018.
[2] "About Michele's List." www.micheleslist.org/pages/1 (March 15, 2020).
[3] Hindman 2018.

not relevant. We classified the remaining sites as including news or politics, or not. Our coding was generous; if any content tapped into local news, we coded it as a "yes." This includes health care or business sites that provide information about elections, new ordinances or regulations, and the like. The data in Figures 2.10 and 2.11 are based on the 400 sites that met these criteria.

Appendix H
The Cooperative Congressional Election Study Data, 2016–2019

The Cooperative Congressional Election Study is a nationally representative survey conducted annually by YouGov and in collaboration with dozens of academic institutions. All CCES respondents – roughly 50,000 per year – answer basic demographic and political questions, which are part of the survey's "Common Content." On the four annual surveys from 2016 to 2019, we included a module of questions regarding news consumption and political engagement. YouGov fielded these modules to a random subset of 1,000 respondents from the overall sample.

Even after sample weighting, respondents to opt-in panels like the CCES tend to be somewhat more knowledgeable about politics and more likely to participate than respondents to face-to-face surveys like the American National Election Study.[1] This can complicate studies of political engagement. But in general, this should create a hard test for news effects. People who are minimally attentive to politics should be able, for instance, to offer an evaluation of local political figures or congressional incumbents, leaving relatively less room for media influence. The extent to which we identify significant media effects in a relatively informed sample suggests the true effect of news coverage may be even larger.

MEASURES OF POLITICAL ENGAGEMENT: 2016–2019

In our examination of local political engagement in the survey modules from 2016 to 2019, we used several different measures: knowledge of the

---

[1] Malhotra and Krosnick 2007.

mayor and local school superintendent, as well as various questions about local political participation. For our mayor and superintendent measures, we categorize as "correct" any substantive response (i.e., a name) to the question. That was necessary because our surveys do not contain information about respondents' city of residence, which means we can't know for sure the name of their mayor or school superintendent. Although we do know respondents' county of residence and zip code, there are often multiple cities and school districts within a single county, and zip codes also cross jurisdictional boundaries. The upshot is that the figures we present in Chapter 4 likely overestimate local political knowledge, since some of the names respondents offered are likely incorrect. This is another reason that our news effects are probably underestimates; offering an answer is easier than knowing the right one.

Despite these caveats, we have reason to believe that our coding of knowledge is quite accurate. On the 2017 CCES, we included a question that asked respondents to name their state's attorney general. Since we know each respondent's state of residence, we were able to check the accuracy of their responses. The vast majority – about three-quarters – said they didn't know (similar to our school superintendent question, incidentally). But among the respondents who offered any name, 86% gave the correct one. And most of the people who got it wrong named a candidate for attorney general or someone who had previously served in the position, suggesting a meaningful level of knowledge. To the extent that the same pattern applies to our mayor and superintendent questions – that is, the respondents who give a name are people who do have relevant knowledge – then coding any name as correct is likely to categorize accurately people who are and aren't knowledgeable about local politics.

Our measure of local participation is based on a question that asked respondents whether they had engaged in one of several different activities within the last year. We use those items to create an index. Table H.1 reports the percentage of respondents who engaged in each activity that comprises the local participation index. Tables H.2 to H.5 present regression models on which various figures in Chapters 4 and 5 are based.

TABLE H.I. *Local political participation among CCES respondents*

	2017	2018	2019
In the past year, have you ... ?			
Voted in a local election	64%	77%	65%
Attended local political meetings (such as school board or city council)	12	12	16
Signed a letter or petition (including over email) about an issue in your community	30	38	35
Used social media to communicate about politics in your community	28	37	34
Contacted a member of your local government (such as the mayor)	14	26	21

Note: Entries indicate the percentage of respondents in each year who reported participating in each activity.

TABLE H.2. *Local newspaper consumption and local political engagement*

	Know Mayor			Know Superintendent		Local Participation		
	2016	2017	2019	2016	2019	2017	2018	2019
Read local newspaper	0.665** (0.251)	0.916** (0.227)	0.516** (0.186)	0.475 (0.338)	0.695** (0.197)	0.738** (0.142)	0.519** (0.091)	0.551** (0.097)
College education	0.462* (0.220)	0.730** (0.242)	0.340 (0.191)	0.449 (0.249)	0.643** (0.208)	0.344** (0.122)	0.136 (0.114)	0.141 (0.110)
Female	0.323 (0.179)	0.023 (0.179)	0.105 (0.149)	0.161 (0.324)	0.437* (0.178)	-0.125 (0.107)	-0.078 (0.093)	-0.028 (0.096)
Age	-0.007 (0.008)	0.015* (0.006)	0.010 (0.007)	-0.019* (0.008)	0.006 (0.008)	-0.006** (0.003)	-0.007 (0.003)	-0.002 (0.003)
White	0.154 (0.320)	-0.168 (0.240)	-0.293 (0.263)	0.183 (0.389)	-0.072 (0.257)	-0.202 (0.120)	0.321 (0.166)	-0.043 (0.218)
Black	0.995 (0.563)	0.633 (0.330)	0.264 (0.392)	0.334 (0.613)	0.832** (0.297)	-0.252 (0.201)	0.023 (0.274)	-0.080 (0.202)
Democrat	0.453 (0.314)	0.826** (0.273)	0.312 (0.291)	0.668 (0.384)	0.221 (0.334)	0.345* (0.140)	0.420* (0.156)	-0.536** (0.154)
Republican	0.297 (0.370)	1.159** (0.337)	0.095 (0.242)	0.721* (0.357)	0.398 (0.312)	0.223* (0.109)	0.206 (0.156)	0.279* (0.133)
Political interest	0.272* (0.129)	0.361* (0.157)	0.325** (0.108)	0.266 (0.167)	0.366* (0.152)	0.438** (0.051)	0.596** (0.048)	0.553** (0.055)
Constant	-1.995** (0.530)	-2.900** (0.460)	-2.054* (0.437)	-3.108** (0.558)	-3.875** (0.618)	0.031 (0.248)	-0.352 (0.247)	-0.485* (0.237)
(Pseudo) R^2	0.062	0.133	0.056	0.041	0.075	0.228	0.287	0.250
Chi-square (F-test)	36.307	108.485	56.924	47.102	39.276	38.624	48.512	55.287
N	747	780	961	933	969	929	839	957

Notes: Cell entries are logistic regression coefficients for knowing the mayor and school superintendent and linear regression coefficients for local political participation. Standard errors are in parentheses. Levels of significance: ** $p < 0.01$; * $p < 0.05$. Data come from modules of the Cooperative Congressional Election Study from 2016 to 2019.

TABLE H.3. *Newspaper reading versus TV viewing and political engagement*

	Know Mayor	Know Superintendent	Local Participation
Read local newspaper	0.413*	0.658**	0.391**
	(0.176)	(0.208)	(0.115)
Watch local TV news	0.188	−0.094	0.026
	(0.118)	(0.151)	(0.082)
College education	0.363	0.634**	0.154
	(0.190)	(0.205)	(0.112)
Female	0.078	0.429*	−0.051
	(0.144)	(0.170)	(0.097)
Age	0.008	0.006	−0.003
	(0.007)	(0.008)	(0.003)
White	−0.324	−0.082	−0.079
	(0.258)	(0.249)	(0.209)
Black	0.187	0.805**	−0.146
	(0.396)	(0.293)	(0.201)
Democrat	0.318	0.242	0.563**
	(0.286)	(0.336)	(0.146)
Republican	0.114	0.417	0.302*
	(0.245)	(0.311)	(0.139)
Political interest	0.339**	0.385*	0.576**
	(0.106)	(0.155)	(0.052)
Constant	2.003**	−3.821**	−0.433
	(0.436)	(0.597)	(0.218)
(Pseudo) R^2	0.054	0.073	0.235
Chi-square (F-test)	58.723	44.329	51.470
N	961	969	957

Notes: Cell entries are logistic regression coefficients for knowing the mayor and school superintendent and linear regression coefficients for local political participation. Standard errors are in parentheses. Levels of significance: ** $p < 0.01$; * $p < 0.05$. Data come from a module of the 2019 Cooperative Congressional Election Study.

TABLE H.4. *The effect of college education on citizens' attention to local and national news*

	Attention to Local News			Attention to National News		
	2017	2018	2019	2017	2018	2019
College graduate	−0.102 (0.063)	−0.052 (0.052)	0.049 (0.074)	0.210** (0.065)	0.245** (0.079)	0.344** (0.071)
Woman	0.145* (0.082)	−0.087 (0.079)	−0.043 (0.061)	−0.248** (0.071)	−0.418** (0.073)	−0.399** (0.064)
Age	0.009** (0.002)	0.011** (0.002)	0.009** (0.002)	0.006** (0.002)	0.010** (0.002)	0.009** (0.002)
White	−0.180* (0.089)	−0.246** (0.084)	0.136 (0.117)	0.245** (0.070)	0.125 (0.094)	0.032 (0.112)
Black	0.011 (0.152)	0.071 (0.011)	0.028 (0.198)	0.127 (0.106)	0.036 (0.155)	−0.196 (0.169)
Democrat	0.370** (0.110)	0.187 (0.119)	0.292** (0.111)	0.508** (0.096)	0.531** (0.107)	0.591** (0.153)
Republican	0.307** (0.103)	0.102 (0.141)	0.137 (0.117)	0.446** (0.133)	0.255** (0.119)	0.327** (0.127)

Constant	2.251**	2.487**	2.225**	2.277**	2.305**	2.353**
	(0.164)	(0.170)	(0.177)	(0.132)	(0.121)	(0.216)
R^2	0.070	0.062	0.053	0.120	0.142	0.162
F Statistic	6.904	7.956	4.592	20.065	20.406	20.767
Observations	963	972	967	962	973	964

Notes: Cell entries are OLS regression coefficients predicting attentiveness to local and national news on a scale that runs from "not closely at all" to "very closely." Standard errors are in parentheses. Levels of significance: ** $p < 0.01$; * $p < 0.05$. Data come from modules of the Cooperative Congressional Election Study from 2017 to 2019.

TABLE H.5. *Effects of reading a local newspaper on engagement,*
by college education, 2019 CCES

	Know Mayor	Know Superintendent	Local Participation
Read local newspaper	0.558**	0.800**	0.803**
	(0.215)	(0.268)	(0.148)
College education	0.328	0.696**	0.375**
	(0.242)	(0.278)	(0.157)
Read local newspaper x college education	0.166	−0.004	−0.224
	(0.253)	(0.291)	(0.241)
Female	−0.038	0.296*	−0.267**
	(0.155)	(0.175)	(0.127)
Age	0.014**	0.010	0.004
	(0.006)	(0.007)	(0.003)
White	−0.205	0.006	0.119
	(0.279)	(0.266)	(0.220)
Black	0.178	0.730**	−0.165
	(0.386)	(0.308)	(0.222)
Democrat	0.431	0.349	0.753**
	(0.290)	(0.317)	(0.143)
Republican	0.192	0.493	0.441**
	(0.247)	(0.306)	(0.132)
Constant	−1.278**	−2.986**	0.677**
	(0.370)	(0.483)	(0.270)
(Pseudo) R^2	0.043	0.061	0.140
Chi-square (F-test)	37.273	46.757	23.744
N	961	969	957

Notes: Cell entries are logistic regression coefficients for knowing the mayor and school superintendent and linear regression coefficients for local political participation. Standard errors are in parentheses. Levels of significance: ** $p < 0.01$; * $p < 0.05$. Data come from a module of the 2019 Cooperative Congressional Election Study.

Appendix I
Mayoral Election Turnout Data

Thomas M. Holbrook and Aaron C. Weinschenk compiled the mayoral election data we use in Chapter 4 for our analysis of the relationship between local newspaper coverage and voter turnout.[1] These data are based on publicly available election returns from localities throughout the United States. We restrict our analysis to data from the 217 elections in 73 cities for which we have both a measure of voter turnout and a measure of local newspaper mayoral coverage. Of the cities for which we have data, 8 are in the Northeast, 22 are in the South, 21 are in the Midwest, and 22 are in the West.

The newspaper coverage measure comes from the content analysis we detail in Chapters 2 and 3. Although our mayoral coverage measure is not specifically about elections, it serves as a good proxy for mayoral election coverage because it includes all stories that mention the mayor; our coding picks up every election story in the lead-up to a mayoral contest. Moreover, any significant story about the mayor in an election year will almost certainly have an electoral frame. In addition, we focus our analysis on the share of the news hole, rather than total volume, so that we have a comparable measure across cities, which are served by newspapers of varying sizes.

We ran several statistical models to provide a more precise estimate of the relationship between turnout and newspaper coverage. These are designed to account for several important features of our turnout data. First, the observations are not "independent" – that is, turnout in a given

---

[1] See Holbrook and Weinschenk 2014.

election in a city is likely related to turnout in that city in previous elections. Second, characteristics of cities are likely to affect turnout in ways that might inaccurately inflate the apparent effect of news coverage. For instance, if more educated cities have higher turnout and newspapers in those cities devote more coverage to local politics – perhaps because of demand from an educated readership – then what appears to be a strong relationship between coverage and turnout might be spurious; education might be causing both to go up. Third, the timing of municipal elections can dramatically affect turnout. When mayoral elections are held in presidential or midterm election years, turnout will be much higher than in off-year elections. As a result, we need a rigorous way to account for these complicated relationships and isolate the discrete effect of news coverage on turnout.

We employ two types of models that help address these complications: (1) fixed-effects models account for unmeasured sources of variation among the cities and years that might affect turnout; and (2) random-effects models allow us to control directly for demographic features of cities that could be relevant for both turnout and news coverage. These include education and income levels, population size, and ethnic compos-ition.[2] Because fixed-effects and random-effects models have different advantages, we estimate both types.[3] In all of these models, we also control for whether the election occurs in the same year as a presidential or midterm campaign, either by estimating year fixed effects or using a dummy variable. Finally, in some analyses, we restrict the data to the 22 cities for which we have at least 4 elections, giving us a greater ability to leverage the changes in newspaper coverage and turnout, while holding constant many city-level variables.

Table I.1 presents the various model specifications, all of which are consistent and demonstrate an independent effect of news coverage on voter turnout. Table I.2 displays models in which we include measures of coverage of other aspects of local government (city government, school board, and county government), none of which is significantly related to mayoral turnout.

---

[2] These measures are drawn from the US Census.
[3] Clark and Linzer 2015.

TABLE I.I. *Mayoral newspaper coverage and voter turnout in mayoral elections*

	All Cities				Cities with at least Four Elections	
Mayoral Share of News Hole	1.23* (0.64)	1.51** (0.61)	1.67** (0.50)	1.82** (0.47)	1.87** (0.87)	1.87** (0.73)
Presidential or Midterm Election	–	5.02 (3.25)	–	8.39** (2.18)	7.92 (4.71)	9.31** (3.41)
Percent Bachelor's Degree	–	–	16.84 (23.35)	12.02 (23.05)	–	54.27 (41.24)
Median Income (in $1,000s)	–	–	−0.14 (0.15)	−0.11 (0.14)	–	−0.53 (0.39)
Population (in 100,000)	–	–	0.04 (0.11)	0.06 (0.11)	–	0.12 (0.10)
Percent Hispanic	–	–	−0.28** (0.09)	−0.31** (0.09)	–	−0.12 (0.14)
City Fixed Effects	Yes	Yes	No	No	Yes	No
Year Fixed Effects	Yes	No	Yes	No	No	No
Random Effects	No	No	Yes	Yes	No	Yes
R^2	0.18	0.15	0.32	0.26	0.17	0.32
Observations	217	217	217	217	92	92

Notes: Data come from Holbrook and Weinschenk's mayoral election returns, 1993–2011. Levels of significance: ** $p < 0.05$; * $p < 0.10$.

TABLE I.2. *Different topics of local government coverage and voter turnout in mayoral elections*

	(1)	(2)	(3)	(4)
Mayoral Share of News Hole	1.92*	1.68*	2.28**	2.08**
	(0.97)	(0.97)	(0.62)	(0.62)
City Government Share of News Hole	−0.68	−0.34	−0.63	−0.47
	(0.89)	(0.85)	(0.57)	(0.56)
School Board Share of News Hole	0.17	0.82	−0.20	0.41
	(1.64)	(1.55)	(1.27)	(1.22)
County Government Share of News Hole	−1.44	−0.88	−1.47	−0.59
	(2.19)	(2.16)	(1.23)	(1.20)
Presidential or Midterm Election	−	5.02	−	8.23
		(3.28)		(23.77)
Percent Bachelor's Degree	−	−	8.77	8.229
			(24.10)	(23.77)
Median Income (in $1,000s)	−	−	−0.13	−0.10
			(0.15)	(0.15)
Population (in 100,000)	−	−	−0.01	0.04
			(0.12)	(0.11)
Percent Hispanic	−	−	−0.28**	0.29**
			(0.10)	(0.10)
City Fixed Effects	Yes	Yes	No	No
Year Fixed Effects	Yes	No	Yes	No
Random Effects	No	No	Yes	Yes
R^2	0.21	0.16	0.34	0.26
Observations	217	217	217	217

Notes: Data come from Holbrook and Weinschenk's mayoral election returns, 1993–2011. Levels of significance: ** $p < 0.05$; * $p < 0.10$.

Appendix J
Google Trends Data

We draw the online search data in Chapter 4 from 50 metropolitan areas indexed in Google Trends, from 2004 (the first year available) through 2016.[1] For each year, we collected data on the popularity of searches about local government that correspond to the terms we used in our content analysis. For mayor, that was "mayor." For city government, "city council" or "town council." For school board, "school board." We do not include county government searches because search volumes are so low in most cities that they are not included in Google Trends results. Within each metropolitan area, we collected data on search popularity for each month, and then calculated the average for each year. This gives us a measure comparable to our content analysis data, which we also aggregated annually.

The data we present in Figure 4.4 are averages across our 50 cities. But the relationship between online search behavior and news coverage varies from city to city. Appendix Figure J.1 plots the regression results from equations in which we predict search scores based on the news coverage for each city.

Before turning to the results, let us take just a moment to explain how to read and interpret the figure. The dots represent the coefficients (or point estimates) for news coverage in each regression equation. The horizontal lines represent the 90% confidence intervals for each coefficient. If the confidence interval crosses the vertical zero line, that means that the variable is not statistically significant; its effect is essentially zero (at $p < 0.10$). Positive point estimates with confidence intervals entirely to the right of the zero-line mean that news coverage predicts search

[1] For more information, see: https://trends.google.com/trends.

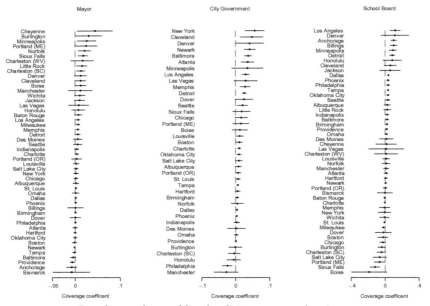

FIGURE J.I. Google searches and local politics coverage, by city
Note: Each dot represents a regression coefficient for newspaper coverage, with 90%
confidence intervals.

behavior. The rare coefficient with confidence intervals entirely to the left
of the zero-line mean that coverage and searches are negative related.
Because each of these statistical models has just 13 observations – one for
each year – there is a lot of uncertainty around these estimates, which
means that most will not achieve statistical significance.

In the mayoral models, 13 of the coefficients are positive and statistically
significant – mayoral coverage strongly predicts changes in mayor searches,
especially in places such as Cheyenne, Burlington, and Minneapolis. Just one
model produces a negative and significant coefficient. In the city government
models, the coverage coefficient is positive and significant in 17 of the
40 cities for which we have data. Again, just one is negative and significant.
In the school board models, 14 coefficients are positive and significant, while
3 are negative and significant. These patterns, while not unequivocal evidence of a connection, are strongly suggestive. Indeed, 90% of the statistically significant results are in the expected direction. Given the small number
of observations, the tendency across measures for reductions in coverage to
lead to reductions in interest points to a connection between the two.

Appendix K
Citizen Engagement in Congressional Elections

The analysis of congressional elections in Chapter 4 relies on a content analysis of local news coverage and measures of citizen engagement from the 2010 and 2014 Cooperative Congressional Election Study.

US HOUSE ELECTION CONTENT ANALYSIS

Very little political science research has sought to analyze media coverage of House elections from more than a handful of districts. Thus, there is no accepted method of identifying the local news outlets that serve a particular House contest. We selected papers based on the method we describe in Appendix C. That is, we focused on the largest circulating paper in each congressional district in 2010 that we could access through one of several electronic databases or the newspaper's online archives. Because of redistricting, as well as shifts in newspaper circulation within districts, we repeated this exercise for every congressional district in 2014. Across election cycles, the average newspaper circulation size in our districts varied greatly; the smallest paper had a readership of only about 5,000, whereas the largest circulation size approximated 1.8 million. The average circulation of the papers in our data set is roughly 178,000.

After choosing a newspaper in each district, we identified every news story in the 30 days leading up to the election that mentioned at least 1 of the 2 major-party House candidates. We included in the sample straight news reports, news analyses, editorials, and op-ed columns. We did not code letters to the editor. We did not restrict the analysis strictly to "campaign" stories because we assume that any information about the House candidates is potentially relevant for voters. As a result, our coding includes a comprehensive analysis of the media coverage to which voters could have been exposed in the lead-up to the election. Our analyses do not include independent and minor-party candidates. Our method produced 6,003 articles in 2010 and 4,524 articles in 2014.

It is important to recognize a limitation when drawing comparisons between House race coverage in 2010 and 2014. In some cases, district boundaries shifted as a result of redistricting, so the largest circulating newspaper in 2010 was not always the largest paper for the district in 2014. In other cases, the paper remained the same but the composition of the district changed. Although these are important considerations, the evidence we have suggests that they do not compromise our analysis.

First, our findings are virtually the same regardless of whether the relevant local paper was different in the two elections, or whether the paper stayed the same. For instance, in districts where the paper changed, the decrease in the number of stories from 2010 to 2014 was 2.4. In same-paper districts, it was 2.9.

Second, changes in the composition of districts do not account for the decline in coverage. Indeed, factors such as electoral competitiveness and newspaper circulation size predict coverage across our two elections in a very similar way, which suggests that redistricting does not explain the over-time changes in the volume of news we observe. Even with the measurement challenges of redistricting, there is little doubt that the total amount of congressional campaign news coverage reported in the largest circulating newspapers in districts across the country was less, and less substantive, in 2014 than in 2010.[1]

THE 2010 CCES AND 2010–2014 CCES PANEL STUDY

The 2010 CCES interviewed more than 55,000 adults who answered a common battery of questions before and after the midterm elections, including the series of questions about House elections we analyze in Chapters 4 and 5. The 2010–2014 panel component of the CCES makes it especially valuable for assessing changes in political engagement over time. For the 2014 wave, YouGov attempted to re-interview 22,346 respondents who had completed both the 2010 and 2012 waves. They successfully completed interviews with 15,252 panelists (68% of those they attempted to re-contact). The 2010–2014 Panel Study includes a

[1] For more details on the content analyses, see Hayes and Lawless 2015; 2018.

subset of 9,500 of these respondents, all of whom were interviewed before and after the 2014 elections. Regression models from the 2010 CCES and the 2010–2014 CCES panel appear in Tables K.1 to K.6.

Although panel attrition is always a concern, on the most relevant measures for our analysis, differences between the base sample and the 2014 panel respondents are small. Moreover, there are no partisan differences in attrition. Importantly, voters were much more likely to be successfully re-contacted compared to nonvoters, but that biases our estimates downward and makes for a more difficult case to uncover media effects.[2]

In addition to the difference-in-difference analysis we present at the end of Chapter 4, we also conducted a cross-sectional analysis, in which we used the 2014 CCES and our 2014 news data to determine whether the volume of House coverage correlates with political engagement. Unlike other cross-sectional analyses, however, we can account for respondents' past knowledge and participation, which are very strong predictors of future engagement.

The regression results reveal significant effects for news coverage, and also the value of panel data. Not surprisingly, people who in 2010 could place the Democratic House candidate to the left of the Republican, rate their House member, and express a preelection vote intention were much more likely than people who couldn't to be able to do those things in 2014 as well. But even accounting for the substantial explanatory power of previous knowledge and participation, we still find significant news effects. As the number of stories about a congressional race increased, respondents were more likely to place the Democratic candidate to the left of the Republican on the ideology scale and to rate the incumbent. If we relax the threshold for statistical significance, then they were also more likely to express a vote intention ($p < 0.11$).[3] Table K.6 presents lagged dependent variable models that show similar news effects for both college-educated and non-college-educated respondents.

[2] For a detailed description of the panel student, re-interview rates, and attrition, see: https://dataverse.harvard.edu/file.xhtml?fileId=2864258&version=6.0.
[3] For details about this analysis and the regression results, see Hayes and Lawless 2018.

TABLE K.I. *Predicting political knowledge and participation in US House elections, 2010*

	Rate House Incumbent	Place Democrat to Left of Republican	House Vote Intention	Placebo Tests	
				Know House Majority	Rate Congress
Number of Stories	0.008*	0.008**	0.004*	0.001	-0.002
	(0.003)	(0.002)	(0.002)	(0.002)	(0.004)
Competitiveness	0.055	0.201**	-0.006	-0.051	0.058
	(0.050)	(0.031)	(0.029)	(0.027)	(0.048)
Open Seat	0.258	-0.151	-0.256**	-0.115	-0.042
	(0.131)	(0.096)	(0.064)	(0.066)	(0.109)
Uncontested	-0.039	—	-0.559**	0.103	-0.014
	(0.151)		(0.095)	(0.081)	(0.153)
Quality Candidate	-0.018	0.144	-0.003	0.009	-0.105
	(0.117)	(0.076)	(0.063)	(0.054)	(0.102)
Democratic Spending	0.011*	0.023**	0.011**	0.004	0.001
	(0.005)	(0.003)	(0.003)	(0.003)	(0.004)
Republican Spending	0.002	0.006**	0.001	0.006**	0.001
	(0.004)	(0.002)	(0.002)	(0.002)	(0.002)
Market Convergence	1.164**	1.224**	0.874**	0.048	0.726
	(0.377)	(0.228)	(0.219)	(0.240)	(0.371)

College Graduate	0.354**	0.459**	0.367**	0.985**	0.679**
	(0.057)	(0.037)	(0.039)	(0.046)	(0.084)
Strength of Partisanship	0.176**	0.170**	0.561**	0.272**	0.303**
	(0.024)	(0.018)	(0.020)	(0.019)	(0.033)
Age	0.041**	0.024**	0.027**	0.029**	0.045**
	(0.002)	(0.001)	(0.001)	(0.002)	(0.003)
Income	0.079**	0.106**	0.103**	0.143**	0.102**
	(0.007)	(0.006)	(0.006)	(0.007)	(0.011)
White	0.385**	0.425**	0.306**	0.385**	0.244**
	(0.069)	(0.053)	(0.049)	(0.051)	(0.085)
Constant	-1.900**	-4.622**	-2.712**	-2.384**	-0.993**
	(0.137)	(0.137)	(0.100)	(0.113)	(0.158)
Pseudo R²	0.111	0.124	0.136	0.139	0.122
Chi-square	994.860	1,134.188	1,793.383	1,650.979	805.555
N	43,740	41,700	44,247	44,181	44,090

Notes: Cell entries are logistic regression coefficients. Robust standard errors clustered on congressional district are in parentheses. Levels of significance: ** $p < 0.01$; * $p < 0.05$, one-tailed.

TABLE K.2. *Predicting changes in political knowledge and participation in US House elections: A difference-in-difference analysis*

	Place Democrat Left of Republican	Rate House Incumbent	House Vote Intention
Difference in Number of Stories	0.011**	0.005*	0.008**
	(0.002)	(0.003)	(0.002)
Difference in Total Spending	0.164**	0.024	0.041**
	(0.011)	(0.018)	(0.012)
Constant (cut point 1)	−1.937	−3.536	−2.516
	(0.049)	(0.063)	(0.041)
Constant (cut point 2)	1.437	2.989	2.178
	(0.063)	(0.049)	(0.035)
Pseudo R^2	0.030	0.001	0.004
Chi-square	425.050	8.203	39.523
N	8,083	9,242	9,035

Notes: Cell entries are ordered logistic regression coefficients. Robust standard errors clustered on congressional district are in parentheses. Levels of significance: ** $p < 0.01$; * $p < 0.05$, one-tailed. Independent variables represent the differences in the number of stories about the House race and total spending in the House race in 2014 compared to 2010.

TABLE K.3. *National news viewing and changes in political engagement*

	Place Democrat Left of Republican	Rate House Incumbent	House Vote Intention
Difference in Number of Stories	0.012**	0.007*	0.010**
	(0.002)	(0.004)	(0.003)
Difference in Total Spending	0.177**	0.029	0.036**
	(0.013)	(0.023)	(0.015)
Increase in National TV News Viewing	0.133*	0.014	−0.008
	(0.078)	(0.141)	(0.095)
Difference in Number of Stories × Increase in National TV News Viewing	0.002	−0.006	−0.016 **
	(0.005)	(0.009)	(0.006)
Constant (cut point 1)	−1.918	−3.706	−2.585
	(0.043)	(0.087)	(0.053)
Constant (cut point 2)	1.442	3.078	2.195
	(0.038)	(0.067)	(0.046)
Pseudo R²	0.037	0.002	0.004
Chi-square	340.913	6.874	28.047
N	5,339	6,139	5,960

Notes: Cell entries are ordered logistic regression coefficients. Robust standard errors clustered on congressional district are in parentheses. Levels of significance: ** $p < 0.01$; * $p < 0.05$, one-tailed. Independent variables represent the differences in the number of stories about the House race and total spending in the House race in 2014 compared to 2010. Analyses include only the respondents who indicated in both years that they watched TV newscasts.

TABLE K.4. *Effects of news coverage on engagement, by college education, 2010 CCES*

	Place Democrat Left of Republican	Rate House Incumbent	House Vote Intention
Story Count	0.007**	0.008*	0.003
	(0.002)	(0.004)	(0.002)
Story Count × College Graduate	0.003	−0.001	0.005
	(0.002)	(0.005)	(0.003)
Competitiveness	0.202**	0.055	−0.005
	(0.031)	(0.050)	(0.029)
Open Seat	−0.152	0.258	−0.256**
	(0.096)	(0.131)	(0.064)
Uncontested	–	−0.039	−0.559**
		(0.151)	(0.095)
Quality Candidate	0.144	−0.018	−0.003
	(0.076)	(0.117)	(0.063)
Democratic Spending	0.023**	0.011*	0.011**
	(0.003)	(0.005)	(0.003)
Republican Spending	0.006**	0.002	0.001
	(0.002)	(0.004)	(0.002)
Market Convergence	1.222**	1.163**	0.874**
	(0.227)	(0.377)	(0.220)
College Graduate	0.414**	0.368**	0.300**
	(0.053)	(0.084)	(0.059)
Strength of Partisanship	0.170*	0.176**	0.561**
	(0.018)	(0.024)	(0.020)
Age	0.024**	0.041**	0.027**
	(0.001)	(0.002)	(0.001)
Income	0.106**	0.079**	0.103**
	(0.006)	(0.007)	(0.006)
White	0.425**	0.385**	0.307**
	(0.053)	(0.069)	(0.049)
Constant	−4.608**	−1.903**	−2.698**
	(0.139)	(0.138)	(0.101)
Pseudo R^2	0.124	0.111	0.136
Chi-square	1,144.193	998.468	1,799.301
N	41,700	43,740	44,247

Notes: Cell entries are logistic regression coefficients. Robust standard errors clustered on congressional district are in parentheses. Levels of significance: ** $p < 0.01$; * $p < 0.05$, one-tailed.

TABLE K.5. *Predicting changes in political knowledge and participation in US House elections, by college education: A difference-in-difference analysis*

	Place Democrat Left of Republican	Rate House Incumbent	House Vote Intention
Difference in Number of Stories	0.011** (0.002)	0.009* (0.004)	0.008** (0.003)
Difference in Number of Stories x College Graduate	0.000 (0.003)	−0.012* (0.005)	−0.001 (0.004)
Difference in Total Spending	0.165** (0.011)	0.026 (0.018)	0.040** (0.012)
College Graduate	0.010 (0.048)	−0.003 (0.081)	−0.152** (0.057)
Constant (cut point 1)	−1.929 (0.040)	−3.535 (0.074)	−2.585 (0.049)
Constant (cut point 2)	1.444 (0.036)	2.987 (0.062)	2.102 (0.043)
Pseudo R^2	0.030	0.002	0.004
Chi-square	418.323	11.356	44.161
N	7,948	9,087	8,885

Notes: Cell entries are ordered logistic regression coefficients. Robust standard errors clustered on congressional district are in parentheses. Levels of significance: ** $p < 0.01$; * $p < 0.05$, one-tailed. Independent variables represent the differences in the number of stories about the House race and total spending in the House race in 2014 compared to 2010.

TABLE K.6. *Predicting political knowledge and participation in US House elections in 2014, by college education: A cross-sectional analysis with lagged dependent variables*

	Place Democrat Left of Republican	Rate House Incumbent	House Vote Intention
Lagged Dependent Variable	1.201**	1.767**	1.559**
(from 2010)	(0.059)	(0.132)	(0.077)
Story Count	0.018**	0.019*	0.019*
	(0.005)	(0.009)	(0.008)
Story Count × College Graduate	0.006	−0.015	−0.007
	(0.006)	(0.013)	(0.008)
Competitiveness	0.143*	−0.118	−0.066
	(0.067)	(0.142)	(0.074)
Open Seat	−0.457**	−0.505*	−0.485**
	(0.126)	(0.224)	(0.144)
Quality Candidate	0.413**	0.068	0.268*
	(0.102)	(0.178)	(0.108)
Democratic Spending	0.236**	0.136	0.087*
	(0.044)	(0.094)	(0.048)
Republican Spending	0.092*	0.078	0.026
	(0.036)	(0.063)	(0.022)
College Graduate	0.270**	0.581**	0.169
	(0.080)	(0.175)	(0.115)
Sex (female)	−0.632**	−0.628**	−0.670**
	(0.049)	(0.109)	(0.069)
Strength of Partisanship	0.166**	0.198**	0.457**
	(0.024)	(0.047)	(0.030)
Constant	−1.383**	1.126**	−0.189
	(0.094)	(0.194)	(0.125)
Pseudo R^2	0.146	0.084	0.156
Chi-square	1,200.659	259.583	793.093
N	7,884	9,018	8,803

Notes: Cell entries are logistic regression coefficients. Robust standard errors clustered on congressional district are in parentheses. The "Place Democrat Left of Republican" model is restricted to contested races. Levels of significance: ** $p < 0.01$; * $p < 0.05$, one-tailed.

Appendix L
Arlington and Charlottesville Exit Polls

We conducted two exit polls, the results of which we describe in Chapter 6. Here, we include details about the protocol, questionnaire, and sample of voters.

PROTOCOL

The first exit poll took place in Arlington County, Virginia, on November 6, 2018, the day of the midterm elections. Forty-one exit pollsters worked shifts at 10 different precincts throughout the county. We selected precincts in both North and South Arlington, which have somewhat different demographic profiles. North Arlington is wealthier, more educated, and more white. Although our goal was not to generate a representative sample of the county, drawing data from different areas yielded a somewhat more diverse pool of voters.

The second took place in the City of Charlottesville, Virginia, on November 4, 2019. Virginia has off-year elections, so in odd years, state legislators and local elected officials are on the ballot (gubernatorial elections happen every other off-year cycle). On Election Day, 108 exit pollsters worked shifts at all 12 precincts within the city limits.

The exit pollsters were undergraduates from George Washington University (for Arlington) and the University of Virginia (for Charlottesville). Before Election Day, each pollster participated in a training session, where we instructed them on how to adhere to county election regulations, approach voters, and administer the survey. The protocol included a randomization procedure designed to reduce selection effects in the interview process. We placed the students in teams of two or

193

three and assigned each group a precinct. On Election Day, they worked a three-hour shift.

When a voter agreed to participate, the exit pollster handed the voter a pen and a one-page survey on a clipboard and then stepped away. Respondents completed the survey – which included questions about the federal and county races in Arlington, and state legislative and city elections in Charlottesville – with privacy.

We visited and checked in on each team throughout the day. After their shift, the exit pollsters returned their surveys to our offices. We paid the students for their time.

QUESTIONNAIRE

The exit polls in each location included a series of demographic questions, as well as questions about vote choice. The experiment was embedded in the last question of the survey. The questionnaires printed here include all three experimental conditions. Each respondent, of course, received only one.

ARLINGTON COUNTY EXIT POLL, NOVEMBER 6, 2018

Please answer the following questions by filling in the appropriate box or bubble for each.

Generally speaking, do you usually think of yourself as a Republican, a Democrat, an Independent, or what?

- O   Republican
- O   Democrat
- O   Independent
- O   Other party

How closely would you say you follow politics?

- O   Very closely
- O   Somewhat closely
- O   Not too closely
- O   Not closely at all

What is your gender?

- O   Male
- O   Female
- O   Non-conforming

Are you:

- O   White
- O   Black
- O   Hispanic/Latino
- O   Asian
- O   Other

In what year were you born? [   ]

What is the highest level of education you have attained?

- O   High school diploma
- O   Some college
- O   Bachelor's degree
- O   Post-graduate degree

In the election for U.S. Senate, who did you vote for?

- O   Corey A. Stewart (R)
- O   Timothy M. Kaine (D)
- O   Matt J. Waters (L)
- O   I didn't vote

In the election for U.S. Representative, who did you vote for?

- O   Thomas S. Oh (R)
- O   Donald S. Beyer, Jr. (D)
- O   I didn't vote

In the election for Arlington County Board, who did you vote for?

- O   Matthew D. "Matt" de Ferranti
- O   John E. Vihstadt
- O   I didn't vote

In the election for Arlington School Board, who did you vote for?

- O   Barbara J. Kanninen
- O   Audrey R. Clement
- O   I didn't vote

[Version 1] Are you interested in signing up for a daily digest of local news from ARLNow.com so that you can keep up with what's going on in your community? It won't be used for marketing purposes!

[Version 2] As you probably know, many people think that following local politics and government is an important of being an informed citizen. Are you interested in signing up for a daily digest of local news from ARLNow.com so that you can keep up with what's going on in your community? It won't be used for marketing purposes!

[Version 3] As you probably know, local governments make many decisions that affect your life and the lives of your neighbors. Are you interested in signing up for a daily digest of local news from ARLNow.com so that you can keep up with what's going on in your community? It won't be used for marketing purposes!

- O   Yes. Please write your email address: [   ]
- O   No
- O   I already subscribe to ARLNow.com

CITY OF CHARLOTTESVILLE EXIT POLL, NOVEMBER 4, 2019

Please answer the following questions by filling in the appropriate box or bubble for each.

Generally speaking, do you usually think of yourself as a Republican, a Democrat, an independent, or what?

- O Republican
- O Democrat
- O Independent
- O Other party

How closely would you say you follow politics?

- O Very closely
- O Somewhat closely
- O Not too closely
- O Not closely at all

Are you:

- O White
- O Black
- O Hispanic/Latino
- O Asian
- O Other

What is your gender?

- O Male
- O Female
- O Non-conforming

In what year were you born? [   ]

What is the highest level of education you have attained?

- O High school diploma
- O Some college
- O Bachelor's degree
- O Post-graduate degree

How long have you lived in Charlottesville? [   ]

In the election for State Senate, who did you vote for?

- O Creigh Deeds (D)
- O Elliot Harding (I)
- O I didn't vote in this race

In the election for House of Delegates, who did you vote for?

- O Sally Hudson (D)
- O I didn't vote in this race

[Version 1] Are you interested in signing up for a daily digest of local news from the *Daily Progress* so that you can keep up with what's going on in your community? It won't be used for marketing purposes!

[Version 2] As you probably know, many people think that following local politics and government is an important of being an informed citizen. Are you interested in signing up for a daily digest of local news from the *Daily Progress* so that you can keep up with what's going on in your community? It won't be used for marketing purposes!

[Version 3] As you probably know, local governments make many decisions that affect your life and the lives of your neighbors. Are you interested in signing up for a daily digest of local news from the *Daily Progress* so that you can keep up with what's going on in your community? It won't be used for marketing purposes!

- O Yes. Please write your email address: [   ]
- O No
- O I already receive an afternoon newsletter from the *Daily Progress*.

TABLE L.I. *Characteristics of exit poll samples*

	Arlington	Charlottesville
Partisanship		
Democrat	63%	76%
Independent	23	16
Republican	13	7
Something else	1	1
Political Interest		
Follows politics not closely at all	1	1
Follows politics not too closely	7	9
Follows politics somewhat closely	38	46
Follows politics very closely	55	44
Gender		
Male	45	40
Female	55	59
Non-conforming	<1	1
Race / Ethnicity		
White	74	82
Black	8	9
Hispanic/Latino	6	3
Asian	6	4
Other	4	2
Multiple categories	2	0
Education		
High school diploma	1	6
Some college	6	18
Bachelor's degree	43	33
Post-graduate degree	50	43
Age		
Mean	42 years	46 years
Median	36	45
N	1,068	2,999

SAMPLE

In all, exit pollsters conducted surveys with 1,068 voters as they left the polls in Arlington and 2,999 people who had just cast a vote in Charlottesville. Although we have no reason to believe we did not generate a representative sample of each precinct's voters, it is important to recognize that both Arlington County and Charlottesville are highly educated, Democratic, and politically engaged communities (see Table L.1).

References

Abernathy, Penelope Muse. 2018a. "The Loss of Newspapers and Readers." Chapel Hill, NC: University of North Carolina Hussman School of Journalism and Media. Available online at www.usnewsdeserts.com/reports/expanding-news-desert/loss-of-local-news/loss-newspapers-readers/ (accessed February 24, 2020).

2018b. "The Expanding News Desert." Chapel Hill, NC: University of North Carolina Hussman School of Journalism and Media. Available online at www.usnewsdeserts.com/ (accessed September 10, 2020).

2020. "News Deserts and Ghost Newspapers: Will Local News Survive?" Chapel Hill, NC: University of North Carolina Hussman School of Journalism and Media. Available online at www.usnewsdeserts.com/reports/news-deserts-and-ghost-newspapers-will-local-news-survive/ (accessed October 24, 2020).

Adams, James, Erik Engstrom, Danielle Joeston, Walt Stone, Jon Rogowski, and Boris Shor. 2017. "Do Moderate Voters Weigh Candidates' Ideologies? Voters' Decision Rules in the 2010 Congressional Elections." *Political Behavior* 39(1): 205–27.

Althaus, Scott L. 1998. "Information Effects in Collective Preferences." *American Political Science Review* 92(3): 545–58.

Althaus, Scott L. and Todd Trautman. 2008. "The Impact of Television Market Size on Voter Turnout in American Elections." *American Politics Research* 36(6): 824–56.

Anzia, Sarah. 2014. *Timing and Turnout: How Off-Cycle Elections Favor Organized Groups.* Chicago: University of Chicago Press.

Arceneaux, Kevin, Martin Johnson, and Hermine Maes. 2012. "The Genetic Basis of Political Sophistication." *Twin Research and Human Genetics* 15(1): 34–41.

Arnold, R. Douglas. 2004. *Congress, the Press, and Political Accountability.* New York: Russell Sage Foundation; Princeton, NJ: Princeton University Press.

Atwater, Tony, Frederick Fico, and Gary Pizante. 1987. "Reporting on the State Legislature: A Case Study of Inter-Media Agenda-Setting." *Newspaper Research Journal* 8(2): 53–61.

Baekgaard, Martin, Carsten Jensen, Peter B. Mortensen, and Soren Serritzlew. 2014. "Local News Media and Voter Turnout." *Local Government Studies* 40(4): 518–32.

Barabas, Jason and Jennifer Jerit. 2009. "Estimating the Causal Effects of Media Coverage on Policy-Specific Knowledge." *American Journal of Political Science* 53(1): 73–89.

Bartels, Larry M. 1996. "Uninformed Votes: Information Effects in Presidential Elections." *American Political Science Review* 40(1): 194–230.

Baybeck, Brady. 2014. "Local Political Participation." In *Oxford Handbook of State and Local Government*, Donald P. Haider-Markel (ed.). New York: Oxford University Press.

Bennett, Linda L. M. and Stephen Earl Bennett. 1989. "Enduring Gender Differences in Political Interest: The Impact of Socialization and Political Dispositions." *American Politics Quarterly* 17(1): 105–22.

Bentley, Clyde. 2001. "No Newspaper Is No Fun – Even Five Decades Later." *Newspaper Research Journal* 22(4): 2–15.

Berelson, Bernard. 1949. "What Missing the Newspaper Means." In *Communications Research*, Paul F. Lazarsfeld and Frank N. Stanton (eds.). New York: Harper & Brothers.

Blumler, Jay G. and Elihu Katz. 1974. *The Uses of Mass Communications: Current Perspectives on Gratifications Research*. Sage Annual Reviews of Communication Research volume III. Beverly Hills, CA: Sage.

Campa, Pamela. 2018. "Press and Leaks: Do Newspapers Reduce Toxic Emissions?" *Journal of Environmental Economics and Management* 91 (September): 184–202.

Chadha, Monica and Summer Harlow. 2018. "Bottom Lines and Deadlines: Examining Local Digital News Startups' Content across Different Revenue-Earning Sites." *Journalism Practice* 13(6): 723–41.

Clark, Tom S. and Drew A. Linzer. 2015. "Should I Use Fixed or Random Effects?" *Political Science Research and Methods* 3(2): 399–408.

Clarke, Peter and Susan H. Evans. 1983. *Covering Campaigns: Journalism in Congressional Elections*. Stanford, CA: Stanford University Press.

Cohen, Marty, Hans Noel, and John Zaller. 2004. "Local News and Political Accountability in U.S. Legislative Elections." Paper presented at the annual meeting of the American Political Science Association. Chicago: September 2–5.

Darr, Joshua P., Matthew P. Hitt, and Johanna L. Dunaway. 2018. "Newspaper Closures Polarize Voting Behavior." *Journal of Communication* 68(6): 1007–28.

Delli Carpini, Michael X. and Scott Keeter. 1996. *What Americans Know about Politics and Why It Matters*. New Haven, CT: Yale University Press.

Delli Carpini, Michael X., Scott Keeter, and J. David Kennamer. 1994. "Effects of the News Media Environment on Citizen Knowledge of State Politics and

Government." *Journalism and Mass Communication Quarterly* 71(2): 443–56.

Downs, Anthony. 1957. *An Economic Theory of Democracy*. New York: HarperCollins.

Dubois, Elizabeth and Grant Blank. 2018. "The Echo Chamber Is Overstated: The Moderating Effect of Political Interest and Diverse Media." *Information, Communication & Society* 21(5): 729–45.

Durkin, Jessica, Tom Glaisyer, and Kara Hadge. 2010. "An Information Community Case Study: Seattle." *New America Foundation*. Available online at karahadgeprone.com/s/Seattle-case-study.pdf (accessed June 1, 2021).

Einstein, Katherine Levine, Maxwell Palmer, and David M. Glick. 2019. "Who Participates in Local Government? Evidence from Meeting Minutes." *Perspectives on Politics* 17(1): 28–46.

Eveland, William P. and Dietram A. Scheufele. 2000. "Connecting News Media Use with Gaps in Knowledge and Participation." *Political Communication* 17: 215–37.

Ferrier, Michelle, Gaurav Sinha, and Michael Outrich. 2016. "Media Deserts: Monitoring the Changing Media Ecosystem." In *The Communication Crisis in America – and How to Fix It*, Mark Lloyd and Lewis A. Friedman (eds.). New York: Palgrave Macmillan.

Fiorina, Morris. 2017. *Unstable Majorities: Polarization, Party Sorting, and Political Stalemate*. Stanford, CA: Hoover Institute Press.

Fischer, Sean, Kokil Jaidka, and Yphtach Lelkes. 2020. "Auditing Local News Presence on Google News." *Nature Human Behaviour* 4: 1236–44.

Fiske, Susan T., Richard R. Lau, and Richard A. Smith. 1990. "On the Varieties and Utilities of Political Expertise." *Social Cognition* 8(1): 31–48.

Fogarty, Brian J. 2013. "Scandals, News Coverage, and the 2006 Congressional Elections." *Political Communication* 30(3): 419–33.

Fowler, Erika Franklin, Kenneth M. Goldstein, Matthew Hale, and Martin Kaplan. 2007. "Does Local News Measure Up?" *Stanford Law and Policy Review* 411: 410–31.

Gallup. 1966. Gallup Poll # 1966-0737: Vietnam/Elections. Question 25: USGALLUP.737.Q14A. Cornell University, Ithaca, NY: Roper Center for Public Opinion Research. Available online at https://doi-org.proxygw.wrlc.org/10.25940/ROPER-31087718 (accessed October 15, 2020).

Gao, Pengjie, Chang Lee, and Dermot Murphy. 2020. "Financing Dies in Darkness? The Impact of Newspaper Closures on Public Finance." *Journal of Financial Economics* 135(2): 445–67.

Gentzkow, Matthew. 2006. "Television and Voter Turnout." *Quarterly Journal of Economics* 121(3): 931–72.

Gershon, Sarah. 2012. "Press Secretaries, Journalists, and Editors: Shaping Local Congressional News Coverage." *Political Communication* 29(2): 160–83.

2013. "Voter Reaction to Media Coverage of Anglo, Latino, and African American Congresswomen: An Experimental Study." *Political Research Quarterly* 66(3): 702–14.

Gilens, Martin. 2001. "Political Ignorance and Collective Policy Preferences." *American Political Science Review* 95(2): 379–96.

Gillion, Daniel, Jonathan Ladd, and Marc Meredith. 2020. "Party Polarization, Ideological Sorting, and the Emergence of the U.S. Partisan Gender Gap." *British Journal of Political Science* 50(4): 1217–43.

Gimpel, James, Joshua Dyck, and Daron Shaw. 2006. "Location, Knowledge, and Time Pressures in the Spatial Structure of Convenience Voting." *Electoral Studies* 25: 35–58.

Goldenberg, Edie and Michael Traugott. 1984. *Campaigning for Congress.* Washington, DC: Congressional Quarterly Press.

Hajnal, Zoltan L. 2009. "Who Loses in American Democracy: A Count of Votes Demonstrates the Limited Representation of African Americans." *American Political Science Review* 103(1): 37–57.

Hajnal, Zoltan L. and Paul Lewis. 2003. "Reviving Local Democracy: Institutional Solutions to Low Voter Turnout." *Urban Affairs Review* 38 (5): 645–68.

Hajnal, Zoltan L. and Jessica Trounstine. 2005. "Where Turnout Matters: The Consequences of Uneven Turnout in City Politics." *Journal of Politics* 67(2): 515–35.

Hamilton, James T. 2016. *Democracy's Detectives: The Economics of Investigative Journalism.* Cambridge, MA: Harvard University Press.

Harlow, Summer and Monica Chadha. 2018. "Looking for Community in Community News: An Examination of Public-Spirited Content in Online Local News Sites." *Journalism* 22: 596–615.

Hayes, Danny and Matt Guardino. 2013. *Influence from Abroad: Foreign Voices, the Media, and U.S. Public Opinion.* New York: Cambridge University Press.

Hayes, Danny and Jennifer L. Lawless. 2015. "As Local News Goes, So Goes Citizen Engagement: Media, Knowledge, and Participation in U.S. House Elections." *Journal of Politics* 77(2): 447–62.

2018. "The Decline of Local News and Its Effects: New Evidence from Longitudinal Data." *Journal of Politics* 80(1): 332–6.

Hayes, Danny and Seth C. McKee. 2009. "The Participatory Effects of Redistricting." *American Journal of Political Science* 53(4): 1006–23.

Hersh, Eitan. 2020. *Politics Is for Power: How to Move Beyond Political Hobbyism, Take Action, and Make Real Change.* New York: Simon & Schuster.

Higgins, E. Tory and G. King. 1981. "Accessibility of Social Constructs: Information Processing Consequences of Individual and Contextual Variability." In *Personality, Cognition, and Social Interaction*, N. Cantor and J. Kihlstrom (eds.). Hillsdale, NJ: Lawrence Erlbaum Associates.

Hindman, Matthew. 2009. *The Myth of Digital Democracy.* Princeton, NJ: Princeton University Press.

2015. "Stickier News: What Newspapers Don't Know about Web Traffic Has Hurt Them, Badly – But There Is a Better Way." Shorenstein Center on Media, Politics, and Public Policy. Available online at http://shorensteincenter.org/wp-content/uploads/2015/04/Stickier-News-Matthew-Hindman.pdf (accessed August 19, 2020).

2018. *The Internet Trap: How the Digital Economy Builds Monopolies and Undermines Democracy*. Princeton, NJ: Princeton University Press.

Hoffman, Lindsay H. and William P. Eveland. 2010. "Assessing Causality in the Relationship between Community Attachment and Local News Media Use." *Mass Communication and Society* 13(2): 174–95.

Holbrook, Thomas and Aaron C. Weinschenk. 2014. "Campaigns, Mobilization, and Turnout in Mayoral Elections." *Political Research Quarterly* 67(1): 42–55.

Hopkins, Daniel J. 2018. *The Increasingly United States: How and Why American Political Behavior Nationalized*. Chicago: University of Chicago Press.

Hsiang, Iris Chyi and Yee Man Margaret Ng. 2020. "Still Unwilling to Pay: An Empirical Analysis of 50 U.S. Newspapers' Digital Subscription Results." *Digital Journalism* 8(4): 526–47.

Iyengar, Shanto and Donald R. Kinder. 1987. *News That Matters: Television and American Opinion*. Chicago: University of Chicago Press.

James, Oliver. 2011. "Performance Measures and Democracy: Information Effects on Citizens in Field and Laboratory Experiments." *Journal of Public Administration Research and Theory* 21(3): 399–418.

Jennings, Jay and Meghan Rubado. 2019. "Newspaper Decline and the Effect on Local Government Coverage." Annette Strauss Institute for Civic Life. Available online at https://moody.utexas.edu/sites/default/files/Strauss_Research_Newspaper_Decline_2019–11-Jennings.pdf (accessed January 25, 2020).

Jerit, Jennifer, Jason Barabas, and Toby Bolsen. 2006. "Citizens, Knowledge, and the Information Environment." *American Journal of Political Science* 50(2): 266–82.

Kang, Seok and Sherice Gearhart. 2010. "E-Government and Civic Engagement: How Is Citizens' Use of City Web Sites Related with Civic Involvement and Political Behaviors?" *Journal of Broadcasting & Electronic Media* 54(3): 443–62.

Kettering Foundation. 1979. Gallup/The Kettering Foundation Poll # 1979-POS955: 11th Annual Survey of the Public's Attitudes toward the Public Schools. Question 8: USGALLUP.955POS.Q008. Cornell University, Ithaca, NY: Roper Center for Public Opinion Research. Available online at https://doi-org.proxygw.wrlc.org/10.25940/ROPER-31089498 (accessed October 15, 2020).

Kim, Young Mie. 2016. "Algorithmic Opportunity: Digital Advertising and Inequality in Political Involvement." *The Forum* 14(4): 471–84.

Knight Foundation. 2019. "State of Public Trust in Local News." Available online at https://knightfoundation.org/reports/state-of-public-trust-in-local-news/ (accessed July 18, 2020).

Krosnick, Jon A. and Donald R. Kinder. 1990. "Altering the Foundations of Support for the President through Priming." *American Political Science Review* 84(2): 497–512.

Larreguy, Horacio, John Marshall, and James M Snyder, Jr. 2020. "Publicising Malfeasance: When the Local Media Structure Facilitates Electoral Accountability in Mexico." *The Economic Journal* 130(631): 2291–327.

Larson, Stephanie Greco. 1992. *Creating Consent of the Governed: A Member of Congress and the Local Media.* Carbondale: Southern Illinois University Press.

Lassen, David Dreyer. 2005. "The Effect of Information on Voter Turnout: Evidence from a Natural Experiment." *American Journal of Political Science* 49(1): 103–18.

Lee, Angela M. 2013. "News Audiences Revisited: Theorizing the Link between Audience Motivations and News Consumption." *Journal of Broadcasting & Electronic Media* 57(3): 300–17.

Lee, Sangwon. 2019. "Connecting Social Media Use with Gaps in Knowledge and Participation in a Protest Context: The Case of Candle Light Vigil in South Korea." *Asian Journal of Communication* 29(2): 111–27.

Levine, Adam S. and Reuben Kline. 2019. "Loss-Framed Arguments Can Stifle Political Activism." *Journal of Experimental Political Science* 6(3): 171–9.

Malhotra, Neil and Jon A. Krosnick. 2007. "The Effect of Survey Mode and Sampling on Inferences about Political Attitudes and Behavior: Comparing the 2000 and 2004 ANES to Internet Surveys with Nonprobability Samples." *Political Analysis* 15(3): 286–323.

Manheim, Jarol B. 1974. "Urbanization and Differential Press Coverage of the Congressional Campaign." *Journalism Quarterly* 51(4): 649–53.

Marschall, Melissa and John Lappie. 2018. "Turnout in Local Elections: Is Timing Really Everything?" *Election Law Journal: Rules, Politics, and Policy* 17(3): 221–33.

Martin, Gregory J. and Joshua McCrain. 2019. "Local News and National Politics." *American Political Science Review* 113(2): 372–84.

McLeod, Jack M., Katie Daily, and Zhongshi Guo. 1996. "Community Integration, Local Media Use, and Democratic Processes." *Communication Research* 23(2): 179–209.

McLeod, Jack M., Dietram A. Scheufele, and Patricia Moy. 1999. "Community, Communication, and Participation: The Role of Mass Media and Interpersonal Discussion in Local Political Participation." *Political Communication* 16(3): 315–36.

Mondak, Jeffrey J. 1995. "Newspapers and Political Awareness." *American Journal of Political Science* 39(2): 513–27.

Moskowitz, Daniel J. 2021. "Local News, Information, and the Nationalization of U.S. Elections." *American Political Science Review* 115(1): 114–29.

Napoli, Philip M., Sarah Stonbely, Kathleen McCollough, and Bryce Renninger. 2017. "Local Journalism and the Information Needs of Local Communities: Toward a Scalable Assessment Approach." *Journalism Practice* 11(4): 373–95.

Nicholson, Stephen P. and Ross A. Miller. 1997. "Prior Beliefs and Voter Turnout in the 1986 and 1988 Congressional Elections." *Legislative Studies Quarterly* 50(1): 199–213.

Nielsen, Rasmus Kleis. 2015. *Local Journalism: The Decline of Newspapers and the Rise of Digital Media*. London: I. B. Tauris.

Oliver, J. Eric, Shang E. Ha, and Zachary Callen. 2012. *Local Elections and the Politics of Small-Scale Democracy*. Princeton, NJ: Princeton University Press.

Orman, John. 1985. "Media Coverage of the Congressional Underdog." *PS: Political Science and Politics* 18(4): 754–9.

PEN America. 2019. "Losing the News: The Decimation of Local Journalism and the Search for Solutions." Available online at https://pen.org/local-news/ (accessed October 1, 2020).

Peterson, Erik. 2019. "Not Dead Yet: Political Learning from Newspapers in a Changing Media Landscape." *Political Behavior* 43: 336–61.

        2021. "Paper Cuts: How Reporting Resources Affect Political News Coverage." *American Journal of Political Science* 65(2): 443–59.

Petre, Caitlin. 2015. "The Traffic Factories: Metrics at Chartbeat, Gawker Media, and the *New York Times*." New York: Columbia University Tow Center for Digital Journalism. Available online at www.cjr.org/tow_center_reports/the_traffic_factories_metrics_at_chartbeat_gawker_media_and_the_new_york_times.php (accessed January 26, 2020).

Pew Research Center. 2012. "How People Get Local News and Information in Different Communities," September 26. Available online at www.journalism.org/2012/09/26/how-people-get-local-news-and-information-different-communities/ (accessed January 25, 2020).

        2019a. "Newspaper Fact Sheet," July 9. Available online at www.journalism.org/fact-sheet/newspapers/ (accessed February 24, 2020).

        2019b. "Internet/Broadband Fact Sheet," June 12. Available online at www.pewinternet.org/fact-sheet/internet-broadband/ (accessed February 24, 2020).

        2019c. "Local TV News Fact Sheet," June 25. Available online at www.journalism.org/fact-sheet/local-tv-news/ (accessed March 20, 2020).

        2019d. "For Local News, Americans Embrace Digital, but Still Want Strong Community Connection," March 26. Available online at www.journalism.org/2019/03/26/for-local-news-americans-embrace-digital-but-still-want-strong-community-connection/ (accessed April 2, 2020).

        2019e. "The Importance of Local News Topics Often Does Not Align with How Easily the Public Can Find Information about Them," March 26. Available online at www.journalism.org/2019/03/26/the-importance-of-local-news-topics-often-does-not-align-with-how-easily-the-public-can-find-information-about-them/ (accessed January 26, 2020).

Poepsel, Mark. 2021. "Community and Small-Town Journalism." In *The International Encyclopedia of Journalism Studies*, T. P. Vos, F. Hanusch, D. Dimitrakopoulou, M. Geertsema-Sligh, and A. Sehl (eds). Available online at https://doi.org/10.1002/9781118841570.iejs0120 (accessed June 1, 2021).

Price, Vincent and John Zaller. 1993. "Who Gets the News? Alternative Measures of News Reception and Their Implications for Research." *Public Opinion Quarterly* 57(2): 133–64.

Prior, Markus. 2005. "News v. Entertainment: How Increasing Media Choice Widens Gaps in Political Knowledge and Turnout." *American Journal of Political Science* 49(3): 577–92.

2007. *Post-Broadcast Democracy: How Media Choice Increases Inequality in Political Involvement and Polarizes Elections*. New York: Cambridge University Press.

2009. "The Immensely Inflated News Audience: Assessing Bias in Self-Reported News Exposure." *Public Opinion Quarterly* 73(1): 130–43.

2019. *Hooked: How Politics Captures People's Interest*. New York: Cambridge University Press.

Putnam, Robert D. 2000. *Bowling Alone: The Collapse and Revival of American Community*. New York: Simon & Schuster.

Rubado Meghan E. and Jay T. Jennings. 2020. "Political Consequences of the Endangered Local Watchdog: Newspaper Decline and Mayoral Elections in the United States." *Urban Affairs Review* 56(5): 1327–56.

Ryfe, David, Donica Mensing, Hayreddin Ceker, and Mehmet Gunes. 2012. "Popularity is Not the Same Thing as Influence: A Study of the Bay Area News System." *International Symposium on Online Journalism* 12(2): 144–61.

Schaffner, Brian F., Jesse H. Rhodes, and Raymond J. La Raja. 2020. *Hometown Inequality: Race, Class, and Representation in American Local Politics*. New York: Cambridge University Press.

Scheufele, Dietram and David Tewksbury. 2007. "Framing, Agenda Setting, and Priming: The Evolution of Three Media Effects Models." *Journal of Communication* 57(1): 9–20.

Schulhofer-Wohl, Sam and Miguel Garrido. 2011. "Do Newspapers Matter? Short-Run and Long-Run Evidence from the Closure of the *Cincinnati Post*." Working Paper 686. Minneapolis, MN: Federal Reserve Bank of Minneapolis.

Schudson, Michael. 1981. *Discovering the News: A Social History of American Newspapers*. New York: Basic Books.

Scott, James K. 2006. "'E' the People: Do U.S. Municipal Government Web Sites Support Public Involvement?" *Public Administration Review* 66(3): 341–53.

Seamans, Robert and Feng Zhu. 2014. "Responses to Entry in Multi-Sided Markets: The Impact of Craigslist on Local Newspapers." *Management Science* 60(2): 476–93.

Shaker, Lee. 2014. "Dead Newspapers and Citizens' Civic Engagement." *Political Communication* 31(1): 131–48.

Sinclair, Betsy. 2012. *The Social Citizen: Peer Networks and Political Behavior*. Chicago: University of Chicago Press.

Skocpol, Theda. 2003. *Diminished Democracy: From Membership to Management in American Civic Life*. Norman: University of Oklahoma Press.

Snyder, James M. and David Strömberg. 2010. "Press Coverage and Political Accountability." *Journal of Political Economy* 118(2): 355–408.

Southwell, Brian G., Suzanne Dolina, Karla Jimenez-Magdaleno, Linda B. Squiers, and Bridget J. Kelly. 2016. "Zika Virus–Related News Coverage and Online Behavior, United States, Guatemala, and Brazil." *Emerging Infectious Diseases* 22(7): 1320–1.

Stevens, Daniel, Dean Alger, Barbara Allen, and John L. Sullivan. 2006. "Local News Coverage in a Social Capital Capital: Election 2000 on Minnesota's Local News Stations." *Political Communication* 23(1): 61–83.

Sullivan, Margaret. 2020. *Ghosting the News: Local Journalism and the Crisis of American Democracy.* New York: Columbia Global Reports.

Sung, Woo-Yoo and Homero Gil-de-Zúñiga. 2014. "Connecting Blog, Twitter, and Facebook Use with Gaps in Knowledge and Participation." *Communication & Society* 27(4): 33–48.

Tidmarch, Charles M. and Brad S. Karp. 1983. "The Missing Beat: Press Coverage of Congressional Elections in Eight Metropolitan Areas." *Congress & the Presidency* 10(1): 47–61.

de Tocqueville, Alexis. 1969. *Democracy in America.* Garden City, NY: Doubleday.

Tolbert, Caroline J. and Ramona S. McNeal. 2003. "Unraveling the Effects of the Internet on Political Participation?" *Political Research Quarterly* 56(2): 175–85.

Trussler, Marc. 2020. "Get Information or Get in Formation: The Effects of High-Information Environments on Legislative Elections." *British Journal of Political Science.* DOI: https://doi.org/10.1017/S0007123419000577.

Vermeer, Jan Pons. ed. 1987. *Campaigns in the News: Mass Media and Congressional Elections.* Westport, CT: Greenwood Press.

Vinson, Danielle C. 2003. *Local Media Coverage of Congress and Its Members: Through Local Eyes.* Cresskill, NJ: Hampton Press.

Vliegenthart, Rens and Stefaan Walgrave. 2008. "The Contingency of Intermedia Agenda Setting: A Longitudinal Study in Belgium." *Journalism & Mass Communication Quarterly* 85(4): 860–77.

de Vreese, Claes H. and Hajo Boomgaarden. 2006. "How Content Moderates the Effects of Television News on Political Knowledge and Engagement." *Acta Politica* 41: 317–41.

Warshaw, Christopher. 2019. "Local Elections and Representation in the United States." *Annual Review of Political Science* 22(1): 461–79.

Weeks, Brian and Brian G. Southwell. 2010. "The Symbiosis of News Coverage and Aggregate Online Search Behavior: Obama, Rumors, and Presidential Politics." *Mass Communication and Society* 13(4): 341–60.

Weinschenk, Aaron C. and Christopher T. Dawes. 2017. "The Relationship between Genes, Personality Traits, and Political Interest." *Political Research Quarterly* 70(3): 467–79.

Wenger, Debora and Bob Papper. 2017. "Local TV News and the New Media Landscape," *Knight Foundation.* Available online at https://knightfoundation.org/reports/local-tv-news-and-the-new-media-landscape (accessed March 15, 2020).

Zaller, John R. 1992. *The Nature and Origins of Mass Opinion.* New York: Cambridge University Press.

1994. "Elite Leadership of Mass Opinion: New Evidence from the Gulf War."
In *Taken by Storm: The News Media, U.S. Foreign Policy, and the Gulf War*,
Lance Bennett and David Paletz (eds.). Chicago: University of Chicago Press.
Zingher, Joshua N. and Jesse Richman. 2019. "Polarization and the
Nationalization of State Legislative Elections." *American Politics Research*
47(5): 1036–54.

Index

Other Books in the Series (continued from page iii)

For EU product safety concerns, contact us at Calle de José Abascal, 56–1°,
28003 Madrid, Spain or eugpsr@cambridge.org.

www.ingramcontent.com/pod-product-compliance
Ingram Content Group UK Ltd.
Pitfield, Milton Keynes, MK11 3LW, UK
UKHW010250140625
459647UK00013BA/1778